"In this absorbing and well-argued book, Adam Couchman relocates worship from something we do to something fundamentally going on beyond us, in the Son's communion with the Father, in which we participate by the Spirit. In this he subtly critiques a widespread assumption that worship is an anthropological category and defines it squarely as a theological process. Furthermore, he shows the significant consequences of this apparently recondite argument, leaving the whole church greatly in his debt."

—SAMUEL WELLS, VICAR OF ST MARTIN-IN-THE-FIELDS

"*Liturgia Dei* offers an original and thought-provoking contribution both to Christology and liturgical studies alike by pushing to its logical conclusion the claim that Jesus is both fully human and divine. If the human and divine natures are not to be pitted against each other, then Jesus worships as a human being and also as God. The concept of God as a worshipper is a fresh and challenging insight that takes us into the theo-drama enacted within God and within the life and witness of the church. I highly recommend this book, richly creative, even daring, in its theological claims and in the wisdom of its insights."

—GLEN O'BRIEN, PROFESSOR OF CHRISTIAN THOUGHT AND HISTORY, UNIVERSITY OF DIVINITY, MELBOURNE, AUSTRALIA

"This book presents an argument that is as compelling as it is pertinent today. Relying on a wide variety of both classical and contemporary sources, Couchman makes a radical, yet subtle case for God-centeredness in understanding liturgy. For indeed, all too often, worship is approached with the help of mere anthropological categories, the risk of which is that the divine agency is no longer theorized. Christian liturgy, however, is all about a sharing in the life of the Trinity and the encompassing work of God's redemption. Couchman's work is a very welcome voice in the growing choir of theologians of the liturgy who seek a proper balance between what the humanities can offer and the theological tradition."

—JORIS GELDHOF, VICE-DEAN FOR RESEARCH, KU LEUVEN

"Adam Couchman articulates the consequences of conceiving of the liturgy as formative theological practice. Worshippers—in, through, and with the high priestly work of the vicarious humanity of Christ—are given to participate within the infiniteness of the self-communicative mystery of the God whose life is life-giving. Human beings, therefore, are irreducibly grounded within the beneficence of divine creativity, and are materially incorporated into relations of mutual responsibility."

—JOHN MCDOWELL, PROFESSOR OF PHILOSOPHY, SYSTEMATIC THEOLOGY, AND MORAL THEOLOGY, UNIVERSITY OF DIVINITY

Liturgia Dei

Liturgia Dei

Worshiping the Worshiping God

ADAM COUCHMAN

PICKWICK *Publications* · Eugene, Oregon

LITURGIA DEI
Worshiping the Worshiping God

Copyright © 2025 Adam Couchman. All rights reserved. Except for brief quotations in critical publications or reviews, no part of this book may be reproduced in any manner without prior written permission from the publisher. Write: Permissions, Wipf and Stock Publishers, 199 W. 8th Ave., Suite 3, Eugene, OR 97401.

Pickwick Publications
An Imprint of Wipf and Stock Publishers
199 W. 8th Ave., Suite 3
Eugene, OR 97401

www.wipfandstock.com

PAPERBACK ISBN: 979-8-3852-3629-9
HARDCOVER ISBN: 979-8-3852-3630-5
EBOOK ISBN: 979-8-3852-3631-2

Cataloguing-in-Publication data:

Names: Couchman, Adam, author.

Title: Liturgia dei : worshiping the worshiping God / Adam Couchman.

Description: Eugene, OR : Pickwick Publications, 2025 | Includes bibliographical references and index.

Identifiers: ISBN 979-8-3852-3629-9 (paperback) | ISBN 979-8-3852-3630-5 (hardcover) | ISBN 979-8-3852-3631-2 (ebook)

Subjects: LCSH: Theology, Doctrinal. | Liturgics.

Classification: BT75.2 .C2025 67 (paperback) | BT75.2 .C67 (ebook)

10/08/25

Scripture quotations are taken from the New Revised Standard Version Updated Edition. Copyright © 2021 National Council of Churches of Christ in the United States of America. Used by permission. All rights reserved worldwide.

For Sonia

It is interesting to ponder how the Christian community's self-definition would be changed if it took as its beginning point, 'We are a community for whom Jesus prays."

—Gail O'Day

Contents

Acknowledgments | xiii

List of Abbreviations | xvii

1. The Curtain Raiser | 1
   On Trinitarian Nomenclature | 6
   The Need for a Clear Definition of "Worship" | 8
   A Survey of Existing Definitions | 11
   David Fagerberg's Theocentric Definition | 15
   Defining "Glory" | 16
   Conclusion | 19

2. Mise-en-Scène | 21
   Scenes | 22
   The Working Relationship of Balthasar and Speyr | 22
   Balthasar's Theo-drama | 27
   Vanhoozer's Drama of Doctrine | 31
   Performance Theory | 34
   Improvisation | 40
   Participation? | 45
   Scene: Peter Sellars's *St. Matthew's Passion* | 47
   The Role of Scripture Within the Theo-drama | 49
   Fitting Performance | 55
   Conclusion | 56

3. The Protagonist—Jesus Christ (Part One) | 57
   Tracing the Threads from Paul's "the Gospel" to the Creeds | 60

From "the Gospel" to *Regulae Fidei* | 61
From *Regulae Fidei* to the Creeds | 64
The Hypostatic Union | 65
Perichoresis | 68
Communicatio Idiomatum | 70
Scene—Improvising to Emmaus and Back | 73
Jesus' Identity Is Revealed in Performance | 76

4 The Protagonist—Jesus Christ (Part Two) | 78
Jesus Worshiping from His Humanity | 78
Scene—John 17 | 85
Scene—The Last Supper as a Performance of the Passover | 87
Jesus Worshiping from His Person | 88
Scene—Gethsemane in Performance | 89
Toward a Theocentric Definition of Worship | 93
Conclusion | 95

5 The Protagonist(s)—The Trinity | 97
Adrienne von Speyr | 97
David Fagerberg | 101
Scene: Basil's *On the Holy Spirit* | 102
God as Creator | 105
God as Personae | 108
God as Performer | 109
God as Audience | 110
God as Creator, Personae, Performer, and Audience | 113
Philippians 2—The Father and Son Reveal the *Liturgia Dei* | 114
Roman 8—Mother Spirit Reveals the *Liturgia Dei* | 118
Conclusion | 121

6 The Company of Worshipers | 123
Liturgical Anthropology | 123
Homo Liturgicus Before James K. A. Smith | 125
Homo Liturgicus According to James K. A. Smith | 129
Humans as the *Imago Dei* | 132
The Intersection of *Homo Liturgicus*, the *Imago Dei*, and the *Liturgia Dei* | 134

The Human Performance of Eternal Glorification | 137
Conclusion | 139

7 The Characterization of the Company | 140
The Call for Liturgical Renewal | 140
Scene—*Societas Liturgica* and the Tension of the Final Eucharist | 141
Paul's Concerns Regarding the Lord's Supper in Corinth | 145
The *Liturgia Dei* and Feminist Liturgical Critique | 149
Scene—Feminist Protest Hiding in Plain Sight | 152
John Wesley's Open Table | 155
A New Perspective on an Old Problem | 158
Conclusion | 163

8 The Final Curtain | 164
Being of the Same Mind | 165
Scene: Improvisation on an Improvisation | 166
An Open Invitation to Join in the Performance | 169

Credits | 173

Name (Author) Index | 185

Subject Index | 187

Scripture Index | 189

Acknowledgments

I ACKNOWLEDGE THE TRADITIONAL owners of the land on which this research was conducted. Primarily, this was the land of the Wurundjeri people of the Kulin nation. I also acknowledge the Yagera and Turbul peoples on whose land I now live. This is their sovereign land that was stolen and never ceded. I pay my respects to their elders past and present and commit myself to a more just future with all Aboriginal people.

No book emerges in isolation. This one is certainly no different. This book comes from my doctoral thesis, and so my first thanks go to my supervisors, Rev. Prof. Glen O'Brien and Rev. Assoc. Prof. John Capper. They have provided timely and accurate guidance along the way and have been a tremendous source of encouragement to me. The past six years have been tumultuous, to say the least, and the only thing that has remained constant through it all has been working on this thesis. Glen and John have been constant companions throughout it all, the good and the bad—writer's block, imposter syndrome, marriage breakdown, ministry loss, unemployment, remarriage, moving house four times, re-employment, and eventually finding my feet, and my voice, once again. Throughout it all, I have had the privilege of the generous and kind support of these two godly men. It seems a cliche to say I wouldn't have made it without them, but the reality of that statement is far too true to measure. I am forever grateful.

I have enjoyed the opportunity to share the journey with amazing colleagues and friends. At the commencement of this research, at Eva Burrows College. In the end, at Yarra Theological Union, and now beyond it at St. Francis College. I am grateful for the support of Rev. Dr. Chris Monaghan CP, Rev. Dr. Ross Fishburn, Prof. John McDowell, Rev. Assoc. Prof. Michael Kelly CSsR, Lt.-Col. Dr. Terry Grey, Major Andrew Walton, Dr. Carmel Posa SGS, Dr. Jill O'Brien SGS, Rev. Dr. Matthew

Beckmann OF, Rev. Dr. Ruth Matheison, Assoc. Prof. Peter Klein, and a host of other faculty, staff, and students. They have all encouraged and supported me in my research, and I am so grateful for their generosity and personal interest in me. One faculty member, in particular, deserves special mention. Dr. Robyn Reynolds OLSH was known for her encouraging and supportive care for everyone. She always took a special interest in my research, and I was always happy to share with her stories of my progress. Sadly, Robyn died just a few months before I submitted this thesis. While she never saw the finished project, her belief in me along the way ensured that it did, in fact, get finished.

The staff at the University of Divinity have been a great support throughout my time as a student. In the beginning, Prof. John McDowell and Dr. Suman Kashyap provided guidance and administrative support. For the latter part of the thesis, Assoc. Prof. Liz Boase has been a critical source of guidance as the dean of the School of Graduate Research. The confirmation panel that included Prof. Wendy Mayer and Assoc. Prof. Geoff Thompson was a crucial moment in my candidature. Their critical and thoughtful advice provided a necessary focus for my research, and it is a better product because of it.

It would be remiss to forget to mention the important role that Thesis Bootcamps and Writing Days have performed throughout my studies. Initially held under the watchful gaze of Dr. Fotini Toso, I came to value and ultimately rely upon these dedicated days where distractions were limited so I could focus on writing. Thanks also to the fellow students who joined at various points along the way. In particular, Anne Pate and Leonie Bird joined me in running the final stretch together.

I am also grateful to the University of Divinity for the provision of two research grants to attend the *Societas Liturgica* Congresses in 2019 and 2023. These funds enabled me to test and refine my ideas among a group of world-leading liturgical scholars. The research is a better product because of these opportunities. I am also grateful for two awards that were granted along the way. First, the Leatherland Prize was awarded by the Australian Academy of Liturgy and the University of Divinity in my first year of candidature (2018). Second, the New and Emerging Scholar Prize was awarded by the Australian and New Zealand Association of Theological Schools (ANZATS) in my final year of candidature (2023).

Finally, to my family, I am forever grateful for your love and support. To my mother, Helen, father, Phil, and my step-children, Kaja, Gabe, and Rory. Thank you for being you and for being a grounding force while my head has been in the clouds. To my wife Sonia who is my greatest encourager, proofreader, sounding board, and cheerleader. I am eternally thankful for your presence in my life. I'm so glad you have been with me as I've been writing, and I'm so glad it is you who will be next to me all along.

To my daughters, Brielle and Annabelle, may this be one additional sign of my unending love for you.

List of Abbreviations

Ap	"The Apostles' Creed." In *Creeds and Confessions of Faith in the Christian Tradition*, edited by Jaroslav Pelikan and Valerie Hotchkiss, 1:667–69. New Haven, CT: Yale University Press, 2003.
APBA	Anglican Church of Australia. *A Prayer Book for Australia*. Mulgrave: Broughton, 1995.
BCP	*The Book of Common Prayer and Administration of the Sacraments and Other Rites and Ceremonies of the Church According to the Use of the Church of England*. London: Oxford University Press, 1662.
Chal	"The Definition of Faith of the Council of Chalcedon." In *Creeds and Confessions of Faith in the Christian Tradition*, edited by Jaroslav Pelikan and Valerie Hotchkiss, 1:172–81. New Haven, CT: Yale University Press, 2003.
N-CP	"The Niceno-Constantinopolitan Creed." In *Creeds and Confessions of Faith in the Christian Tradition*, edited by Jaroslav Pelikan and Valerie Hotchkiss, 1:160–63. New Haven, CT: Yale University Press, 2003.
TD	Hans Urs von Balthasar. *Theo-Drama*. Translated by Graham Harrison. 5 vols. San Francisco: Ignatius, 1988–98.
TSA	The Salvation Army

1

The Curtain Raiser

It is 9:55 a.m. on Sunday morning at Holy Name of Jesus Anglican Church in Vermont South, in the eastern suburbs of Melbourne, Australia. The bell above the church is rung, calling the community to worship. Inside the church, the same ringing bell signals to the gathering worshipers that it is time for the conversations to cease and silent attention to be turned to the drama that is about to unfold. In reality, the worshipers have been preparing all morning, all week, indeed, for much of the congregation, all of their lives. They follow the same patterns, the same routines, and the same habits that they perform each week as they "go to church." The ringing bell, though, marks that moment in time when individual preparations converge into shared communal ones, at this particular time and in this particular place. A reverent hush descends upon the congregation in this local parish of The Anglican Church of Australia.

As the clock passes over the hour, the vicar calls for the congregation to stand together and sing the processional hymn. The lead performers slowly and deliberately process toward the altar. Cross, candles, and canon converge at the center of the congregation as "church" begins. From here the liturgy follows the pattern outlined in *A Prayer Book for Australia (APBA)*,[1] the script authorized for use within parishes of the Anglican Church in Australia.

In commonality with many other parishes and local churches around Australia, and the world, this congregation uses the *Revised*

---

1. Anglican Church of Australia, *Prayer Book for Australia.*

Common Lectionary to select which passages of Scripture are read aloud.[2] It is the seventh Sunday of Easter in Year A and, as usual, when the time comes to proclaim the Gospel reading, the congregation stands while the text is carried to the center of the worship space. It is declared that this is "A reading from the gospel of our Lord Jesus Christ, according to St. John 17:1–11." The people respond together "Glory to you, Lord Jesus Christ."[3] Then the text is read aloud in the midst of the people.

> After Jesus had spoken these words, he looked up to heaven and said, "Father, the hour has come; glorify your Son so that the Son may glorify you, since you have given him authority over all people, to give eternal life to all whom you have given him. And this is eternal life, that they may know you, the only true God, and Jesus Christ, whom you have sent. I glorified you on earth by finishing the work that you gave me to do. So now, Father, glorify me in your own presence with the glory that I had in your presence before the world existed.
>
> I have made your name known to those whom you gave me from the world. They were yours, and you gave them to me, and they have kept your word. Now they know that everything you have given me is from you, for the words that you gave to me I have given to them, and they have received them and know in truth that I came from you, and they have believed that you sent me. I am asking on their behalf; I am not asking on behalf of the world but on behalf of those whom you gave me, because they are yours. All mine are yours, and yours are mine, and I have been glorified in them. And now I am no longer in the world, but they are in the world, and I am coming to you. Holy Father, protect them in your name that you have given me, so that they may be one, as we are one." (John 17:1–11 NRSVUE)[4]

To conclude the reading, the text is held high in the air and the reader declares, "This is the Gospel of the Lord." The congregation join in response, "Praise to you, Lord Jesus Christ."[5] Following the reading of the Gospel, a sermon is given on the text.

Later, as a part of the authorized liturgy, the congregation voices together its shared faith using the words of the Niceno-Constantinopolitan

---

2. English Language Liturgical Consultation, "RCL Tables."

3. *APBA*, 103.

4. Unless otherwise stated all Scripture references are taken from the New Revised Standard Version—Updated Edition.

5. *APBA*, 103.

Creed (N-CP).[6] On other occasions, the congregants will use the Apostles' Creed (Ap)[7] or another authorized creedal confession. Through these shared, historic, and authorized creeds they affirm together the faith which they individually confessed at their baptismal entry into the church, which they share in common with each other and with Christians throughout time and the world. They confess their belief in one God, the three persons of the Trinity: Father, Son, and Mother Spirit,[8] and the full humanity and divinity of Jesus Christ. Following this confession, the congregation shares together in the Lord's Supper. This microform of the cosmic drama of salvation concludes with the people being dismissed to love and serve the Lord. The gathered community becomes the scattered community. They move out into the world and anticipate returning the next Sunday to share in another performance all over again. The script will be the same, yet the performance will inevitably be different.

The events described above are nothing particularly unique regarding Christian worship. This particular Sunday, and this particular reading, though, raise questions that are perhaps so obvious that they are given little consideration, the theological wood preventing us from seeing the trees. In commenting upon the text above from John 17, Gail O'Day suggests that "it is interesting to ponder how the Christian community's self-definition would be changed if it took as its beginning point, 'We are a community for whom Jesus prays.'"[9]

Reworking O'Day's provocative thought, it is also interesting to ponder how the Christian community's definition of *worship* would be changed if it took as its beginning point "Jesus worships." This Jesus is the same Jesus the church confesses to be fully human and fully divine, and yet *he worships*. He asks the Father to glorify him with the glory he had in his presence before the world existed. While it does not appear in this reading on this occasion, later in John 17 Jesus states that he has also given the same "glory" to his followers.

At one and the same time, in Christian confession, highlighted in N-CP and Ap, this same Jesus is *worshiped* as God. Furthermore, in Christian prayer, Jesus *mediates worship* to God. In Christian Scripture, Jesus is depicted as a *worshiper* of God. The four canonical Gospel narratives all

6. *APBA*, 170; "Niceno-Constantinopolitan Creed," 160–63.

7. *APBA*, 171; "Apostles' Creed," 667–69.

8. The use of the term "Mother Spirit" will be explained in "On Trinitarian Nomenclature" below.

9. O'Day, "Gospel of John," 798.

depict Jesus worshiping in ways that are consistent with a faithful, first-century Jewish male. This immediately reveals the problem that this book is seeking to address. The Jesus who was baptized in the Jordan by John some two thousand years ago is the same Jesus who is worshiped today as God, one with the Father and Mother Spirit. As such, worship is offered *to* Jesus, who is the Christ. Larry Hurtado suggests that this "cultic devotion" that is given to Jesus, that was usually reserved for the God of Israel, is one of the "most striking" innovations of earliest Christianity.[10] Following on from this, the risen and ascended Christ performs the function of "High Priest" (e.g., Heb 5:1–10), acting as the mediator between God and humanity. He advocates on behalf of the people to God and on behalf of God to the people.[11] Therefore, as worship is offered *to* Christ it is also offered *through* Christ. Yet the same Christ *to* and *through* whom worship is offered, is himself a worshiper. As such, worship is offered *to*, *through*, and *with* Christ. It is necessary, therefore, that any definition of worship that is offered applies simultaneously to Jesus Christ in these three ways—*to*, *through*, and *with* him. It must take account of the hypostatic union of the divine and human natures in Jesus Christ, the perichoretic relationship of the Trinity, and finally the implications of both of those doctrines for the church's ongoing worship of God today. This book seeks to offer such a definition of worship.

The research questions this book seeks to address are as follows. How should worship be defined in the light of its performance by Jesus Christ? How is his performance of worship to be understood in the light of the church's confession that he is both fully divine and fully human? What is revealed about the relationship between the divine and human natures in the person of Jesus Christ when he performs worship? What is revealed about the inner relations of the three persons of the Trinity by Jesus' worship, and the worship offered by the Father and Mother Spirit? How does humanity reflect (*imago Dei*) the God who worships (*liturgia Dei*)? In what ways does this investigation impact the church's performance of worship?

In responding to these questions this book will argue that *to*, *through*, and *with* the fully divine and fully human person of Jesus Christ glory is given to God the Father through the embodied, theo-dramatic performance of God the Son. This embodied performance within the person of

---

10. Hurtado, *How on Earth Did Jesus Become a God?*, 197.
11. Jungmann, *Place of Christ in Liturgical Prayer*, xx.

Jesus Christ reveals that worship is much more than something humans perform out of themselves toward the divine. Etymologically, Λειτουργία (*leitourgia*—from *laos* and *ergon*) is either the work *of* the people or the work *for* the people. What will be suggested here, though, is that the worshiping Jesus reveals that Λειτουργία is primarily the work of the *persons*, the three persons of the Trinity. From a theo-dramatic viewpoint, the glory of God that is given and received by Jesus is not a static, motionless photograph of the inherent worth and splendor of the divine, but rather a dynamic, dramatic, audience-engaging, performative glory that is eternal, ongoing, and inherent to the very nature of God. To summarize this eternal divine worship the term *liturgia Dei* is introduced here. The term is intentionally opaque with the possibility of being translated "the worshiping God" and "the worship of God." It will be demonstrated that both meanings are intended. The *liturgia Dei* is essential to the divine nature, wherein the worshiping God worships God.

While the opening focus of this book is upon Jesus' worship, it will also be argued that Scripture reveals glimpses of the Father and Mother Spirit performing the *liturgia Dei* upon the stage of the world. Such glimpses support the argument that worship is essential to the divine nature. For example, Jesus' request to the Father in the passage cited above, "glorify your Son, that your Son may glorify you" (John 17:1) and "glorify me in your presence with the glory I had with you before the world began" (John 17:5). Similarly, the Spirit joins in the groan-filled prayers of creation and God's people when words cannot be found (Rom 8:22–26), and God exalts the Son and gives him the name that is above all names (Phil 2:9–11). In these examples, acts of worship are performed by all three persons of the Trinity. This book argues that this is more than a matter of anthropomorphic writing on the part of the authors of the texts. Rather, it is evidence that supports the argument that worship itself is of the essence of God's nature. God worships God. This observation has significant implications for how worship itself is defined. This book proposes a theocentric and trinitarian definition of worship, the *liturgia Dei*, as follows: worship is the eternal glorification of God that extends from, and returns to, the eternal relations of Father, Son, and Mother Spirit. The church joins in worship *to*, *through*, and *with* Jesus Christ.

In focusing on the canonical accounts of Jesus' worship it is necessary, in accordance with the Definition of Faith of the Council of Chalcedon

(Chal),[12] to apply this definition without confusing or dividing the two natures, thus preserving the hypostatic union. Also, the performance of worship by the church today must be taken into consideration. It will be shown how the *liturgia Dei* relates to the way humans worship. Theo-dramatic terminology will assist, since the church's worship is engaging in the single performance of the theo-drama that extends from creation through the incarnation and on to cosmic consummation. The worship that takes place in the church today is not independent of the *liturgia Dei*. Rather it is both fully dependent upon and a theo-dramatic performance of it.

ON TRINITARIAN NOMENCLATURE

The ongoing use of the nomenclature of "Father, Son, and Spirit" has been increasingly challenged, particularly concerning the gender-specific language of "Father" and "Son." Kay Bonikowsky notes that "when the experience of men is normalized, God is imagined as male, arranging women into the subordinate role in the spiritual world as well as the physical."[13] This is not just a "tangential 'woman's issue'" but, as Mary Collins notes, a "radical theological and ecclesial question."[14] The premise of Christians gathering to worship is not the unknowability of God but rather the opposite. When Christians gather to worship God, they assume that God can be known and therefore named. The problem is determining what name(s) are to be used to address God in worship and beyond. As Collins rightly asks, "who among us knows with confidence how best to name this God of Jesus Christ today? 'Our Father?' 'Our Mother?' 'Loving Parent?'"[15]

Marjorie Procter-Smith articulates the nature of this theological problem when she suggests that "traditional Christian public prayer (and, by extension, private and personal prayer) is based on problematic assumptions about the nature of God, about the nature of human life and need, about the necessary rituals which surround the act of prayer."[16] As a result, the language chosen to name and describe the three persons of the Trinity is a critical choice, particularly as it relates to Christian worship.

---

12. "Definition of Faith of the Council of Chalcedon," 172–81.
13. Bonikowsky, "Also a Mother," 20.
14. Collins, "Naming God," 292.
15. Collins, "Naming God," 293.
16. Procter-Smith, *Praying with Our Eyes Open*, 9.

As will be discussed below the church's beliefs are founded on the church's worship (*ut legem credenda lex statuat supplicandi*). At the same time, there are biblical and historical precedents to consider as well as the fundamental relationality of the divine persons that the traditional terms of "Father" and "Son" seek to express. Substituting "Father, Son, and Spirit" for "Creator, Redeemer, and Sanctifier," for example, removes the gender-specific nature of the first two names but loses the relationality that they bring with them. This relationality is critical to a right contemplation of the Trinity. As Gregory of Nazianzus stated,

> No sooner do I conceive of the One than I am illumined by the Splendor of the Three; no sooner do I distinguish Them than I am carried back to the One. When I think of any One of the Three I think of Him as a Whole, and my eyes are filled, and the greater part of what I am thinking of escapes me. I cannot grasp the greatness of That One so as to attribute a greater greatness to the Rest. When I contemplate the Three together, I see but one torch, and cannot divine or measure out the Undivided Light.[17]

A further problem of naming the three persons as Creator, Redeemer, and Sanctifier lies in assigning one particular attribute to only one of the persons, risking the loss of the trinitarian foundation of each activity. For example, the first person of the Trinity is named as Creator and so the second and third persons are not. The use of attributes of God's character as names for the three persons limits the given attribute to one person and so serves to distinguish the three from the one. As a result, while the problem of gendered language is overcome, a theological shortfall is encountered in the process. This theological shortfall is significant to this book, given the argument being presented here that Jesus at worship reveals God at worship.

This book seeks to draw upon the relationality that the traditional terms bring while recognizing that they insufficiently express, and even distract from, the fullness of the divinity that lies beyond them. Attempts to broaden the meaning of these terms, or find appropriate alternatives, are ongoing and this is a necessary inclusion to the continuing theological conversation.[18] Sarah Coakley suggests that:

---

17. Gregory of Nazianzus, "Oration 40: On Holy Baptism," §41.

18. On Jesus as the embodiment of Woman-Wisdom see Douglas, *Early Church Understandings of Jesus as the Female Divine*.

> Neither the straightforward obliteration of "Father" language, nor the "feminization" of the Spirit (or indeed of the Son), constitute in themselves satisfactory strategies in the face of the profound feminist critique of classical Christian thought forms and patterns of behavior. These problems can only be met satisfactorily by an ascetic response which attacks idolatry at its root.[19]

While Coakley warns against the "feminization" of the Spirit, others, such as Bonikowsky in her summary of Asian feminist theology, suggest thinking of the Trinity as "family." As such, Bonikowsky highlights benefits in recognizing God as both "Father" and "Mother." It "deepens our own experience of God's presence with us. As the baby in her mother's womb is aware of the all-encompassing presence of her mother, so the biblical language and imagery of the Spirit as Mother reveals God to be near, intimate, and permeating all creation."[20]

There is a balance to be struck here given Gregory of Nazianzus's warning that we should not consider God to be male since the term "Father" is used to name the first person.[21] Introducing the use of "Mother" to describe the third person risks the same problem of unnecessarily gendering one person over and against the others. However, the use of *only* male pronouns to describe two of the three persons over a long period, particularly in the church's worship, leaves a shortfall regarding the feminine attributes of God. To recognize and respond to this problem, this book will retain the historical terms of "Father" and "Son" for the first and second persons of the Trinity and utilize the term "Mother Spirit" for the third person of the Trinity. In no way is this to be seen as a solution to the problem named above. Rather, it is hoped that an appropriate balance may be struck between honoring the historical and biblical foundations of trinitarian terminology while also pointing to the need to move beyond the disproportionate use of patriarchal conventions within worship and theology.

THE NEED FOR A CLEAR DEFINITION OF "WORSHIP"

Throughout history and throughout the church today Christians gather to give glory to God. In cathedrals, churches, homes and hotels, around

---

19. Coakley, *God, Sexuality and the Self*, 53n1.
20. Bonikowsky, "Also a Mother," 24.
21. Gregory of Nazianzus, "Oration 31: On the Holy Spirit," §7.

campfires and kitchen tables, with and without the protection of local laws, in full view of the world around them, or hidden away to avoid intense religious persecution, they worship as individuals, as families, and in formal gatherings of thousands of people. Under these and many other conditions, the church has gathered and continues to gather for a purpose broadly called "worship." Yet what is meant by this term?

The term has been used in a variety of ways. Predominantly the term is understood to mean an offering of reverence or adoration given from humans to the divine. The term has also had other uses for reverence or adoration between humans, including in the marriage ceremony of the *Book of Common Prayer* (*BCP*) and the first form of marriage in *An Australian Prayer Book*, where the bride and groom pledge to "worship" their spouse with their body.[22] The fact that *A Prayer Book for Australia* (*APBA*) has removed the term from its first form of marriage replacing it, instead, with "I wed you with all that I am and all that I have; I honor you,"[23] indicates that the meaning of the word "worship" was seen as problematic in this setting. This change alone highlights the need for a clear definition of the term. Similarly, the honorific "Your Worship" was used historically in legal settings, as a sign of respect toward the judge or other person in a position of authority. The focus of this book is on the meaning of "worship" in Christian vernacular. While its predominant meaning is given to the acts and attitudes of humans toward the divine, this book suggests that it is first and foremost a divine activity.

A key component of N-CP is that Jesus Christ is "of one substance [essence] with the Father."[24] This confession is made, either implicitly or explicitly, in historic continuity with the church universal. The confession affirms that Jesus Christ is truly and properly divine and truly and properly human. According to Chal he is:

> one and the same Christ, Son, Lord, Only-begotten, acknowledged in two natures which undergo no confusion, no change, no division, no separation; at no point was the difference between the natures taken away through the union, but rather the property of both natures is preserved and comes together into a single person and a single subsistent being.[25]

---

22. *Book of Common Prayer* (1662), 172; Anglican Church of Australia, *Australian Prayer Book*.

23. *APBA*, 649.

24. N-CP, 163.

25. Chal, 181.

This union is such that every action of Christ is at one and the same time truly and properly divine and truly and properly human. In theo-dramatic terms, this union is *performed* in the life of Jesus Christ. The nature of this performance is such that the two natures cannot be confused or separated. Rather, every moment in the life of Jesus Christ is a dramatic performance of the union of the two natures. Every action of the God-human is a performance of the divine and human natures united within his person, perfectly expressing the character of both Jesus of Nazareth and the *Logos*.

Throughout the canonical accounts of the gospel this same God-human is depicted as a worshiper. From an early age he joins in Jewish festivals at the temple (Luke 3), he is baptized in the Jordan River (Matt 3:13-17; Mark 1:9-11; Luke 3:21-22), he participates in Jewish worship in the temple (e.g., Luke 2:46; Luke 20:1), the synagogue (Matt 4:23; Luke 4:16-27), and in festivals such as Passover (Luke 22:8). He prays (Luke 6:12; John 17) and teaches his disciples to do the same (Matt 6:5-15; Luke 11:1-4). These observations prompt the investigation being undertaken and raise questions regarding what the worshiping Christ reveals about God and the ongoing performance of worship within the theo-drama today.

In Jesus Christ, theo-dramatic performance is observed in its most definitive form. As the second person of the Trinity, he is the divine *Logos* (e.g., John 1:1-18) and, importantly, a *Logos* that is not just spoken but enacted. His character is revealed through embodied performance. He is the Word-Act. Through this incarnated embodiment of the *Logos*, the divine and human natures are united in performance and so both natures are truly and properly seen via this protagonist among the *dramatis personae*.

Moving from this broader Christological viewpoint to focus on a more specific examination of Jesus' own worship, the embodied performance of the divine *Logos* becomes even more significant. His own worship is a continuation of the theo-dramatic self-revelation of God. Thomas F. Torrance asserts that "what God is toward us in Jesus Christ on earth and in time, he is antecedently and eternally in himself, and that everything that God is in himself he is toward us in Jesus Christ."[26] This assertion will be applied to Jesus as a worshiper in this book. Since Jesus is God, and Jesus worships, then God worships. If, in Jesus Christ, God is worshiping, then something about divinity and the nature of worship is revealed through Jesus the worshiper. As a result, a clear definition of "worship" is required.

---

26. Torrance, *Incarnation*, 258.

A SURVEY OF EXISTING DEFINITIONS

David Peterson suggests that any definition of worship "must apply to Jesus himself, since he is a worshiper, and as such must include reference to his divinity."[27] This will function as a guiding principle throughout this book. Similarly, in *Worship: Its Theology and Practice*, Jean-Jacques von Allmen emphasizes the Christological foundations of Christian worship. He acknowledges that even a "superficial" reading of the New Testament shows that Jesus' life was, indeed, "liturgical."[28] In this regard, Christian worship is unique among all other forms of worship, given the founder of this faith receives worship as God, mediates worship for others, and performs the worship of God, at one and the same time (*to*, *through*, and *with* Jesus). This unique feature of Christian worship is reflected in *APBA*; "As one body and one holy people, may we proclaim the everlasting gospel of Jesus Christ our Lord, *through whom, with whom, and in whom*, in the unity of the Holy Spirit, all glory is yours, eternal God, now and for ever."[29]

While this feature appears in the two examples above, existing definitions of Christian worship fail to account for this unique feature of Christian belief and, as a result, tend to be anthropocentric. In short, worship is viewed as a unidirectional activity that proceeds from humanity (or more broadly, creation) toward the divine. Anthropocentric definitions of worship are unable to account for the hypostatic union of the worshiping Jesus since they fail fully to account for the fact that worship occurs *to*, *through*, and *with* Jesus. As a result, the tension of holding together the full divinity and full humanity of Christ risks being lost when those definitions are applied to the worshiping Jesus, as the hypostatic union is unintentionally but inevitably divided.

Some definitions focus upon those acts performed by humans toward God in response to the divine initiative. Daniel Block asserts that "true worship involves reverential *human acts* of submission and homage before the divine Sovereign in response to his gracious revelation of himself and in accord with his will."[30] Similarly, Donald Bloesch suggests that "worship is a *creative response* to God's gracious act of condescension in Jesus Christ, a response that takes the form of praise, proclamation,

---

27. Peterson, *Engaging with God*, 17.
28. Allmen, *Worship*, 21.
29. *APBA*, 132. Emphasis added.
30. Block, *For the Glory of God*, 65.

recollection and prayer."[31] Karl Barth similarly focusses upon human acts in his lengthier definition:

> "Liturgy" means the proclamation of the mighty acts of God by which the congregation is established and in the celebration of which it permits itself to be established anew, again and again. By participation in this worship—to which belong in the broad sense also the instruction of youth, brotherly discipline, pastoral and other forms of care—and from this worship, built upon it and active in it, the Christian congregation lives, its members serve each other and together serve their Lord, and with their witness serve the world.[32]

Others take this anthropocentricity to an ontological conclusion, suggesting that "to be human is to worship."[33] In this regard, James K. A. Smith asserts that "we are what we love"[34] and so describes humans as *homo liturgicus*. That is, we are "liturgical animals—embodied, practicing creatures whose love/desire is aimed at something ultimate."[35] He suggests that *all* people love/desire someone or something ultimate and that liturgical practices within the church serve the purpose of directing those desires toward the God of Jesus Christ. Smith's philosophical anthropology will become critical later in this book as it will be argued that *homo liturgicus* is a reflection of the *liturgia Dei* via the *imago Dei*. At this point, it is important to acknowledge that Smith grounds his ontological view of worship within the human person. To worship is to be human. As such, *homo liturgicus* remains an anthropocentric view of worship. Even so, this book will work with Smith's findings to provide the necessary trinitarian grounding that is lacking.

Other scholars situate this anthropocentricity within a teleological framework. For example, Ben Witherington III claims, echoing *The Westminster Shorter Catechism*, that "the chief end of humankind . . . is the proper worship of God by all creatures."[36] It is worth highlighting here that Witherington's definition of worship includes all of creation,

---

31. Bloesch, *Church*, 119. Emphasis added.
32. Barth, *God Here and Now*, 96.
33. Block, *For the Glory of God*, 1.
34. Smith, *Desiring the Kingdom*, 40.
35. Smith, *Desiring the Kingdom*, 40.
36. Witherington, *We Have Seen His Glory* 18. Cf. the first question of the Catechism: "man's chief end is to glorify God and to enjoy him forever." "Westminster Shorter Catechism," 652.

a move that Nils Alstrup Dahl extends to include heavenly worship as well. According to Dahl, when Christians worship, "they participate in the heavenly worship of the angels and of the perfect saints."[37] This last definition broadens this anthropocentricity as far as is possible, including the angels and saints, yet it does not go so far as to suggest that God is a worshiper as well. As a result, it still fails to account for Jesus' divinity in his performance of worship.

Susan J. White suggests that the "story of the church's worship, like the story of the church itself, is a human story."[38] From this anthropocentric view of worship, White outlines the foundations of Christian worship by summarizing it in terms of "theology, Bible, history and the human sciences."[39] This outline forms the content of her first chapter, from which the outworking of the rest of the work flows.

In summarizing differing theologies of worship, White provides a brief outline of six different theological models that Christians have used to define worship. These include worship as service to God, worship as the mirror of heaven, worship as affirmation, worship as communion, worship as proclamation, and worship as the arena of transcendence.[40] Each model is summarized, and criticisms or shortfalls are offered. White acknowledges that the models are "not mutually exclusive" but operate interdependently so that, for example, the worshiper is at one and the same time offering service to God while doing so in the communion of the church.[41]

While building upon an anthropocentric view of worship, White acknowledges that the worship that takes place in church is mirroring that which is taking place in heaven. This view is predominantly emphasized in Orthodox liturgy and brings to the forefront that worship is the "ultimate human destiny" and an "eternal vocation" and so "when we enter into Christian worship . . . we enter into a different dimension of time and space, a cosmic dimension, where we can gradually attune ourselves with the ceaseless praises of the heavenly hosts."[42] In this way, White emphasizes that the worship taking place within the church is bigger than its temporal reality, yet the use of the term "mirror" suggests that there

---

37. Dahl, "New and Living Way," 409.
38. White, *Groundwork*, x.
39. White, *Groundwork*, 1.
40. White, *Groundwork*, 2–16.
41. White, *Groundwork*, 15.
42. White, *Groundwork*, 4.

remains a qualitative distinction between worship on earth and worship in heaven; the two are similar but still fundamentally different. An opportunity exists to connect the two via the priestly work of Christ, but it is an opportunity that White does not take. Further, when she recounts the biblical foundations of the study of worship no mention is given of the fact that Jesus himself is a worshiper. These two omissions combined bring to the fore how anthropocentric definitions of worship lead to failures to account for Jesus' own performance of worship, the connection between the ongoing worship of the church and the eternal worship of heaven within the high priesthood of Christ, and the place of worship in the ongoing theo-drama.

In his text *Prayerbook of the Bible*, Dietrich Bonhoeffer emphasizes the humanity of the praying Jesus. He states that prayers are "human words" and so interprets Jesus' performance of prayer from this basis.[43] As a result, he suggests that "in Jesus' mouth the human word becomes God's word."[44] In regard to the two natures of Christ, Bonhoeffer does not account for the divine nature, nor the hypostatic union, when it comes to Jesus the worshiper. Rather he states that the "truly human Jesus Christ prays in this psalm [22] and takes us into his prayer."[45] He suggests that Jesus demonstrates that he has taken upon himself all that it means to be human. As such, worship, for Bonhoeffer, is a human activity and so Jesus' performance of prayer does not stem from his divinity, nor is it needed for his humanity, but rather enacts his mediatorial role on our behalf. In doing so he "shows himself to be the true Son of God."[46] The mediatorial role of Christ continues when Christians pray. Bonhoeffer interprets Christian prayer as an action through which "Christ brings us before the face of God."[47] Christian prayer, specifically praying the prayers of the Bible, is not firstly about the person in prayer, but rather Christ who prays it on their behalf.

Two significant factors are missing from Bonhoeffer's account of prayer. First, a trinitarian framework. For example, when Christians pray, they do so to the Father, through the Son, in Mother Spirit, or to the Father, with the Son, and Mother Spirit.[48] Second, for Bonhoeffer,

43. Bonhoeffer, *Prayerbook*, 156.
44. Bonhoeffer, *Prayerbook*, 157.
45. Bonhoeffer, *Prayerbook*, 166.
46. Bonhoeffer, *Prayerbook*, 172.
47. Bonhoeffer, *Prayerbook*, 157.

48. This trinitarian framework for prayer will be expanded below in "God as Creator."

the divinity of Christ is inactive as he prays and so the two natures are divided. Instead, this book argues that when Jesus prays, he does so as truly human *and* truly divine. Christ does not set aside his divinity to pray as a human, rather his divinity and humanity are fully revealed as he prays. When Christians pray, their offering is joined to Christ's by Mother Spirit and in so doing the prayer is presented to the Father by Christ. Prayer is made *with* Christ.

This summarizes the problem that this book seeks to address. Existing definitions fail fully to consider the full divinity and humanity of Jesus Christ within his acts of worship. That is, they remain human actions that flow from creation toward the divine. Furthermore, such definitions fail to consider the glimpses of the Father and Mother Spirit at worship.

DAVID FAGERBERG'S THEOCENTRIC DEFINITION

David Fagerberg offers a definition of liturgy that comes closest to overcoming this problem, when he defines it as "the Trinity's perichoresis kenotically extended to invite our synergistic ascent into deification."[49] It is necessary to take time to unpack this definition to show why it comes close to overcoming the problem this book is seeking to address yet ultimately does not achieve it entirely.

Fagerberg argues that liturgy is a revelation of God and as such is an "activity done by God."[50] Worship, and liturgy as its formal performance, are first and foremost "the work of God."[51] Furthermore, it is an action performed by the "whole Christ (*Christus totus*)," that is, Christ and the church together.[52] He emphasizes the primary divine work in the liturgy. In theo-dramatic terms it is firstly God's performance, not the performance of the church. He cites Virgil Michel to affirm that worship is the "action of the Trinity in the Church. The Church in her liturgy partakes of the life of the divine society of the three persons in God."[53] In all this, Fagerberg emphasizes the central role of the Trinity in the liturgy. Joris Geldhof notes how this definition lacks any vocabulary

49. Fagerberg, "Liturgical Theology," 12; Fagerberg, "Liturgy, Signs, and Sacraments," 455; Fagerberg, *Liturgical Mysticism*, 12.

50. Fagerberg, "Liturgical Theology," 9.

51. *Catechism of the Catholic Church*, n1069.

52. *Catechism of the Catholic Church*, nn1136 and 795.

53. Fagerberg, "Liturgical Theology," 11, citing Virgil Michel, *The Liturgy of the Church* (New York: MacMillan, 1937), 40.

associated with social sciences and anthropology. Instead, Fagerberg "opts for weighty theological notions with a significant history and multilayered meanings."[54] It is the "Trinity's perichoresis"—the interpenetrating movement from person to person within the Godhead—that is extended toward the church "kenotically." The church is "invited" to join in this movement through "synergistic ascent" which leads to "deification."[55] What Fagerberg contributes with this definition is a shift away from anthropocentric definitions of worship that emphasize liturgy as a primarily human activity toward a theocentric emphasis primarily upon the Trinity. What is missing is an emphasis upon the mediatorial role of Christ within the synergistic ascent, the *through* Jesus. More specifically, the hypostatic union of the divine and human natures is lost altogether. As a result, the definition fails to be applicable to Jesus the worshiper. Specifically, Jesus' humanity is missing in this definition. There is a distinction between the divinity of Christ, as it is included in the "Trinity" in his definition, and human performance of liturgical acts. The word "our," in particular, suggests a distinction between that which is taking place in the Trinity and that which Christians do. This distinction has been overcome in the incarnation, and the hypostatic union is the location where the two are united. Fagerberg's definition falls short at this point.

Instead, this book proposes a theocentric definition of worship that considers the human and divine natures of Jesus Christ, the performance of the Father and Spirit in acts of worship, and also how the church joins in this worship. This is a definition that takes seriously the *to, through*, and *with* nature of worship and applies to Jesus Christ in his divinity and his humanity at one and the same time. That is, it applies to his person. Furthermore, the church is invited to join in the performative nature of worship as an eternal attribute of the divine.

DEFINING "GLORY"

A key term in this book is "glory" and its cognate, "glorification," and so it is essential to clarify its use here. N-CP uses the term in reference to the Trinity. Mother Spirit is "co-worshipped and co-glorified with the Father

---

54. Geldhof, *Monotheism in Christian Liturgy*, 2.

55. Fagerberg, "Liturgical Theology," 12; Fagerberg, "Liturgy, Signs, and Sacraments," 455; Fagerberg, *Liturgical Mysticism*, 12.

and the Son"[56] and so its meaning is critical to this book. The English term "glory" is used to translate δόξα (*doxa*). Kittel notes that, in non-biblical use, δόξα has a basic meaning of "what one thinks," "opinion," or "the opinion others have of me."[57] In short, this refers to someone's reputation. As it was employed in the LXX the term came to take on a theological meaning. "The term always speaks of one thing. God's power is an expression of the 'divine nature,' and the honor ascribed to God by man is finally no other than an affirmation of this nature. The δόξα θεοῦ is the 'divine glory' which reveals the nature of God in creation and in His acts, which fill both heaven and earth."[58]

In Ezek 43:1–5 (LXX) δόξα θεοῦ (*doxa theou*) is much more than the reputation or opinion of the divine. It is dynamic and moving. It can be seen and heard, and it occupies space as it fills the temple. Paul follows the LXX usage in employing the term to refer to the divine nature. In 2 Cor 4, δόξα θεοῦ is seen in the face of Christ. So, already in Scripture, from Ezekiel to Paul, there is a progression from a general term describing a person's reputation to a specific one used in reference to God, and then to Christ as the image of God (2 Cor 4:4). In this way the term itself is an example of theological interpretation and the progression of meaning for a given term as a result. All of this is taking place *within* Scripture. Importantly, Kittel also notes how the New Testament authors progressed the use of the term by applying it to Christ in the same manner as it applied to God.[59] For example, Paul refers to Christ as the "Lord of glory" (1 Cor 2:7).

In a similar manner, the term is also applied to people and the church. For example, Paul speaks in Rom 8:30 of the predestined being justified and glorified. In 2 Cor 3:18 Christians grow from glory into glory, and this transformation comes through Mother Spirit. Significantly, Paul refers to men (specifically) as the "image and reflection of God" and women as the "reflection of man" in 1 Cor 11:7. It is no small matter that this passage is one of the "texts of terror" that has historically been used to subjugate women in the church and beyond. It is important, therefore, to join with feminist theologians and others in acknowledging that these texts "justify oppression, yet we are working for liberation."[60] As we at-

56. Pelikan and Hotchkiss, *Creeds and Confessions*, 1:163.
57. Kittel, *Theological Dictionary of the New Testament*, 2:233–34.
58. Kittel, *Theological Dictionary of the New Testament*, 2:246.
59. Kittel, *Theological Dictionary of the New Testament*, 2:248.
60. Slee, *Praying Like a Woman*, 36–37.

tempt here to demonstrate the evolving use of "glory" as a theological term in the New Testament and beyond, we seek to liberate it from this gendered application. What is important at this point is that the term has shifted from being one applied to God alone to one that is also applied to humans.

The evolution of the use of "glory" continued beyond the New Testament authors. Irenaeus famously stated that the glory of God is a human fully alive[61] but also that the glory of humans is God.[62] The reciprocity of this "glory," moving from God to humanity and back again, suggests that it is dynamic and given from one to another. Gregory of Nyssa describes this movement taking place within the Trinity.

> You observe the circular course traced by glory, always going through things that are like. The Son is glorified by the Spirit; again the Son has glory from the Father and the Only Begotten becomes the glory of the Spirit. For by what else will the Father be glorified save by the true glory of the Only Begotten? Again, in what else shall the Son be glorified, save in the greatness of the Spirit? And so again the argument goes round in a circle, glorifying the Son through the Spirit and the Father through the Son.[63]

This movement from one person of the Trinity to another describes the concept of *perichoresis*, the mutual indwelling of all three persons of the Trinity within the divine nature. Thus, we can suggest that the divine glory is God's self. This glory is given from Father to the Son in begetting him, to Mother Spirit as she proceeds forth from Father [and the Son], then on to creation which is born out of God's very nature. Importantly, Balthasar, in his comprehensive exposition of *The Glory of the Lord*, notes that the divine glory is hidden as well as seen. "Δόξα (*doxa*) signifies, not various realities, but one single reality in different aspects. This single reality is disclosed ... as the eternal trinitarian love that has come into the world."[64] It is eschatological but also "present proleptically in the lowliness and hiddenness."[65] Gregory of Nyssa similarly refers to the hiddenness of God's glory as "luminous darkness," a "seeing that consists in not

---

61. Irenaeus, "Against Heresies" 4.20.7.

62. Irenaeus, "Against Heresies" 3.20.2.

63. Gregory of Nyssa, "Against the Macedonians" (GNO III.1.108.33), cited in Meredith, *Gregory of Nyssa*, 42. Meredith's translation.

64. Balthasar, *Glory of the Lord*, 7:260.

65. Balthasar, *Glory of the Lord*, 7:260.

seeing," since it transcends all human knowledge and knowing.[66] Nicola Slee echoes Gregory's apophatic emphasis upon the darkness of God;

> For the darkness of God will lighten every sadness
> and the splendor of divine darkness will dazzle every eye
> And the fullness of divine glory will overshadow every longing
> and the secret of divine beauty will satisfy every desire.[67]

Glory, herein, describes all of God's acts toward and within creation; it is God's very self being revealed upon the stage of creation. It refers both to all that is seen, heard, and known of the divine, as well as that which is unseen, unheard, and unknown. It is given and received but, since God's nature is infinite and unbounded, it is not something that can be controlled or fully apprehended. The glory of God becomes the glory of humans through the Lord of glory and Mother Spirit. This "glorification" moves beyond what Kevin Vanhoozer suggests: "the communication of God's glory, the publication of God's excellence."[68] Vanhoozer's definition restricts "glorification" to the original meaning of "reputation." Instead, in following the evolution of the use of the term through the New Testament and beyond, glorification is much more than this. It is God giving and receiving God's self. Importantly, as Gregory of Nyssa has suggested above, the giving and receiving of the glory of God occurs in both an *ad intra* and *ad extra* way.

CONCLUSION

This chapter has introduced the problem being addressed in this book. Namely, anthropocentric definitions of worship fail fully to account for the divine and human natures in the person of Jesus Christ. Jesus is a worshiper. Jesus is fully human and fully divine, and the two natures are hypostatically united within his person. When Jesus worships, therefore, his divine nature is worshiping. Further, there are glimpses of the Father and Mother Spirit performing worship in Scripture as well. This suggests that worship is something that is of the essence of the divine nature, not just the offering of reverence or adoration from humans to the divine. Anthropocentric definitions of worship cannot account for the worship

---

66. Gregory of Nyssa, *Life of Moses*, 80–81.
67. Slee, *Praying Like a Woman*, 57.
68. Vanhoozer, *Faith Speaking Understanding*, 76.

that is taking place between the divine persons. As a result, there is a need for a thoroughly theocentric definition of worship.

The task of this book, then, is to offer a definition of worship (*liturgia Dei*) that incorporates the hypostatic union of the divine and human natures in Jesus Christ, the perichoretic relationship of the Trinity, and explores the implications of both of those doctrines for the church's ongoing worship. This will be achieved through an investigation of the worshiping Jesus Christ in the light of the church's confession that this one person is fully human and fully divine. Worship is eternally taking place between the divine persons of Father, Son, and Mother Spirit. A theocentric definition of worship is offered: the eternal glorification of God that extends from, and returns to, the eternal relations of Father, Son and Mother Spirit. The church joins in this worship *to, through,* and *with* Jesus Christ.

In outline, the research questions being addressed throughout this book are as follows. How is Jesus' performance of worship to be understood in the light of the church's confession that he is both fully divine and fully human? What is revealed about the relationship between the divine and human natures in the person of Jesus Christ when he performs worship? These questions will be addressed in chapter 3. What is revealed about intra-trinitarian relations when Jesus performs worship? This question will be addressed in chapter 4. How does humanity reflect (*imago Dei*) the God who worships (*liturgia Dei*)? This question will be addressed in chapter 5. In what ways does this investigation impact the church's performance of worship? This question will be addressed in chapter 6.

Prior to answering those questions, though, the task moves to outlining how these goals will be achieved. That is a question of method, or, in theo-dramatic terms, dramaturgy. Vanhoozer suggests that the role of the dramaturge is "to help those involved in the production, particularly the director, come to a better understanding of the play so that the performance will stay true to the playwright's intent."[69] So, this book now moves to outlining how the research questions will be addressed.

---

69. Vanhoozer, *Drama of Doctrine*, 251.

2

Mise-en-Scène

THE DRAMATIC ARTS HAVE been drawn upon in a variety of ways to aid theologians in their task of effectively describing the mystery of God's drama of salvation. From Paul's costumed-based exhortation to "put on the Lord Jesus Christ" (Rom 13:14) to the employment of the term *persona* to describe Father, Son, and Mother Spirit within trinitarian terminology, theatrical terms have provided a fruitful source of theological language. Jesus' worship is embodied in performance, and so this book will draw upon categories within theo-dramatic theology and performance theory to formulate a response to the problem being addressed. These categories have proven to be useful to several theologians in a variety of ways. Hans Urs von Balthasar drew upon the categories of drama at length in his *Theo-Drama* (*TD*).[1] Kevin Vanhoozer's *The Drama of Doctrine* outlined his "canonical-linguistic theology," wherein he utilized Balthasar's term "theo-drama" to present his methodology within a Protestant and Evangelical framework.[2] Similarly, the emerging discipline of Biblical Performance Criticism is also providing useful insights into the formation and interpretation of the biblical texts themselves.[3] Such approaches are drawing upon the dramatic arts and performance theory to engage new means of interpreting the Bible and constructing theology.[4]

1. Balthasar, *Theo-Dramatik*; English translation: Balthasar, *Theo-Drama*, trans. Harrison.
2. Vanhoozer, *Drama of Doctrine*.
3. See, for example, Rhoads and Dewey, "Performance Criticism."
4. Schechner, *Performance Theory*.

This book will draw upon the work of Balthasar's *TD*, Vanhoozer's *The Drama of Doctrine*, and the categories offered by performance theory in order to answer the research questions posed.

This theo-dramatic methodology is suited to this book since the research questions being asked focus upon the performance of worship by Jesus and the meaning that can be drawn from it. In outline, theology is expressed in terms drawn from the world of theatre and performance theory to emphasize the theo-dramatic nature of revelation. Scripture is interpreted using a theological hermeneutic where the creeds are the lens through which the text is read. Finally, the purpose of the task is aimed toward ongoing, fitting performances within the theo-drama by the church.

SCENES

Throughout this book, "scenes" will be used as illustrative material to demonstrate how the theoretical aspects have been observed or applied in practical settings. Some of these are drawn from my own life and experience. Others are observations taken from theatrical and musical productions. Still others are theo-dramatic retellings of biblical stories. They are each illustrative in nature and seek to demonstrate how this book has implications beyond its publication. The scenes are visually distinguished from the main body of the book; however, they are not to be considered supplementary material to the book, as an appendix might be. Rather, these are substantial demonstrations of the argument being contested at the points where they are given.

THE WORKING RELATIONSHIP OF BALTHASAR AND SPEYR

Theo-dramatic theology will provide the methodological framework for this book; however, before moving further into greater detail into what is meant by this, it is critical to note that Hans Urs von Balthasar's theology was formed in partnership with Adrienne von Speyr. A short excursus is needed here to summarize the effect of this on their combined work.

Balthasar devoted the text *Our Task* to their common work. The opening sentences of the introduction declare how close he understood their partnership to be.

This book has one chief aim: to prevent any attempt being made after my death to separate my work from that of Adrienne von Speyr. It will show that in no respect is this possible, as regards both theology and the developing Community [of St. John]. At the same time, it is worth saying that no one should expect this to be a biography of Adrienne or my own autobiography. It is concerned solely with our common work. During Adrienne's lifetime, there were repeated warnings that the work entrusted to us might later be endangered.[5]

Speyr was born into a Protestant family in Switzerland in 1902. She met Balthasar in 1940 at a time when she was actively seeking to convert to Catholicism. Speyr, a medical doctor, was baptized by Balthasar, a Jesuit priest, on All Saints Day in 1940, and he became her spiritual director and confessor.[6] Over the next twenty-seven years, until she died in 1967, they would work together, in both theology and ministry. Together they formed the Community of St. John, a secular institute for spiritual formation that they had hoped would receive official sanction by the church. Instead, Balthasar would need to leave the Jesuits to continue his work with Speyr. They each wrote prolifically, with Balthasar acting as amanuensis for many of Speyr's writings due to her failing eyesight and eventual blindness. He would later give credit to her influence upon him when he suggested that "on the whole I received far more from her, theologically, than she from me."[7]

Johann Roten has provided a thorough summary of where their theology intersects on topics such as their theologies of mission, history, and holiness.[8] Roten suggests that their "common work" was based upon their "common mission" and highlights how Balthasar's later works, in particular, rely almost exclusively upon Scripture and Speyr's writings.[9] Of particular importance to this book is the interdependence of their thought evident throughout *TD*, volume 5. In a prefatory note to that volume, Balthasar writes that he wants to "show the fundamental consonance between her views and mine on many of the eschatological topics discussed here."[10] In volume 5, more than any other in the trilogy, he writes in a style

5. Balthasar, *Our Task*, 1.
6. Sutton, *Heaven Opens* 2.
7. Balthasar, *First Glance at Adrienne Von Speyr*, 13.
8. Roten, "Two Halves," 76–77.
9. Roten, "Two Halves," 71, 76n31.
10. Balthasar, *TD*, 5:13.

that deliberately obscures his own voice to amplify hers. Citation after citation from Speyr is linked together with barely any context or comment from Balthasar. The reliance upon Speyr's work may seem excessive; however, Jennifer Martin suggests that this style of writing is utilized "in order to indicate their speaking in *una voce*."[11] That is, he is not over-citing Speyr at the expense of himself. Rather, he is seeking to demonstrate how they speak together with a common theology, mission, and voice.

An example of this is the section headed "The Absolute Quality of Prayer." There, citing a variety of Speyr's works, Balthasar states the following:

> When God stands before God we can say "that God shows honor to God" "in a reciprocal glorifying," "in an eternal, reciprocal worship." "Worship as we know it is a grace that comes from the triune worship. Nothing is more rooted in God than worship." "All worship has its primary basis in the other's otherness. Where there is mere oneness, worship is not possible. The Son does not worship the Father because the Father is like him; that would mean that the Son found himself worthy of worship and that he worshipped himself. Worship is a relation to a Thou, a relation so strong and pure that only the Thou is of any account. Thus worship does not rest on a need, but in the being (and the 'being-thus') of God for God and for creatures."[12]

The themes and content of this quote are central to this book and will be expounded in greater detail below. For now, it is given as an example of how lengthy sections of *TD* volume 5 are constructed from a string of direct quotations from Speyr's works with little to no commentary or interpretation from Balthasar in between. Of the more than one hundred and eighty words in the quote above only the first eight are Balthasar's own words. It is important to keep in mind, though, his stated intent cited above that there is a "fundamental consonance between her views and mine."[13] Balthasar cites Speyr not as someone with a different voice to his own, but rather to join his voice to hers and hers to his, to speak *una voce*.

Although Balthasar acknowledged the lasting impact that Speyr had on his theology and expressed the desire that their work would never be

---

11. Martin, *Hans Urs Von Balthasar*, 122.

12. Balthasar, *TD*, 5:96. In this quote Balthasar cites from multiple texts from Adrienne von Speyr. Respectively, these are *Kath. Briefe*, vol. 1, 319; *Philipper (Dient der Freude)*, 20; *Objektive Mystik*, 82; and *Welt des Gebetz* [*World of Prayer*], 56, 209.

13. Balthasar, *TD*, 5:13.

separated, there has been a wide variety of reactions to this claim. Some reject the suggestion that Speyr had any influence at all on Balthasar's theological development. Kevin Mongrain suggests that the impact "was deforming rather than constructive, derived rather than original ... [and] completely dispensable for theologically understanding him."[14] Paul Peterson expresses doubt based upon the contrast in their education.

> Balthasar had already completed his theological study, written various book[s] and engaged with much of modern theology, literature and philosophy before meeting her or seeing her conversion. It is difficult to imagine that she, as a new convert, without any significant theological or philosophical education, was to have an important influence upon his intellectual development.[15]

Others harshly dismiss her writings outright as *"pseudomystischen Humbug* [pseudo-mystical humbug]."[16]

On the other side of the spectrum are those who are more generous in their reception of Balthasar's claims. Rodney Howsare notes how the "unity of person and mission in Balthasar's Christology" is positively developed alongside his working relationship with Speyr. At the very least, he suggests, "she kept his theology from becoming merely intellectualistic and abstract."[17] Jennifer Martin similarly argues that Balthasar's claims of interdependence with Speyr "really ought to be trusted."[18] Howsare responds by suggesting that "it is Speyr—who had no formal training in theology—who served as Balthasar's most influential teacher, a flesh-and-blood tutor in matters of mystical theology, ecclesiology, and, most vitally, prayer."[19]

More specific and pointed is the suggestion that Speyr is "denied [her] rightful place in history . . . by the curious machinery of sexual politics and hierarchical tradition."[20] Peterson suggests that "Balthasar was attempting to introduce the *Renouveau Catholique* and the *Nouvelle Théologie*, as well as mystical figures into a context which was not

14. Mongrain, *Systematic Thought of Hans Urs Von Balthasar*, 11–12.
15. Peterson, *Early Hans Urs Von Balthasar*, 300.
16. Züfle, "Braucht Hans Urs von Balthasar eine Heiligsprechung?," 320, in Peterson, *Early Hans Urs Von Balthasar*, 299.
17. Howsare, *Balthasar*, 23.
18. Martin, *Hans Urs Von Balthasar*, 122.
19. Murphy, *Theology of Criticism*, 33.
20. Murphy, *Theology of Criticism*, 33.

welcoming to these new pieties and theologies. The authority structure did not accept his projects."[21] Peterson highlights that Balthasar's suggestion that his writings be read in concert with Speyr's was a specific point of conflict in this context.

Matthew Sutton notes that Speyr's writings are "beyond classification."[22] Her mystical experiences, translated into theological texts with the aid of Balthasar, cross multiple disciplines, and demand that existing structures either make way, deny entry, or more insidiously, simply ignore her. Her experiences, her style of writing, her lack of theological training, and here it is argued her gender, became a stumbling block to the accepted processes of the academy, for it is easier to reject the unfamiliar and strange than to change a rigidly formed opinion to make a way in for it.

A key example of authors ignoring her work is found in *The Cambridge Companion to Hans Urs von Balthasar*. In their introduction, editors David Moss and Edward T. Oakes cite Balthasar's claim from *Our Task* above: "[I want] to prevent any attempt being made after my death to separate my work from that of Adrienne von Speyr."[23] In doing so Moss and Oakes state that "one must come to terms with his insistence that his own theology is *directly* derived from hers."[24] Throughout the eighteen essays that comprise the book, though, only two authors engage with Speyr's theology beyond a brief citation.[25] Furthermore, part 4 of *The Companion* is devoted to "Contemporary Encounters." The first two of three chapters are entitled "Balthasar and Karl Barth"[26] and "Balthasar and Karl Rahner."[27] The third chapter, from editor Edward T. Oakes himself, is devoted to the future reception of Balthasar's theology. While there is no doubt that both Barth and Rahner had significant interactions with Balthasar, theirs in no way compares to the twenty-seven-year working relationship with Speyr. The omission of an essay dedicated to Balthasar and Speyr's working relationship is a stark editorial oversight,

21. Peterson, *Early Hans Urs Von Balthasar*, 299.
22. Sutton, *Heaven Opens*, 2.
23. Balthasar, *Our Task*, 1.
24. Oakes and Moss, *Cambridge Companion*, 5. Emphasis in original.
25. Rowan Williams, "Balthasar and the Trinity," in Oakes and Moss, *Cambridge Companion*, 37–50; Geoffrey Wainwright, "Eschatology," in Oakes and Moss, *Cambridge Companion*, 113–28.
26. John Webster, "Balthasar and Karl Barth," in Oakes and Moss, *Cambridge Companion*, 241–55.
27. Karen Kilby, "Balthasar and Karl Rahner," in Oakes and Moss, *Cambridge Companion*, 256–68.

specifically, since the editors had already noted Balthasar's desires in their introduction. There is little evidence that the editors have taken seriously their own claim that "one must come to terms with his insistence that [Balthasar's] theology is *directly* derived from hers."[28]

Despite the ongoing criticism of Balthasar's claims of interdependence, the fundamental reliance of Balthasar's thought upon Speyr's must not be ignored. Instead, this book will accept, and therefore take seriously, Balthasar's claim that Speyr's work should not be separated from his own. As a result, both Speyr and Balthasar will remain key interlocutors throughout this book. Most importantly for this book, Speyr and Balthasar emphasize that worship is eternally taking place within the Godhead, an argument central to this book.[29] Worship is eternally present in the Trinity and subsequently made available for creation to join in via the incarnation of the *Logos* and the ongoing work of Mother Spirit. This will be unpacked further below but, for now, it is enough to note this is a central theme in Speyr and Balthasar's combined work.

BALTHASAR'S THEO-DRAMA

Balthasar's choice to draw upon the dramatic arts for theological expression is an attempt to blur the lines between what is *said* about God's dealings with the world and what is *done* in response.

> The *good* which God does to us can only be experienced as the *truth* if we share in *performing* it (Jn 7:17; 8:31f.); we must "do the truth in love" (*aletheuein en agape* [Eph 4:15]) not only in order to perceive the truth of the good but, equally, in order to embody it increasingly in the world, thus leading the ambiguities of world theatre beyond themselves to a singleness of meaning that can come only from God.[30]

Balthasar seeks to emphasize the dramatic nature of God's dealings with the world. From creation through to the eschaton, all that God says and does, and all that humanity says and does in response, is a part of the dramatic revelation of God, the *theo-drama*. At the center of this theo-drama is the person of Jesus Christ, God's Word. Importantly, the Word is a person, the second person of the Trinity hypostatically united within

---

28. Oakes and Moss, *Cambridge Companion*, 5. Emphasis in original.
29. Speyr, *World of Prayer*, 28; Balthasar, *TD*, 5:96.
30. Balthasar, *TD*, 1:20. Emphasis in original.

a human being in the incarnation. The Word was with God in the beginning, created all things, and in the incarnation comes as God and reveals God through embodied performance upon the stage of creation. This performance reveals the creator of the theo-drama; "It tells us who the Author is by telling us what he has done."[31] What is revealed about God through the incarnation of the Word is a genuine, reliable, and true revelation of the nature of God.

Balthasar draws upon the contrast between "epic" and "lyric" theatre to contrast the distinction between the objective and subjective approaches to the theo-drama. The epic standpoint seeks to be objective, standing on the outside of the action looking in. The lyric standpoint seeks to be subjective; remaining within the action reporting out. In methodological terms, epic theology seeks to categorize and summarize God's acts in systematic ways that keeps the author at arm's length from those very acts. In contrast, lyric theology summarizes a spirituality that takes as its starting point the experience of those acts of God. Rather than dismissing each viewpoint, or creating an either/or scenario, Balthasar seeks to bring both together theo-dramatically. He focuses this bringing together upon the concept of a "witness," one who bears witness to the acts of God with their whole existence. An example of this is given in the lives of the apostles.

> The Apostles are witnesses of the Resurrection and of the whole life of Jesus that underlies it; the form of their objectivity coincides with the form of their witness. They are not uninvolved (or even "interested") reporters, but with their lives they vouch for the testimony they must give. Scripture, for its part, testifies to their giving of testimony. The two coincide entirely when Paul writes a letter and in it, testifies with his whole life to the truth of revelation, putting God's action at the center but including himself (who was taken over by this action, once for all, in Damascus); he pulls out all the stops of his existence in order to convince those to whom he is writing that they too are drawn into this action just as much as he is. Here it is irrelevant whether he's speaking more "lyrically" or more in "epic" terms, for in both respects, above all, he's speaking dramatically: he shows how the drama comes from God, via Christ, to him, and how he hands it on to the community, which is already involved in the action and must bring it into reality.[32]

---

31. Balthasar, *TD*, 2:11.
32. Balthasar, *TD*, 2:57.

Balthasar blurs the lines between "epic" and "lyric." It is not enough to stand on the outside looking in describing what is seen, indeed, it is impossible. Nor is it sufficient to rely upon an insider's account of their existential experience. It is not either-or; rather, theo-dramatic theology is both-and.

Furthermore, Scripture plays a role within the theo-drama.

> It does not stand at some observation post outside revelation. And insofar as it is part of a greater whole, it points beyond itself to its content, and its content is the *pneuma*, which is always more than the *gramma*, the letter; indeed, it contains the letter within it, a vessel that is too small ("the world itself could not contain the books that would be written"—Jn 21:25; cf. 20:30f.). The great unwritten acts of God and Jesus are also part of the drama of world salvation.[33]

In this sense, Scripture is a record of the theo-drama (*transcript*) and a guide for future performance within it (*script*). Furthermore, many of the texts, such as those recognized as sermons, were written to support ongoing performance of the theo-drama, not just as a record of its performance(s).

> The purpose of these remarks has been to refute the superficial idea that, in theo-drama, Scripture plays the part of a somehow uninvolved spectator and reporter who can survey the whole process and can "tell in advance who the murderer is." In all its aspects, scripture is something quite different; it is part of the drama itself, moving along with it.[34]

How this book understands the function of Scripture within the theo-drama will be developed below. For now, it is important to highlight Balthasar's view that Scripture is part of the theo-drama itself.

Balthasar divides the theo-drama into five acts. The first act is the "court of judgment" whereby God pronounces punishment for sin. The second act is where God sends his Son as "Advocate (witness) of the accused." The third act is where the resurrected Jesus introduces something completely different to the scene, "something that has no analogy." The fourth act is the sending of the Spirit to unite God's people with the Son so that they are "coheirs with him." Finally, the fifth act is the "visible manifestation of salvation."[35]

---

33. Balthasar, *TD*, 2:58–59.
34. Balthasar, *TD*, 2:112.
35. Balthasar, *TD*, 2:156.

Christ is center stage within theo-dramatic theology. While Christ appears as a performer on the stage, Balthasar emphasizes that it is Christ who is the "very condition that renders the play possible."[36] In Christ we observe true humanity and divinity; he reveals his true self as the incarnated God-Human, and does so dramatically. He does not play the role of another character; rather he performs the role of himself. He is who he is. That is to say, the fully human and fully divine natures are lived out authentically, genuinely, in theo-dramatic performance, to reveal his true identity. He is the Messiah (John 4:26), the Son of Man (e.g., Mark 10:45), and the one whom others confess to be the Son of God (e.g., John 11:27), which includes the Father as well ("This is my Son," Matt 3:17; 17:5; etc.). Thus, in Jesus Christ,

> We have, in the terms of real life, the truth of what is found on the stage, that is, the utter and total identification of the character as a result of his utter and total performance of his mission. Thus, in theo-drama, he is not only the main character but the model for all other actors and the one who gives them their own identity as characters.[37]

This book emphasizes that Jesus' acts of worship—his prayer, his worship, his giving and receiving of glory—are critical aspects of the revelation of who he is. It is insufficient to suggest that Jesus worships from his humanity while setting aside his divinity. He performs everything as the incarnated *Logos* and he is effective in all that he does because he is both human and divine.[38] This reveals something of both true humanity and true divinity. From the revelation of the true identity of Jesus Christ, the roles that he gives to those who follow him to perform are not separated from his own. Those who share in his mission are joined to his person by Mother Spirit and so "share in his function of revealing God."[39] The church lives out in ongoing theo-dramatic performance the life and character of the divine *Logos*. The church's worship is an ongoing performance of Jesus' worship, which is an incarnated performance of divine worship. It is the *liturgia Dei* lived out in the life of the church.

Finally, we return to the contrast between "epic" and "lyric" and Balthasar's effort to unite the two theo-dramatically. Specifically,

---

36. Balthasar, *TD*, 3:41.
37. Balthasar, *TD*, 3:201.
38. Balthasar, *TD*, 3:520.
39. Balthasar, *TD*, 3:258.

consideration needs to be given to God's place within the theo-drama. Balthasar poses the question as to "whether God is a spectator or a fellow actor." If just the former, then God remains distinct from creation, aloof, separated, and distant. If the latter, then the risks of pantheism and panentheism need to be avoided. In responding to this challenge, Balthasar suggests that God is "*above* the play in that he is not trapped in it but *in* it insofar as he is fully involved in it."[40] Furthermore, he emphasizes God's triune nature as it is revealed in the sending of the Son and Mother Spirit. While this act suggests that the Father remains "above the play," instead the sending of the Son and Mother Spirit reveals that the Father is also *in* it.[41] In all respects, "theo-drama . . . can only be trinitarian."[42]

VANHOOZER'S DRAMA OF DOCTRINE

In conjunction with Balthasar and Speyr, this book also draws upon Kevin J. Vanhoozer's *The Drama of Doctrine* and its follow up text, *Faith Speaking Understanding*, as another example of engaging the categories of theatre, drama, and performance to address the research problem under investigation.[43] Vanhoozer invokes a methodology that draws upon the dramatic metaphors to connect doctrine to church practices involving more than just "theoretical beholding." An audience in a theatre is more than a group of "passive observers" and so theology, framed in dramatic terms, "insists on audience participation."[44] Furthermore, Vanhoozer suggests that "thinking of doctrine in dramatic rather than theoretical terms provides a wonderfully engaging and integrative model for understanding what it means to follow—with all our mind, heart, soul and strength—the way, the truth, and the life embodied and enacted in Jesus Christ."[45]

The approach adopted in Vanhoozer's methodology is intimately connected to the life of the church. In line with the historical theological ordering of *lex orandi, lex credendi*, or more fully *ut legem credenda lex statuat supplicandi*, doctrines emerge from core liturgical practices of the

---

40. Balthasar, *TD*, 3:514.
41. Balthasar, *TD*, 3:514.
42. Balthasar, *TD*, 5:57.
43. Vanhoozer, *Drama of Doctrine*; Vanhoozer, *Faith Speaking Understanding*.
44. Vanhoozer, *Drama of Doctrine*, 16.
45. Vanhoozer, *Drama of Doctrine*, 16.

church.⁴⁶ The longer form of this theological saying emphasizes that the beliefs of the church are established (*statuat*) by the prayer of the church. A simple example of this is Thomas's confession to the risen Jesus, "My Lord and my God!" (John 20:28). Thomas's worship-filled confession at his encounter with Jesus challenges the long-held monotheistic belief of Judaism. It was not that Thomas was contradicting this belief, but it was essential for the early church to wrestle with the problem of the identity of Jesus Christ. While they did so, the church continued to join with Thomas in worshiping Jesus as God, even while they wrestled with the question of Jesus' identity. There are significant questions regarding the nature of the early church's worship here. Namely, "did the early Christians worship Jesus because they believed he was divine? Or did they believe he was divine because they worshipped him?"⁴⁷ As important as these questions are, resolving them does not impact upon the historical ordering of the relationship between the liturgical practices and the articulated beliefs of the church that is important to this book. The beliefs of the church were established by the prayer of the church.

Embedded within Vanhoozer's method is a norming norm, something beyond the interpretative community that directs, informs, corrects, and validates the understanding that is sought in faith.

> Through its proclamation, narration, and teaching, the canon reveals who God is, informs us of what God has done, and directs our response. As such, the canon has theo-dramatic authority: it is the supreme norm for identifying the divine *dramatis personae* and for understanding the theo-dramatic action. The canonical Scriptures have *primal* and *final* authority because just these communicative acts and practices are the chosen media the Spirit uses to inform us of Christ, and to form Christ in us so that we may speak and act in our own situations to the glory of God.⁴⁸

Referring to Scripture as "communicative acts and practices" demonstrates a recognition that the Scriptures do not sit outside of the unfolding theo-drama but rather they perform a function within it. As Ben Quash also notes (citing Balthasar), "Scripture does not 'stand at some observation post outside.' It is inside the drama as well. Its content points beyond itself

---

46. Vanhoozer, *Drama of Doctrine*, 13.

47. Joshua Cockayne and Gideon Salter, "Liturgical Anthropology," *TheoLogica* 6.1 (2021) 90.

48. Vanhoozer, *Drama of Doctrine*, 237.

to the Spirit who makes the drama present and alive in each new scene. Scripture mirrors the drama which is manifested by the Spirit, and Scripture 'can only be understood in reference to' this drama."[49] Both Quash and Vanhoozer are in agreement with Balthasar on this point. The role of scripture within the theo-drama will be expanded in more detail below.

Vanhoozer seeks to preserve a commitment to the Protestant principle of *sola scriptura* while retaining a necessary emphasis upon communal interpretation. He recognizes that theology is not just a matter of rightly articulating a set of abstract ideas. Rather, it involves reflection on theo-dramatic performance, specifically, the divine performance of God. Furthermore, reflection upon past performances is always with a view toward present and future performances. Theological reflection upon past performances, and here the performance of worship by Jesus is at the forefront, leads to further performances both as imitation and improvisation.[50]

Vanhoozer provides an entry point into expressing theology in theo-dramatic terms. In drawing upon Balthasar's framework here Vanhoozer argues that theology should be understood as the task of articulating "God in communicative action."[51] The focal point of God in communicative action is in the person of Jesus Christ, the *Logos*. In theo-dramatic perspective, Jesus Christ is not just the Word, but rather the incarnated Word-*Act*. In this respect, Balthasar's emphasis upon "perception," "utterance," and "act" above is echoed in Vanhoozer's emphasis upon God in communicative action in the person of Jesus Christ. In Jesus, the church perceives, hears, and observes God's self-revealing, communicative action through the incarnation of the *Logos* upon the stage of creation. Theo-drama is a useful metaphor in this respect since it "refers to the real and historical drama of God in interaction with humanity on the world stage, and 'drama' on its own carries connotations of plot, interaction of characters, conflict, and resolution."[52] Furthermore, when the creeds regarding the divine and human natures of Christ and the relationship between the persons of the Trinity become the lens through which the theological task is viewed it can be seen that "God's self-communicative action in history via the acts of Father, Son, and Spirit—*dramatically represents* the immanent Trinity, God's own inner life."[53] Jesus' acts of

49. Quash, *Theology and the Drama of History*, 45, citing Balthasar, *TD*, 2:58.
50. Samuel Wells, foreword to Lugt, *Living Theodrama*, 10.
51. Vanhoozer, *Drama of Doctrine*, 62.
52. Lugt and Hart, *Theatrical Theology*, 8.
53. Lugt and Hart, *Theatrical Theology*, 15. Emphasis in original.

worship are part of God's self-communicative and performative action in history and, as such, dramatically reveal God's inner life. This action as it is seen in the worship of Jesus is central to the *liturgia Dei* and will be the focus of chapters 3 and 4.

PERFORMANCE THEORY

Performance theory emerged in the late twentieth century as a means of studying and describing human behavior. Richard Schechner suggests that performance is "everywhere in life, from ordinary gestures to macrodramas."[54] Max Hermann defines performance as "a game in which everyone, actors and spectators, participates."[55] As it applies to theatre and drama, Schechner defines key terms in the following way; "the drama is what the writer writes; the script is the interior map of a particular production; the theater is the specific set of gestures performed by the performers in any given performance; the performance is the whole event, including audience and performers (technicians, too, anyone who is there)."[56]

It is significant that Schechner distinguishes a "performance" from a simple "gathering" of people "by the presence . . . of a theatrical event guided by a script—something planned, designed for presentation, following a prescribed order."[57] This will prove helpful in the consideration of Jesus Christ as a worshiper. This understanding of performance and its relationship to a script informs, both directly and indirectly, important theological terms such as theo-drama, Scripture, worshipers, and congregation.

A helpful example of the theological use of performance theory is Damaskinos Olkinuora's analysis of Andrew of Crete's *Canon of Lazarus*. He suggests that "some Orthodox theologians are particularly cautious of the term 'performance' in a liturgical context." Instead, he notes that the "communality of ritual is emphasized" over and against the descriptors of "performers" or "audience."[58] In contrast, though, Olkinuora demonstrates that performance theory, and the broader use of the term "performance," is useful for the analysis of an aesthetic text such as the *Canon*

---

54. Schechner, *Performance Theory*, loc. 5240.
55. Cited in Fischer-Lichte, Mosse, and Arjomand, *Routledge Introduction to Theatre and Performance Studies*, 18.
56. Schechner, *Performance Theory*, loc. 1536.
57. Schechner, *Performance Theory*, loc. 1549.
58. Olkinuora, "Performance Theory," 8.

of Lazarus and Byzantine liturgy more broadly. According to Olkinuora, this usefulness is not just anthropological but theological.[59]

By examining hymnography as a form of aesthetic communication, Olkinuora demonstrates that hymns are created with the intent that they be performed, and reperformed, by soloists, choirs, and the gathered congregation. Schechner describes such performance and reperformance as "restored behavior" or "twice-behaved behavior."[60] The hymnwriter creates the script of the hymn with the primary intention that it be sung upon a particular stage: the liturgical setting of Christian worship. The act of composition is the *first* behavior and is, in itself, a kind of performance, although it does lie outside Schechner's definition since at this stage there is no audience other than the *intended* audience in the mind of the creator. Secondly, the choir, soloist, and/or congregation perform the hymn in its congregational and liturgical setting. This is the second, or twice-behaved, performance. In theatrical terms, it is likened to rehearsals. Each rehearsal is a preparation for the public staging but is also a performance in its own right. Similarly, public staging is a performance but is also a rehearsal for future public staging. The behaviors are repeated, refined, re-scened, restaged, and re-enacted. They are restored, or twice-behaved. In the case of theatre, this refers to the scenes of the play. Returning to the hymn, it is sung again and again, alongside other elements of the liturgy, and each performance, though *like* the previous one, is new every time. On each occasion, the performer, the audience, the stage, the occasion, the setting, is different, even if only in a minor way. The combination of each variation of time, space, and audience makes each performance unique.

Olkinuora also refers to the sermon as a "rewritten Bible," a term borrowed from Bogdan Bucur.[61] Both Olkinuora and Bucur acknowledge that the term "rewritten Bible" was first applied in Jewish scholarship by Geza Vermes in 1961, but they suggest that it also applies to their analyses of Byzantine hymns and homilies.[62] The intention of a "rewritten Bible," according to Bucur, is not to superimpose a new reading of the text upon the original but rather to put into liturgical practice that which is observed in the Gospel narratives, "not to abolish the Law or the prophets (Matt

59. Olkinuora, "Performance Theory," 10.

60. Schechner, *Performance Theory*, loc. 5195; Schechner, *Between Theater and Anthropology*, 35–116.

61. Olkinuora, "John Damascene's Homily," 34; Bucur, "Rewritten Bible?"

62. Bucur, "Rewritten Bible?," 109.

5:17), but to reinterpret them in light of the fundamental assumption that Christ is the *telos* of the Law (Rom 10:4)."[63] Applied to hymns and homilies Bucur encourages "hymnographic exegesis" that recognizes "hymns first and foremost as Christological proclamation in the context of the charismatic-prophetic community's liturgical self-actualization."[64] That is, in Schechner's terms, they are dramatic texts that are written by the preacher or hymnographer according to an interior script (it will be argued below that the script is the *Logos*), performed in a theatre (the church) with a specific set of gestures in a performance that includes audience (congregation) and performers (cantors, choir, preacher, clergy, congregation, etc.). Each reading of the text functions as a twice-behaved performance of Scripture. So, Scripture readings, sermons, and other liturgical elements are never fixed because they are always performed by different performers (or performers who are different), to a different audience (or an audience who is different), upon a different stage (or upon a stage that is different). Every performance is new. Every moment of worship is new.

An example of this view of performativity is evident in John Damascene's homily on the withered fig tree. The preacher at one point performs as Christ, assuming his character and words as his own, using the rhetorical device of *ethopoeia*.

> Behold, I myself, the Son and Inheritor, am present! Stand in awe of my Sonship! Reverence my worthiness of the fatherly nature! "I am in the Father and He is in me": even if I came to you, for the sake of my vineyard; even if I descended on earth, I dwell in the bosom of my Father. Hand over to me the fruit of the vineyard![65]

In this example, the preacher performs in the character of Christ, using the words of Christ's original performance as it is transcribed in Scripture. Christ functions as the writer, the text of Scripture as the script, the preacher as the *performer*, and the listening congregation as the *audience*. Of course, the preacher is *not* Christ but John Damascene performing as Christ. Yet at the same time, he is *not-not* Christ. These are Christ's words being heard anew by the audience as if Christ really speaks to them in that moment. This is comparable to the prayer that is prayed "in

---

63. Bucur, "Rewritten Bible?," 110.
64. Bucur, "Rewritten Bible?," 112.
65. John Damascene, *In ficum arefactam* (Kotter 1988), 107:4, 34–38, in Olkinuora, "John Damascene's Homily," 40. Olkinuora's translation.

Christ's name." Such prayer is offered by one who is *not* Christ, yet as it is offered in faith in the name of Christ, it is *not-not* Christ who prays. Schechner notes that all effective performances share this "not-not" and "not" quality. He describes this as a "paradigm of liminality."[66] Barry Stephenson describes that liminality as the "space where normal 'rules' do not apply."[67] Effective prayer is offered in Christ who mediates on behalf of the one(s) who pray, and he mediates between human and divine, creature and creator. Mediation functions in the liminal space of prayer.

Furthermore, in the specific category of "transformation performances," the performance itself enacts a change upon the audience or at least some part of the audience.[68] At a wedding, the groom and bride *become* husband and wife. Family and friends become witnesses to the transformation and take on a performative role of contributing to the marriage's success. New relationships are created, and existing ones are changed into a different kind, all through the transformation performance of the wedding ceremony.

Stephenson suggests,

> Liturgy has a digital quality to it; you either do it or not. Unlike, say, sports, where one can play a good game one week and perform poorly the next, liturgy either happens, or not; on, or off. If you overthrow the receiver, playing poorly, you are still playing the game. But if the host is not consecrated in a communion service; if the wedding ring is forgotten at home; if the young man refuses to read from the Torah at Bar Mitzvah—in such cases we do not have a poorly executed rite, but rather we have no rite at all.[69]

This book, and specifically the definition of worship that it offers using the term *liturgia Dei*, suggests otherwise. Liturgy has, as its foundation, the nature of God. As such, it is being performed eternally. As the church joins in the performance of liturgy it does so in the liminal space of mediation, *to*, *through*, and *with* Christ. While performers make every effort to effectively complete the actions prescribed in the liturgical texts there remains a liminal quality to any such performance. If this liminal quality were removed, it would remain an act of magic by which the actors manipulate and control the divine through the correct performance of the rite. Instead, the liturgy

---

66. Schechner, *Between Theater and Anthropology*, 123.
67. Stephenson, "Ritual as Action, Performance, and Practice," 39.
68. Schechner, *Between Theater and Anthropology*, 127–33.
69. Stephenson, "Ritual as Action, Performance, and Practice," 48.

relies upon the mystery of the God who is wholly other but invites humans to join in theo-dramatic performance in Christ, by Mother Spirit. The right performance is Christ's, not the church's. Epic and lyric are united within his performance. Since liturgy relies upon Christ's right performance it is *always* effective, even if, for example, the host is not consecrated in strict accordance with the prescribed rite, the wedding ring is missing from the ceremony, or the priest mistakenly misspeaks the prescribed words.[70] To a certain extent the doctrine of *ex opere operato* is an attempt to point in this direction. It is not, however, that the work works itself and is therefore effective, but rather that the divine performer (Christ) performs the performance, and therefore it is perfectly performed.

Sermons, such as the one in Olkinuora's analysis above, seek to do something to and for the congregation, to bring about some sort of change. In performing as Christ, John Damascene seeks for the congregation to be transformed into the likeness of Christ. This likeness is embodied in the congregation and brings about further performances of Christ as they in turn perform his likeness in their lives in the theatre of the world. In this way, "via the oral medium of preaching, scripture is both transformed and transformative as it is given voice by the preacher and as it encounters and is encountered by the listener."[71] Wendy Mayer categorizes this type of preaching as "logo-therapy, a form of rational speech-based correction aimed at the soul-sickness of the audience. It works by bringing about in the soul of the hearer the proper order and balance in the human person. This is achieved by having the correct *gnōmē* or mindset in the rational part of the soul."[72]

Olkinuora provides a further example of this in Gregory Palamas's *Homily 53, on the Entrance of the Theotokos into the Temple*, where he asks the audience to participate in the creation of the sermon:

> So come forward, divine audience, holy spectators, the choir [that sings] in harmony with the heavenly Spirit, and co-operate with me in the homily and come together, so that you would not only listen and give your attention, but help me with your sincere prayer, so that also the Logos of the Father would co-operate with me in my writing in the honor of his Mother. May

---

70. Liam Butterworth presents a view that contrasts with what is suggested in this book, reporting on a pastor who performed thousands of baptisms incorrectly. Butterworth, "Pastor Resigns."

71. Mayer, "Homiletic Audience," 12.

72. Mayer, "Homiletic Audience," 14.

it not fail completely, but may He rather help me to finish it harmonically for the [good of the] God-loving audience.[73]

For Olkinuora, hymns and homilies become a "performance of an act where *creators, personae, performers,* and *audience* contribute."[74] There is a complex interconnectedness between the four roles. They are all performed by all the people, even those outside of the gathered church.

> The overlapping of all the four roles of performance creates such a complex network of linkage between us (the believers), God, His saints, and even our enemies, that a strict division between a "performative audience" and "narrative audience" does not seem tenable to me. Each church-goer has his or her own associations provoked by the hymn; each believer reflects on it according to his own background, and a strict theoretical division would do injustice to Byzantine hymnography's multiform semiotics.[75]

Drawing upon these four categories, this book demonstrates that behind and within the visible performance of the church's liturgy there is a God who exists as all four of these roles—*creator, personae, performer,* and *audience*. As such, any performance of liturgy in the church is a joining with the eternal performance of the *liturgia Dei*. Chapter 5 below will demonstrate how these four roles are observable in the divine persons of the Trinity in the theo-drama. Balthasar notes that, in the theo-drama, "God cannot stand at the periphery of the play; he must be at its center."[76] Thus, it is God who is the *creator* with the three persons of the Trinity the primary *personae*, yet the church is invited and enabled to join in, in Christ by Mother Spirit. Together, *performers* and *audience* intersect and interact, interchanging roles, receiving and giving in the action. There is a "fluid transition between auditorium and stage."[77] The *audience* is invested in the success of the drama with *performers* seeking for the *audience* to become an active part of the action; to join with them in the performance. The eternal worship of the divine (*liturgia Dei*), the worship of Jesus, and the worship performed in churches are all part of the same theo-drama. A theo-drama that commences with, reveals, points toward,

---

73. Homily 53, subsection 5, cited in Olkinuora, "Performance Theory," 15.
74. Olkinuora, "Performance Theory," 14.
75. Olkinuora, "Performance Theory," 26.
76. Balthasar, *TD*, 3:505.
77. Balthasar, *TD*, 5:534.

and finally concludes in the God who is simultaneously above and in it: *creator, personae, performer,* and *audience.*

IMPROVISATION

Improvisation is important within the world of theatre. Far from making things up on the spot, there are rules of engagement and different approaches that make it engaging for both the actors and the audience alike. Anthony Frost and Ralph Yarrow suggest that "improvisation is fundamental to all drama."[78] In every performance there are subtle changes made by actors in response to different stimuli that occur in the moment. An audience member laughs, a prop falls to the floor, or another actor forgets a line. In those moments the actor responds differently to the previous performance, and the one that follows, contributing to the uniqueness of each performance. In this way, improvisation aids in the creation of meaning in a performance. Indeed, the meaning is created in the performance, in that moment.[79] Improvisation is about the creation of meaning.[80] Vanhoozer, in adopting drama as a "handmaiden" for theology, suggests that improvisation is an appropriate way of understanding the process of judging how to speak and act in new situations.[81] Improvisors react and speak in ways that are fitting for the given situation. Thus, they need to be able to read and understand the context, be mindful of the past as well as the present, and engage wisely with good "canon sense." That is, they have an awareness of the plot of the theo-drama and their place within it at any given moment. With an intimate knowledge of the *creator* of the theo-drama, and confidence in Mother Spirit to lead, direct, and equip them with the right words to say (Matt 10:19), they perform the theo-drama in the given context, accepting the offer that is given to them from wherever and whomever it comes.[82]

The dramatic term "offer" is important at this point. In improvisation, an offer is a gift from one actor (or even the audience) to another to carry on the story into a new context, that creates new meaning. There are three categorical responses that are possible in response to an offer:

78. Frost and Yarrow, *Improvisation*, 1.
79. Frost and Yarrow, *Improvisation*, 165.
80. Frost and Yarrow, *Improvisation*, 179.
81. Vanhoozer, "One Rule," 84, 88.
82. Vanhoozer, "One Rule," 88–89.

to say "no," "yes," or "yes, and." To say "no" to an offer is to immediately block the offer being made.

> A: "It's another beautiful day outside."
> B: "No it's not."

Blocking inhibits the development of the story and the performance, and therefore the creation of meaning ceases. This example is an active form of blocking: to stop the performance from progressing in the direction that the one making the offer (A) intended.

To say "yes" is to accept the offer that is made but to do nothing with it. As a result, a "yes" on its own, or a "yes, but," are passive forms of blocking. They accept the offer to develop the story, or the performance, but fail to enact it. So, the creation of meaning ceases.[83]

> A: "It's another beautiful day outside."
> B: "Yes, it is."

The third, and preferred option, is to say "yes, and." In this way, the actor accepts the offer given and develops the story, and therefore creates new meaning(s) in that moment. In accepting the offer and developing it, a more interesting story is created with each actor contributing to the creation of meaning in that moment.[84]

> A: "It's another beautiful day outside."
> B: "Yes, and it's an amazing opportunity to explore the forest outside town."

An example of each of these categories can be found in the story of the Canaanite woman in Matt 15:21–28 and its synoptic parallel of the Syrophoenician woman in Mark 7:24–30. The pericope commences with Jesus traveling to the region of Tyre and Sidon. A woman from the region approaches him crying out to him to heal her daughter. Despite being Canaanite, she uses the same language as other Jewish *personae*, "Lord, Son of David, have mercy on me" (15:21; see also 9:27; 20:30–31; 17:15). The language she uses to call upon Jesus is liturgical in nature.[85] Anita Monro highlights how the woman, in her many differences, breaks societal, theological, and liturgical conventions for the sake of her daughter. "Theologically addressing a Jew in his own terms, a lone woman yet prior

---

83. Frost and Yarrow, *Improvisation*, 110–11.
84. Leep, *Theatrical Improvisation*, 15.
85. Wainwright, *Towards a Feminist Critical Reading*, 228.

resident of the region and of the claimed homeland of the addressee, shouting in the public arena but in the careful words of a Jewish religious devotee, the character of the Canaanite woman breaks the power of binary opposition as dichotomy."[86]

In theo-dramatic terms, and specifically as an example of improvised performance, the woman's differences disrupt the expected arc of the story. She addresses Jesus *out* of character. Initially, Jesus' response is to block her, bluntly and abruptly refusing her offer by ignoring her; his silence functions as a "no." The woman persists by trying an alternative offer through the disciples. They, following Jesus' lead, reject her offer as well. However, she continues and so the disciples report this to Jesus. It is unclear from the text who Jesus responds to, the woman or the disciples; however, the result is the same. He acknowledges the offer, but the response seeks to return the story back to the direction it was heading previously; "I was sent only to the lost sheep of Israel" (15:24). This functions as a "yes"; the offer is acknowledged but no new meaning is created. Once more the woman persists, this time embodying her request by kneeling before Jesus. She cries out in desperation, "Lord, help me!" (15:25). A second time Jesus responds and this time it functions as a "yes, but" as he seeks to return the story, and his journey, back to its original direction; "It is not right to take the children's bread and toss it to the dogs" (15:26). Rather than stop her attempts to move the story in a direction that will see her daughter healed, the woman does something quite remarkable. She rejects Jesus' attempt to block her by transforming his insult into an *offer*, thereby redirecting the story, and the *personae* within it, toward the direction that *she* seeks. Jesus' reference to "dogs," which can only be interpreted as an insult toward her, is accepted and dramatically reframed by the woman; "Even the dogs eat the crumbs that fall from their master's table" (15:27). New meaning is created in this moment.

The performative elements of the story are also significant to note. The woman's body position—kneeling before Jesus—embodies the position of a scavenging dog (she begs Jesus in Mark's account—7:26) and so she embodies the insult in front of Jesus, forcing him to see her humanity despite her begging, dog-like posture.[87] In doing so, her verbal acceptance of Jesus' insult is matched by her humble physical stance. In turning what was intended as a block into an offer, she causes Jesus to change

---

86. Monro, "Alterity and the Canaanite Woman," 41.
87. Rhoads, "Jesus and the Syrophoenician Woman," 351.

his mind.[88] In changing his mind, he changes his response. The "no" is transformed into a "yes, and," and her daughter is healed.

What is remarkable in this pericope is how the roles of *personae* within the narrative shift the direction of the narrative and, in doing so, reveal something of the story and its *creator*. In a dramatic twist, it is the Canaanite woman making the offer, and Jesus initially blocking and then accepting, which leads the story forward in a new direction. The woman in this story represents outsiders in many intersecting ways (she is a Canaanite/gentile woman, she is indigenous to the area but living in occupied land, she speaks out of turn, she cries out in public to a Jewish man, and so on). Jesus, on the other hand, represents insiders on this occasion (a Jewish male among a group of Jewish males, a representative of the occupying class, one with the right to speak in public but who refuses to do so, and so on). What is remarkable is that both the woman and Jesus act *out* of character, she as a Canaanite woman, and he out of step with the way the character of Christ has been depicted so far in Matthew's Gospel. She breaks all accepted conventions assigned to her by society and, in so doing, places herself in the center of the story, in a place where Jesus is forced to see her. The choice for Jesus shifts from whether he will acknowledge her or not, to whether he will respond to her request or not. In terms of improvisation, will he respond again with a "no," a "yes, but" or a "yes, and"?

A comparison can be made with this story and the interaction between Jesus and the centurion (Matt 8:4–13). The centurion, also addressing Jesus as "Lord," asks Jesus to heal his servant. Jesus offers to come and heal him, but it is the centurion who tells Jesus that his presence isn't necessary, only that he give an order and it will happen. Like the Canaanite woman Jesus praises the faith of the gentile centurion, and there is also a parallel with those who are expected to be a part of the kingdom. As with the Canaanite woman's daughter, the centurion's servant is healed from a distance and is made well "in that hour" (8:13). What is contrasting, though, is Jesus' willingness to go with the centurion but not the Canaanite woman, the difference being that the centurion was one who held a position of power over Jesus and so *could* have forced Jesus to come with him, but he does not. Whereas Jesus is the one in the position of power over the woman and so he refuses to go with her, despite her desperate pleas toward him.

Further, a wider connection can be made between the woman and the scope of Jesus' mission. When the disciples are sent out in Matt 10

---

88. Rhoads, "Jesus and the Syrophoenician Woman," 352.

their mission is restricted to the "lost sheep of Israel" (10:6). The same phrase is used by Jesus regarding the scope of his own mission in his encounter with the Canaanite woman; "I was sent *only* to the lost sheep of Israel" (15:24; emphasis added). This mother, an indigenous gentile woman, changes Jesus' mind not only regarding her daughter but regarding his broader mission as well. When Jesus sends the disciples out to make disciples following his resurrection, no longer are they only to go to the lost sheep of Israel but to "all the nations" (28:19). Significantly, he does so from a mountain in "Galilee" (28:16) which Matthew, citing Isaiah, had previously identified as "Galilee of the Gentiles" (4:15).

Monro highlights how the pericope of the Canaanite woman has an enormous impact upon Matthew's depiction of the *personae* of Christ. Indeed, it is the woman who "performs the role of Christ herself."[89] Much like the prophet Nathan's dramatic confrontation of King David in which he tells a story that has the effect of holding up a mirror to David, exposing David to himself (2 Sam 12), the Canaanite woman embodies the character of Christ to Jesus. As a result, Jesus is confronted by the need to reassess his own self-identity, namely, his own views of who he is as a first-century Jewish male, who his intended *audience* is, transforming it from exclusively the house of Israel to including even a Canaanite woman, and from there the entire world, and then his ongoing role as the Christ within the theo-drama. The persistent response of the woman expands Jesus' vision of the scope of his mission. Her improvised and embodied acceptance of Jesus' insult turns the narrative in a new direction. New meaning is created at that moment and, as a result, Jesus' mind and missional direction are changed.

In summary, the pericope of the Canaanite woman demonstrates how improvisation functions within the theo-drama. *Personae* interrelate in ways that take the arc of the story forward into new contexts and incorporate new characters. Offers are made and then either accepted or blocked. The story is developed, and *personae* are transformed as they perform, but improvised performances rely upon the *personae* to know and embrace the story, even as it moves in unexpected directions.

---

89. Monro, "Alterity and the Canaanite Woman," 41.

PARTICIPATION?

In turning to consider how performance theory relates to theology, consideration must be given to the term "participation." Is this an appropriate term to describe what is taking place? Christina Gschwandtner suggests that the question of the relationship between human and divine, invisible and visible, heavenly and earthly, was a crucial question for patristic authors. They were confident that "the two realms relate to each other, participate in each other, and depend on each other."[90] The word "participation" has commonly been used to aid in articulating this relationship. For example, Kathryn Tanner suggests,

> Participating in God is just what it means to be a creature. God is (for example) life itself, life through itself, while everything else receives its life from God, without simply being it, in and of itself. Any creature therefore has life in some degree or fashion and can lose it. Expressing much the same thing in a Thomistic way, one could say God does not participate in being but *is* it: to be *God* just is to *be*; in God there is no distinction between what God is (essence) and the fact that God is (existence).[91]

Here Tanner argues that the ground of being is God's very self. The distinction between creature and God is centered upon this theological reality. God *is* and, therefore, does not "participate" in something that God *is not*. For creatures, on the other hand, they exist only within God and so, in contrast, "participate" in God. In this way, Tanner retains a qualitative distinction between God and creature. "To participate in being is, by definition, not to be it, if participation means participating in what one is not; and therefore, with participation arises a distinction between essence and existence, the very constitution of created things."[92]

This distinction between creator and creature is theologically significant, and participation language remains useful to a point. The point where it ceases to be useful, though, is when considering the incarnation. The incarnation, by creedal definition, is the union of creator and creature in the person of Jesus Christ; fully human and fully divine hypostatically united in the one person. As a result, participation, and specifically Tanner's definition of it above, breaks down at this point. Christ is not

---

90. Gschwandtner, "Mimesis or Metamorphosis?," 10.
91. Tanner, "Image of the Invisible," 130.
92. Tanner, "Image of the Invisible," 130.

"participating in what [he] is not."[93] Rather, he is performing who he is. This is important for this book as it relates to Jesus' acts of worship. The term "participation" fails in that it suggests that Christ is becoming something different, something other than fully divine and fully human.

In an attempt to overcome this problem, the term "performance" is helpful. Instead of participating in worship, Jesus is *performing* worship. He does so *as* the incarnate *Logos*, acting out his *personae*. He is living out who he is—the *Logos*, the second person of the Trinity hypostatically united to the humanity of Jesus of Nazareth. He performs *in character*, revealing his divine and human natures in all their fullness. It is the context where Jesus performs worship that is new, and therefore his performance is improvised. However, as he improvises, he reveals the character which is already his; even if, as has been shown above, his improvised performances lead to changes in his own attitude and direction. He is not participating in something he has never been or known before. He is performing something eternal.

This brings us back to the focus of this book, namely, to offer a definition of worship that incorporates the hypostatic union of the divine and human natures in Jesus Christ and the perichoretic relationship of the Trinity, and considers the implications of both of those doctrines for the church's ongoing worship. The categories offered by performance theory, and utilized by Olkinuora, will aid in this task and help to move beyond the sticking point that "participation" presents. It is suggested here that God exists as *creator, personae, performer,* and *audience*. This is true for both the immanent and the economic Trinity. Furthermore, Richard Schechner's analysis of performers in the theatre is helpful; "each function is meaningful only in terms of the whole set."[94] In this regard the "whole" is God, and so in liturgy, it is God who performs for the audience of God. The *personae* are the three persons of the Trinity, each one creating and performing the theo-drama. The complex interrelationships between *creator, personae, performer,* and *audience* are grounded in God's nature. Furthermore, when Christ performs worship, he does so in both an intra-trinitarian and extra-trinitarian sense, as one person who is fully human and fully divine.

Richard Schechner offers an analysis of the Elema tribe of New Guinea, focusing upon their dance of the Hevefe. He discusses how the

---

93. Tanner, "Image of the Invisible," 131.
94. Schechner, *Performance Theory,* loc. 416.

performance of the dance relates to the belief structure of the tribe. After months of preparation, and a month-long rite involving dancing with the Hevefe mask on each night, the performance culminates with the shooting of the masks, marking the death of the spirit that possesses the wearer throughout the performance. Schechner notes that "their performances are not impersonations, but possessions and exchanges; the spirit and the man interpenetrate each other without either losing his identity."[95] This example points toward what is happening in the person of Jesus Christ. When Jesus performs worship there is a union of the divine and human natures within his person without the loss of the fullness of either divinity or humanity. The *liturgia Dei* is on full display in one vivid performance.

Christ's own life provides, not just the pattern of a new human way of life for our imitation, but the cause of that pattern in us, by our assimilation within it. The second person of the Trinity not only shows forth the true image in human form by becoming incarnate but makes us like that image by uniting human nature thereby with the very incomprehensibility of the divine life. It is by being bound to the incomprehensible in and through Christ—and thereby gaining a new identity in him apart from anything one is oneself—that one comes to live a boundlessly full and good life.[96]

When Jesus worships he performs such acts out of the fullness of his divinity and the fullness of his humanity. Each prayer, each sermon, each act of glorification of the divine is an act that is fully human and fully divine. He acts *in character* and so does not "participate" in something that is new. Rather, he "performs" out of his eternal divine nature upon the stage of creation.

SCENE: PETER SELLARS'S *ST. MATTHEW'S PASSION*

In 2010 and 2013 the Berlin Philharmoniker, under the musical direction of Sir Simon Rattle, presented a semi-dramatically staged performance of Johann Sebastian Bach's *St. Matthew's Passion BWV 244*. In contrast to the traditional performance of the work where singers and musicians perform upon a stage to an audience, here, the vocalists dramatically embodied the roles that they were performing while moving in and about the *audience*. This included the main *personae* of Matthew the evangelist, Jesus, Pilate, Mary Magdalene, Peter, Judas, and so on, as

---

95. Schechner, *Performance Theory*, loc. 855–56.
96. Tanner, "Image of the Invisible," 135.

well as the chorus. There are times when the characters interact with the musicians to enact the connectedness of everyone on stage. The performance took advantage of the venue's minimized architectural distinction between stage and *audience* with *performers* fluidly moving in and out of the audience. Some of the seating for the audience is immediately next to musicians and vocalists alike, reducing and even eliminating the imaginary "fourth wall."

Traditionally the work is performed with vocalists and musicians on a stage, or within a designated central section of a church/cathedral, where a distinction exists between *performers* and *audience*. In Sellars's staging, the vocalists and musicians enact the role of the characters they are performing, attempting to embody the story beyond a traditional musical performance of the work. The exception within the performance, though, is the vocalist portraying Jesus. Where other characters move about, up and down the stage, in and out of the audience, Jesus stands in one position singing his assigned lines much like in a traditional performance. In addition, while the lines of Jesus are sung by this stationary actor, the embodiment of those words is portrayed by Matthew the Evangelist as he performs his account of the passion narrative. As the vocalist sings about the flogging of Jesus, for example, it is Matthew whose hands are bound above his head and the agony of being scourged by the Roman soldiers is enacted by him. This portrayal demonstrates the *not-not* quality of this performance. The vocalist performing as Jesus is *not* Jesus but is also *not-not* Jesus in that moment. But, in an additional layer of dramatic development, the vocalist performing the evangelist is not Matthew, but Jesus, or more specifically Matthew performing his account of the gospel of Jesus. As such, he is also *not-not* Jesus.

This captures, in dramatic form, what occurs in the liturgy of *APBA* each week, specifically as it relates to the reading of the Gospel. There, the reading is announced with "The Gospel of our Lord Jesus Christ according to [Matthew chapter . . . verse . . .]."[97] In the liturgy, the reader embodies Matthew's account of Jesus' words. Like the actors and vocalists above, the reader is *not* Jesus, but in embodying his words they are also *not-not* Jesus.

The director takes theatrical license when portraying the flogging of Jesus, as the musical score has a female vocalist, in this setting an alto

---

97. *APBA*, 122.

portraying Mary Magdalene, lyrically depicting the scene before her. The combined effect of the subjective portrayal of Jesus by the two vocalists depicting Jesus and Matthew-as-Jesus, alongside the objective portrayal of what is happening by Mary Magdalene, draws the audience into the moment. Mary's words in this moment are a prayer asking God to intervene. Through this performance, the audience is drawn in to pray the prayer with Mary as well.

Erbarm es Gott!	Have mercy, God!
Hier steht der Heiland angebunden.	Here stands the Savior bound.
O Geißelung, o Schläg, o Wunden!	O scourging, o blows, o wounds!
Ihr Henker, haltet ein!	You executioners, stop!
Erweichet euch	Are you not softened by
Der Seelen Schmerz,	The soul's agony,
Der Anblick solches Jammers nicht?	The sight of such misery?
Ach ja! ihr habt ein Herz,	Ah yes! You have a heart
Das muß der Martersäule gleich	That must be like the post used for torture,
Und noch viel härter sein.	
Erbarmt euch, haltet ein!	An even far harder still.
	Have mercy, stop!

THE ROLE OF SCRIPTURE WITHIN THE THEO-DRAMA

In this book the canon will be read as Scripture, with biblical readings supporting this interpretive approach. For the sake of clarity and emphasis, the terms "Bible" and "Scripture" will be applied differently throughout this book. "Bible" will refer to the text as it is approached as a library of texts, each of which was written by historical authors to historical audiences within historical contexts. "Scripture," on the other hand, will refer to the text as it is approached in the context of faith, that is, as an authoritative text believed by the church to be given by God for revelatory and communicative effect.[98] Such a confessional view of the text is seen in, for example, article 6 of the Anglican *Articles of Religion*:

---

98. For a dramatic account of this distinction using the terms "academic Bible" and "scriptural Bible," see Legaspi, *Death of Scripture*, v–vii.

"Holy Scripture containeth all things necessary to salvation."[99] As such to read the text in liturgy, and to expound upon it in sermons, "is not to operate on a dead text but rather to be caught up into a communicative movement of triune life."[100] In theo-dramatic terms, though, there are a number of models for understanding the role of Scripture as it relates to the theo-drama, namely, script, transcript, prescript, and prop. Each of these will be considered below with the Lord's Prayer used as an example.

Scripture as Script

Vanhoozer has suggested that Scripture should be considered the "script" within the theo-drama, "for those who wish to understand, and participate in, the divine drama."[101] The text, in this model, functions as the content of the theo-drama in each context. Performance is tightly connected to the text and improvisation is limited. That is to say, the authority of Scripture outweighs the cultural context as the performance focuses upon repeating past performances, with only minor local variation. In this view, Scripture has an objective role within the theo-drama as *performers* memorize their lines in rehearsal but ultimately put the text aside on the day of the performance.

The Lord's Prayer in this understanding of Scripture was given by Jesus as a scripted prayer for use by his disciples. The prayer is therefore repeated as it has been received in accordance with the text, from the disciples who passed it on. Improvisation of the prayer is limited to translating the text into local languages. Where the Lord's Prayer is recited verbatim in the liturgy, for example, it functions as a script in this way.[102]

Scripture as Transcript/Prescript

In contrast, Lugt has suggested that Scripture is both a "transcript" of past performances of and a "prescript" of performances to come. He suggests that God has a "plan for the whole play, partly hidden and partly revealed,

---

99. *APBA*, 826.
100. Vanhoozer, "Triune Discourse," 78.
101. Vanhoozer, *Drama of Doctrine*, 149.
102. See, for example, *APBA*, 141. The *APBA* uses the translation provided by the English Language Liturgical Consultation (ELLC). See English Language Liturgical Consultation, "Lord's Prayer."

which is accomplished by inspiring the actors to write a transcript of improvised performances that in turn serves as a prescript for further performance, a unique body of writing Christians call Scripture."[103] The role of improvisation, here, is elevated as current contexts are given more prominent consideration. As Christians live as members of the body of Christ upon the stage of the world, they improvise the text into their cultural setting. Performance is more loosely connected to the text on the page and improvisation is more freely employed. Scripture is read as a record (transcript) of only part of the ongoing theo-drama which then provides an authoritative guide (prescript) for improvisation. Such improvisation is not only assumed but expected as a continuation of the same theo-dramatic plotline, drawing upon Scripture as a prescription of what constitutes faithful performance. In this model, the text operates objectively concerning the theo-drama itself, but subjectively concerning the *performers*. They must immerse themselves in the text and be guided by the director, Mother Spirit, to know the plot that has come before and how to perform it into their own context. The *performer* improvises upon what is known from the text, but the text does not have a performative role of its own. It remains a text that sits *outside* of the theo-drama.

In this model the Lord's Prayer is an example of how disciples should pray. Where the prayer invites the disciples to pray for "daily bread," and the context includes people living in poverty, the *performer* may improvise on the theme of provision, asking God to intervene in the situation to meet the needs of God's people. While the prayer may still be prayed verbatim, it is not essential that this be done. The prayer is *prescripted* but not *scripted*. Mother Spirit sanctifies the imagination of the present company of performers, revealing through the *transcript* what has come before in the theo-drama and, by this, providing the *prescript* for fitting performance in the present.[104]

Scripture as Neither Script Nor Transcript/Prescript

In contrast, Rafael Rodríguez states that "performances of the Jesus tradition neither depended upon *script* nor left behind *transcript*."[105] Instead, he argues against reading the text in such a binary way. His argument is

103. Lugt, *Living Theodrama*, 84.
104. Vanhoozer, *Drama of Doctrine*, 189.
105. Rodríguez, *Structuring Early Christian Memory*, 4. Emphasis in original.

focused primarily on the milieux within which the texts themselves were produced. That is, in the time surrounding the production of the written texts the Jesus tradition was transmitted via oral performances shared among the followers of Christ. Such oral performances instilled the plot of the theo-drama into the collective memory of the earliest Christians, and it is out of this collective memory that the written texts were produced, shared, and then performed. Indeed the production of the written texts were performances in their own right.[106] As has been shown above, "performances are not simply repetitions of what has gone before, but are semi-autonomous events in themselves, events that are apprehended in reference to the tradition."[107] Each reading of the text, each sermon, each liturgical event, is something new. The result of this approach, according to Rodríguez, renegotiates the authoritative role the texts play within the church since they could be considered one performance of the theo-drama among many.

The textual performance of the theo-drama within the predominantly oral culture of the time of their production means that the authoritative force of a written text was less pronounced than in the literary cultures that emerged later. The written texts served the purpose of aiding ongoing oral performances, that is they were a *script*, but a script that functioned to aid improvisation. As such, the relationship between the written text and the performance is more dynamic than either of the models above. The text served performances and performances then determined what was contained in the text.

Nevertheless, over time, oral culture was replaced by literary culture, leading to formal canonization of what constitutes "the text." The result of this is that performances of the text have become something else altogether. The text has become an authoritative account of authoritative performances of the theo-drama; that is, they are a *transcript*. It is from these transcripts that the church seeks to determine what faithful performances are today. In this way, the *transcript* then functions as a *prescript* for improvisation. Rodríguez's insight into the production of the texts themselves within the oral culture of the early church is important. However, the texts, as they are received now, exist within a primarily literary culture. So, how they are used by the church now, particularly in worship, is the primary focus of this book.

---

106. Rodríguez, *Structuring Early Christian Memory*, 4, 97.
107. Rodríguez, *Structuring Early Christian Memory*, 98.

Scripture as Prop, Logos as Script

A third alternative should be considered that shifts the authoritative emphasis away from the text and onto the person of Jesus Christ. In this model, the *script* of the theo-drama is not the text but the *Logos*. As the embodied performance of the divine, the Word-Act, Jesus embodies the perfect performance of both divinity and humanity, the two natures of his one person, in a single, united performance. The church is united to Christ by Mother Spirit, becoming the "body of Christ" (e.g., 1 Cor 12:27). Through this union with Christ the church continues the performance of the divine nature upon the stage of the world. In preferencing *Logos* as *script*, improvisation of the theo-drama has a more important role to play. All Christians "put on Christ" (Rom 13:14) and live out his character within their cultural contexts. They improvise their performances as they live in union with Christ by Mother Spirit. Such embodied performances rely upon the direction of Mother Spirit who has ultimate authority over how the theo-drama is performed and ensures that the divine purposes within it are fulfilled.

This third alternative raises an important question of the relationship between the text and the *Logos*, if *Logos* is the *script*. In this model, the text of Scripture sits under the authority of Mother Spirit, functioning as an aid to her as director of the theo-drama. As such, it is neither *script* nor *transcript/prescript* in the sense offered in the first two models as it is subjectively part of the theo-dramatic action. Rather, Scripture functions as a *prop* used by the *Logos* and Mother Spirit in both performance and direction. There are times when Scripture is a "part of the drama itself,"[108] subjectively functioning *inside* the theo-drama, a "dramatic instrument in the hand of the saving and judging Word."[109] Here it is a *prop* in the hands of the *Logos*, akin to the skull of Yorick in the hand of Shakespeare's *Hamlet*, Wilson the volleyball in the film *Castaway*, or The One Ring in J. R. R. Tolkien's *Lord of the Rings*. In this model, it is impossible to imagine the prop disconnected from the drama itself. To do so would be to dismantle the narrative itself. Similarly, Scripture is a prop in the hands of the *Logos* and Mother Spirit, used by them from within the theo-drama to direct the church's performance and direction of the theo-drama. It is impossible to imagine Scripture as *prop* disconnected from the theo-drama, or alternatively functioning strictly in the

---

108. Balthasar, *TD*, 2:112.
109. Balthasar, *TD*, 2:115.

roles of *script*, *transcript*, or *prescript*. This model subordinates the role of Scripture to a function that is subservient to the authoritative, divine persons of *Logos* and Mother Spirit. This approach avoids the danger of elevating Scripture to a function beyond its intent, to the point where it is anthropomorphized and given authority in its own right. For example, to declare, "The Scriptures say ..." regarding a point of theology gives the text a voice of its own, a voice that risks being given an authority that is different, equal, or even more superior to, the authority of Mother Spirit as theo-dramatic director. Instead, this model subordinates the role of Scripture in a manner that is consistent with N-CP's limited reference to the Scriptures. In the creed, the single reference to "in accordance with the Scriptures" serves to confirm how the resurrection fulfills prophetic references to this central event within the text.[110] That is, the Scriptures serve to confirm the central plot theme revealed in the risen Jesus Christ.

Turning once again to the Lord's Prayer, with *Logos* as the script, the emphasis is placed upon to whom the prayer belongs to, namely *the Lord*. As the church puts on Jesus, it performs his prayer into its current cultural context. Believers pray the prayer of Jesus, as Jesus, into their cultural setting. In reality, the church is *not* Jesus but since it prays his words, and he is the *script*, the church is also *not-not* Jesus. Jesus continues to pray his prayer through the church as the church joins with him, by Mother Spirit, in praying his prayer.

There are limitations to each of the models of Scripture as script or transcript/prescript. There is a danger that either one of these models limits Scripture's role to one *outside* the theo-drama, an "uninvolved spectator and reporter."[111] Alternatively, there is a limitation to the model of Scripture as prop, namely, that it limits Scripture's role to one *inside* the theo-drama. This could eliminate altogether the authoritative function that Scripture has within the church. As a result, a both/and approach is necessary to recognize the objective and subjective functions that Scripture has within the church.

To acknowledge the objective and subjective functions of Scripture within the theo-drama, alongside the roles proposed above, the models of Scripture as both transcript/prescript and prop will ensure it remains integral to the story itself, while retaining its authoritative function within the church, albeit an authority that sits *under* that of the *Logos*

---

110. N-CP, 163.
111. Balthasar, *TD*, 2:112.

and Mother Spirit. It is a prop that is, for example, central to worship wherever Christians gather and is used by Mother Spirit as she directs the theo-dramatic action. The proclamation of Scripture as it is spoken, written, expounded upon, sung, and used in a variety of other forms in worship has a central performative role, yet this role sits under the authority of *Logos* and Mother Spirit. So, with *Logos* functioning as the *script* in the theo-drama, and Scripture functioning as transcript/prescript and prop in the hands of Mother Spirit, attention turns to understanding fitting performance by the church.

FITTING PERFORMANCE

Theo-dramatic theology seeks to give "direction as to how individuals and the church can participate fittingly in the drama of redemption."[112] It has as its goal right performance within the ongoing theo-drama. Performance, as a term, can have a pejorative meaning, especially with regard to liturgy, but it has "nothing to do with hypocrisy, insincerity, or the prideful attempt to achieve salvation by works, and everything to do with active participation in the theo-drama."[113] Performance in theo-dramatic perspective is to "put on the Lord Jesus Christ" (Rom 13:14), an act that involves moving beyond reciting the lines on a page to embodying the life of Christ upon the stage of the world, in union with him, by Mother Spirit. Paul Fiddes has suggested,

> To participate rightly means to join in the missions of the Son and Spirit with our whole being: minds, hearts, and hands. The only way to know and experience the triune God is to participate in those personal relationships that characterize God's being as communion. When we pray to God as Father, for example, we find our address fitting into a movement like that of speech between a son and father.[114]

This is central to the concept of the *liturgia Dei* being put forth in this book. When we pray, we do so *to*, *through*, and *with* Jesus, addressing God as Father, by and in Mother Spirit. Jesus, the Great High Priest, joins us in our prayers so that we might join him in his. Christian prayer is rightly addressed to "Our Father" (Matt 6:9) only because it is performed

---

112. Vanhoozer, *Drama of Doctrine*, 78.
113. Lugt and Hart, *Theatrical Theology*, 8.
114. Fiddes, *Participating in God*, 37.

"in Christ" who prayed to God as "My Father" (e.g., Matt 26:39). Paul Blowers suggests that, for early church theologians, "divine revelation was inexhaustible in its nuances and horizons of meaning, or more to the point, that the divine Logos was always moving and acting through the 'texts' of Scripture and creation to open up new vision."[115] Christian worship, as a performance of the *liturgia Dei*, seeks to be an improvised but fitting performance in the one theo-drama. This worship is given in response to the moving and acting of Christ and, as it occurs, is performed into new and emerging contexts on every occasion.

CONCLUSION

Drawing together what has been outlined above, the theo-dramatic methodology employed in this book is summarized as follows. First, theology is expressed in terms drawn from the world of theatre and performance theory to emphasize the theo-dramatic nature of revelation. Second, within the one ongoing theo-drama, the script is the *Logos* with Mother Spirit performing the role of director. Scripture functions as both a transcript/prescript and a prop. That is, a divine transcript of past performances and a prescript for future performances, and a prop in the hands of the *Logos* that is integral to authentic performance. Interpretation of Scripture will begin with the creeds and move to the text in performance. Given the scriptural basis for the creeds the method functions as a *return* to the text, a text received as canon within the church and used in an ongoing, liturgical manner within the church. Finally, the purpose of the task is aimed toward ongoing, fitting performances within the theo-drama by the church. This methodology is suited to this book since the research questions being addressed call for a method that starts with the confession of the church and moves to the text of Scripture.

---

115. Blowers, *Drama of the Divine Economy*, 377.

3

The Protagonist—Jesus Christ (Part One)

THE FOCUS TURNS NOW to the worshiping Jesus as central protagonist in the theo-drama. But who was and is Jesus? Or more specifically, who does the church confess Jesus to be and how does, or should, that confession relate to the understanding of what is happening when Jesus worships? While it is important to answer this question before proceeding to critical observations regarding the nature of his worship, and therefore worship in general, this book will work with an answer to the question of the identity of Jesus drawn from the ecumenical creeds. It will not seek to establish the identity of Jesus in a new or unique way. As an exercise in liturgical theology, this approach is drawn from liturgy itself wherein Christians gather and, as an ongoing function of their gathered worship, recite creeds together. As people who have already confessed faith in Jesus, and individually and communally accepted as their own the creedal confession that he is fully human and fully divine, they gather to make that confession together again. From the stance of this communal confession, they approach the text as Scripture. The text is read, expounded, and prayed, in worship, *to*, *through*, and *with* Christ. The way the church prays determines the way the church believes, and this also determines the methodology of this book.

The well-known phrase *lex orandi, lex credendi* is foundational to this approach. This phrase is the shorter form of the longer, original format articulated by Prosper of Aquitaine in the fifth century, *ut legem credenda lex statuat supplicandi.*[1] The importance of this longer format lies with the inclusion of the verb *statuat*. Both forms of the phrase seek to emphasize the fundamental link between the church's worship and prayer and the church's articulated confession. The longer form, though, makes clear that the rule of belief is secondary to the rule of prayer.[2] The way the church prays comes before the way the church expresses its belief. Pelikan, following this order, translates *lex orandi, lex credendi* as "the rule of prayer establishes the rule of faith."[3] Elsewhere, Pelikan suggests the following:

> The place that brought together the scholarly exegesis of Scripture and the devotional recitation of Scripture, the technical dogmatic vocabulary of the erudite and the inarticulate affirmation of the simple, was the "melody of theology" in the liturgy. Every doctrine of the orthodox creed was a liturgical doctrine, for the creed was recited in the liturgy. Nevertheless, some doctrines were liturgical in a special sense, because they had been articulated more satisfactorily in worship than in dogma.[4]

The pattern of prayer establishing belief can be observed in the way baptismal formulas were foundational to the wording of the creeds.[5] Similarly, the ongoing theological task of articulating the meaning of what is taking place in the celebration of the Lord's Supper follows on from, and does not precede, the church's ongoing performance of this sacrament. As Fagerberg notes, "liturgical theology receives the *lex orandi* of the Church; it does not create the *lex orandi* of our own desires."[6] Yet it is important to note that the *lex orandi* is not established by a prayer book, a liturgical rite, or historic cultic practice. Rather it is established by Jesus himself who taught his disciples how to pray. More specifically, the establishment of the church's prayer flows from Christ's own performance of prayer (Luke 11:1–4). The church's prayer addressed to "Our Father" occurs *to, through,* and *with* Christ's prayer to "My Father" (e.g., Matt 26:39).

Pelikan notes that "every day for twenty centuries [the church's] petitions have been prayed in more or less the same form by individual

---

1. Pelikan, *Credo*, 166.
2. Kavanagh, *On Liturgical Theology*, 69–70.
3. Pelikan, *Credo*, 99–100.
4. Pelikan, *Spirit of Eastern Christendom*, 137.
5. See, for example, "Creeds of Hippolytus" in Pelikan and Hotchkiss, *Creeds and Confessions*, 1:60–61. Pelikan, *Credo*, 377–83.
6. Fagerberg, "Liturgical Theology," 14–15.

Christians and worshipping congregations everywhere, regardless of confessional affiliation."[7] Before the church's rule of belief was established by the church's rule of prayer, the church's rule of prayer was established by Christ. Therefore, the rule of prayer, which establishes the rule of belief, is itself established by the Christ who prays. The significance of this is highlighted by Pelikan who notes that no creed or confession can authentically "claim to trace the ancestry of its very words directly back to the person of Jesus Christ. . . . But prayer can and does."[8] The relationship between the prayer of the church, being founded upon the prayer of Jesus, and the belief of the church is a cyclical one. This cycle will be important later in this book. Yet, for now, what is important is that the cycle commences with the praying Jesus. This highlights the importance of the questions that this book is seeking to address. In this chapter the following research questions will be addressed: What is revealed about the relationship between the divine and human natures in the person of Jesus Christ when he performs worship? How is his performance of worship to be understood in the light of the church's confession that he is both fully divine and fully human? Articulating what is happening when Christ worships, in the light of the church's creedal confessions that this Christ is fully human and fully divine, will lead to a fuller understanding of what is happening when the church worships.

To address the research questions, this book will use the creeds as an authoritative *regula fidei*, a lens through which Scripture is read, interpreted, and performed. This will highlight the hypostatic union of the divine and human natures within the person of Christ and the relationship of this concept to trinitarian theology active in the worshiping Jesus. The theological concept of *perichoresis*, as first a Christological and second a trinitarian term, will be explored as a means of holding together the paradox of the relationships that exist between the two natures of Christ as well as the three persons of the Trinity. Furthermore, consideration will be given to the unity of work within the person of Christ, taking seriously the suggestion that "what God is toward us in Jesus Christ on earth and in time, he is antecedently and eternally in himself, and that everything that God is in himself he is toward us in Jesus Christ."[9] This is the concept of *communicatio idiomatum*. The hypostatic union, *perichoresis*, and *communicatio idiomatum* will then be tested concerning the

7. Pelikan, *Credo*, 162.
8. Pelikan, *Credo*, 158.
9. Torrance, *Incarnation*, 258.

worship of Jesus Christ. These concepts will provide the foundation for a theological interpretation of selected Scriptures that depict Christ as a worshiper to address the research questions at hand. This chapter will move now to outlining a summary of the creedal confessions regarding Christ by briefly mapping the path that was followed from early confessions regarding Christ to the formal creeds. Following this attention will turn to the worshiping Christ.

TRACING THE THREADS FROM PAUL'S "THE GOSPEL" TO THE CREEDS

A key phrase in Paul's letters is "the gospel." This was, for Paul, a shorthand way of referencing the content of his message, a summary of his teaching. On different occasions, he highlights different aspects of his teaching, depending upon the issue he is addressing. Despite these differences, though, the unifying thread of all of them is the person of Jesus Christ.

In Rom 1, Paul highlights Jesus' genealogical connection to David, emphasizing his humanity combined with the confessional belief that he is "Son of God" because he has been raised from the dead (1:4). In 1 Cor 15, Paul focuses upon the resurrection. It is of "first importance" that Jesus died, was buried, rose again, and appeared to his first followers, including to Paul himself. Using this phrase "the gospel," Paul reminds his audience of what they already know and have come to accept as their own. This is the content of the faith that they have objectively confessed and subjectively believed. Such a reminder aids Paul's various purposes of encouraging, correcting, teaching, warning, and disciplining the recipients.

In 2 Cor 4, Paul highlights that Jesus is the image of God (4:4), the Lord (4:5), and that the glory of God shines through him (4:6). Further, as is common throughout Paul's writing and ministry, the resurrection features prominently (4:13-15). In Galatians, Paul emphasizes the singularity of "the gospel" (1:9), and that its source is Jesus himself (1:12). Further, he suggests that "the gospel" is to be proclaimed to the gentiles and this was declared through Abraham (3:8).

In Philippians Paul emphasizes how "the gospel" needs to be lived out by those who believe it; "live your life in a manner worthy of the gospel of Christ" (1:27). Paul's understanding of "the gospel" was not just about knowing what to believe but also how that belief would impact upon the way the church would live in the world. "Paul wanted the communities he addressed not merely to *believe* the gospel but to *become* the gospel, and in doing so participate in the very life and mission of God."[10] In theo-dramatic terms, the gospel of Jesus was to impact upon the performance of the *personae* as they act out the *script* of the *Logos* upon the stage of the world. Further, the ongoing performance of "the gospel" from these recipients before other *audiences* functions as an invitation to the *audience* to join in the drama as well. *Audiences* become *performers* as they believe and join the performance of "the gospel."

There are key themes about Jesus that are incorporated in Paul's summative phrase "the gospel": the centrality of Jesus, his death and resurrection, and the humanity and divinity of Jesus Christ. These central themes are recalled by Paul's repeated use of "the gospel." These themes, and other central doctrines of Christian belief, form part of a discernible thread woven through the writings of the early church and on to the creeds. This thread highlights the centrality of the Christian confession that Jesus is fully human and fully divine, and this is the lens through which the Scriptures are to be read.

FROM "THE GOSPEL" TO *REGULAE FIDEI*

In much the same way that Paul used the phrase "the gospel" as a shorthand description of the essential content of the faith, *regulae fidei* (rules of faith) also functioned as lenses through which the Scriptures were faithfully interpreted and benchmarks by which to assess that interpretation. Authors have used a variety of terms including "the gospel,"[11] "rule of truth,"[12] and "ecclesiastical rule."[13] What these terms share in common is their function as a "theological catchphrase,"[14] referring to the content of Christian belief and teaching providing a "metanarrative so individual passages [could] be approached in the light of the whole story."[15] Cyril of Jerusalem combined pastoral concern for persons with the overarching need for broad doctrinal consistency when he suggests that, "in order

10. Gorman, *Becoming the Gospel*, 2. Emphasis in original.
11. Clement of Rome, "First Epistle of Clement," 42.
12. Novation, "Treatise Concerning the Trinity," 9.
13. Clement of Alexandria, "Stromata, or Miscellanies" 4.15. Origen similarly uses "ecclesiastical and apostolical tradition"; Origen, "*De Principiis*," Preface.2.
14. Bokedal, "Rule of Faith," 234.
15. Ferguson, *Rule of Faith*, loc. 1024.

that the soul may not perish from ignorance, we comprise the whole doctrine of the Faith in a few lines."[16] These summary forms of the content of the faith, Paul Blowers suggests, "served the primitive Christian hope of articulating and authenticating a world-encompassing story or metanarrative of creation, incarnation, redemption, and consummation."[17] To restate this in theo-dramatic terms, this metanarrative is not just *told* as a story but *performed* as a drama. Here, for simplicity, the term *regula/ regulae fidei* will be used as a summary term for these and other similar terms that functioned in this way.

While the contents of *regulae fidei* were not fixed, nevertheless there remains an observable thread continuing from Paul's "the gospel" on to these *regulae fidei* and then to the ecumenical creeds. In *Against Heresies*, Irenaeus's *regula fidei* functions in an apologetic manner.[18] It provides the necessary order and connection for a faithful interpretation of Scripture. The connectedness of all of Scripture, from creation through to consummation, forms a part of his apology for the faith. Unlike his opponents who contended that Christ revealed a God who was different from the creator, Irenaeus strongly emphasized the oneness of the God of creation with the God revealed in Christ. He insists that the Son is not a different God but rather makes the one, true God visible. "In Jesus Christ there is no new God but a new manifestation of the only God."[19] Christ becomes incarnate for the salvation of all people and, in a similar way to Paul, the life, death, resurrection, ascension and future return of Christ are central themes within Irenaeus's *regula fidei*.[20] Irenaeus suggests that the church is united in its belief in these central doctrines of the Christian faith. The church "believes these points [of doctrine] just as if she had one soul, and one and the same heart, and she proclaims them, and teaches them, and hands them down with perfect harmony, as if she possessed one mouth."[21] Irenaeus is here writing in an apologetic and hyperbolic manner, in order simultaneously to refute false teaching and encourage those believers who share belief in this confession. As such, his claim to church unity on matters of confession and proclamation needs to be read in the light of his apologetic intent. Nevertheless, three points are worth highlighting here.

16. Cyril of Jerusalem, *Catechetical Lectures*, V.12, cited in Heide, *Timeless Truth*, 61.
17. Blowers, "Regula Fidei and the Narrative Character," 202.
18. Irenaeus, "Against Heresies" 1.10.1.
19. Osborn, *Irenaeus of Lyons*, 112.
20. Irenaeus, "Against Heresies" 1.10.1.
21. Irenaeus, "Against Heresies" 1.10.2.

First, there is a broad consistency of content between Paul's "the gospel" and Irenaeus's *regula fidei*, herein described as a common thread. Irenaeus suggests that the rule has been received from "the apostles."[22] In a similar way, and at a similar time to Irenaeus, Tertullian suggests that the "rule . . . was *taught* by Christ."[23] Clement of Rome echoes this when he says that "the Gospel was given to the Apostles for us by the Lord Jesus Christ,"[24] and Hippolytus equally names his *regula fidei* the "tradition of the apostles."[25] Christ is the source and content of the faith, its message and its meaning.

Second, Irenaeus argues that, despite the church being scattered throughout the world, the consistency of confession is evident throughout the whole church. This is evident in the broadly uniform content observable in the various forms of *regulae fidei* across this formative time in the church. This is particularly the case in the focus upon the person of Jesus Christ as fully human and fully divine.[26]

> There is only one Physician—
> Very Flesh, yet Spirit too;
> Uncreated, and yet born;
> God-and-Man in One agreed,
> Very-Life-in-Death indeed,
> Fruit of God and Mary's seed;
> At once impassible and torn
> By pain and suffering here below:
> Jesus Christ, whom as our Lord we know.[27]

Finally, as with Paul's "the gospel," a *regula fidei* is to be lived out by the church. That is, it is performed on the stage of the world by the church, who, through its performance, invites *audiences* to become *performers*, and so hands on the *script* to the next generation of *performers*. In this way, the theo-drama continues. Irenaeus, in *On the Apostolic Preaching*, implores his readers to "keep the rule of faith unswervingly, and perform the commandments of God, believing in God and fearing Him, for He is

---

22. Irenaeus, "Against Heresies" 1.10.1.
23. Tertullian, "On Prescription Against Heresies," 13. Emphasis added. See also Tertullian, "Against Praxeas," 9.
24. Clement of Rome, "First Epistle of Clement," 42.
25. Hippolytus, "Against Noetus," 230.
26. See, for example, Hippolytus, "Against Noetus," 231.
27. Ignatius, "Epistle to the Ephesians," 7.

Lord, and loving Him, for he is Father. Action, then comes by faith."[28] The belief of the church leads to and informs ongoing performance within the theo-drama of God. It is, as Kevin Vanhoozer suggests, that "the direction of doctrine . . . enables us, as individuals and as a church, to render the gospel public by leading lives in creative imitation of Christ."[29] Drawing this together, a *regula fidei* centers upon Christ as the *script* of the theo-drama and equipping the church to interpret Scripture faithfully and therefore perform Christ across the stage of the world. As the church performs *what* it believes it performs *who* it believes.

FROM *REGULAE FIDEI* TO THE CREEDS

Later, with the codification of the creeds and the canonization of the Christian Scriptures, *regulae fidei* took on a fixed, formal, and ecumenically agreed-upon form. What was once a dynamic and fluid narrative, performed and re-performed by Christians, adopted by those new to the faith, functioning as a summary of the gospel that had been passed through the generations, now became a fixed measure of orthodox belief. The creeds became the measure that determined who was officially included among the *personae* and who was not. It is not a side issue that this took place when Christianity "evolved from its position as the schismatic disease of the Empire into an integral part of the design of Imperial identity."[30] Christianity's relocation in the empire from the places of persecution to the positions of power meant that creeds not only served the purpose of aiding the church in the interpretation of Scripture, they also became subject to the purposes of the state.[31] The lines between ecclesiastical and empirical power blurred into one. Despite the political use of the creeds, their theological and liturgical function is the focus of this book.

Following on from Paul's "the gospel" and the various *regulae fidei*, N-CP has, as its central theme, the person of Jesus Christ. Given the debates surrounding the divine and human natures of Christ that prompted the Council of Nicaea (325 CE) and the Council of Constantinople (381 CE), this is not surprising. N-CP emphasizes the divinity of Christ at length; "the only-begotten Son of God, begotten of the Father

---

28. Irenaeus, *On the Apostolic Preaching*, 3.
29. Vanhoozer, *Drama of Doctrine*, 33.
30. Heide, *Timeless Truth*, 60.
31. Heide, *Timeless Truth*, 62.

before all ages, light from light, true God from true God, begotten not made, consubstantial with the Father; through whom all things came to be."[32] Similarly, there is a shorter but no less significant emphasis upon the humanity of Christ; he "became human."[33] Finally, with the reference to Jesus rising "in accordance with the Scriptures," the interdependent relationship between the creed and the text of Scripture is formalized.[34] Further, Pelikan suggests that this direct reference to 1 Cor 15:3 requires "an interpretation of the Old Testament Scriptures as a witness to Jesus Christ, thereby also requiring an interpretation of the Bible 'in accordance with' the creed."[35] And so the cyclical relationship between the prayer of the church and the belief of the church is complete. The relationship commences with the prayer of Jesus gifted to the church which is then expressed in summary form in Paul's "the gospel," the various forms of *regulae fidei*, and finally in the ecumenical creeds.

The creeds have since continued to shape the form and function of Christian worship. The focus of this book is on the ongoing use of creeds as a lens for interpreting Scripture, that is, as an authoritative form of *regulae fidei*. This is particularly relevant given that, in many liturgical settings, a creed is recited or sung as a weekly part of liturgy.[36] In this way, this theological approach to the interpretation of Scripture, with its emphasis on *regulae fidei* shaping and affirming the outcomes of such a reading, constitutes the hermeneutical approach to the scriptural text in this book.

From Paul's version of "the gospel" through the various *regulae fidei*, and onto the ecumenical creeds, retaining a balance is critical when it comes to stating how the two natures of Christ are hypostatically united in one person. Attention turns now to how this informs the way the creeds shape this theological approach to the reading of Scripture.

THE HYPOSTATIC UNION

N-CP emphasizes the divinity of Jesus at length. This reflects the Christological debates that prompted both the Council of Nicaea and the Council

---

32. N-CP, 163.
33. N-CP, 163.
34. N-CP, 163.
35. Pelikan, *Credo*, 142.
36. *APBA*, 103–4, 23, 70–71.

of Constantinople. Each of the elements creates a theological boundary surrounding what is to be considered orthodox Christian belief about Christ, who is said to be "the Only-begotten Son of God, begotten from the Father before all ages, light from light, true God from true God, begotten not made, consubstantial with the Father; through whom all things came to be."[37]

Following the focus on the divine nature, the creed then turns to the incarnation and the humanity of Jesus. In comparison to the detailed exposition of Jesus' divinity, much less is said about his humanity. His conception by Mother Spirit and the Virgin Mary are named and then it states, simply, that he "became human."[38] The brevity of this, again, reflects the nature of the Christological debates that were focused upon the divinity of Jesus and, specifically, the relationship between Father and Son. Regarding his humanity, it was enough simply to state that he was "human." The nature of his humanity was not a concern, nor was the relationship between the divine and human natures mentioned at all in this creed. It is not that this wasn't considered, rather it emphasizes the point that it was not one of the major issues of Christology being debated at the first two ecumenical councils. It would become the topic of debate at later councils, in particular the Council of Chalcedon (451 CE) where the relationship between the two natures was expounded most clearly and definitively.

This council produced Chal, which was seen not as a *new* creed but rather one that clarified the meaning received through N-CP:

> We have driven off erroneous doctrines by our collective resolution and we have renewed the unerring creed of the fathers. We have proclaimed to all the creed of the 318 [The Creed of Nicaea],[39] and we have made our own those fathers who accepted this agreed statement of religion—the 150 who later met in great Constantinople and themselves set their seal to the same creed [N-CP].[40]

Thomas Aquinas emphasizes that later creeds are a development of N-CP: "In every council of the Church a symbol of faith has been drawn up to meet some prevalent error condemned in the council at that time.

---

37. N-CP, 163.
38. N-CP, 163.
39. "Creed of Nicaea," 156–59.
40. Chal, 175.

Hence subsequent councils are not to be described as making a new symbol of faith; but what was implicitly contained in the first symbol was explained by some addition directed against rising heresies."[41]

Pelikan highlights how there is both "continuity and development" in the creeds that needs to be interpreted, "dialectically, in the light of the doctrine of the person of Christ, confessed by the councils and in the creeds as the exemplar both of continuity and of change."[42] The dialectical relationship between continuity and development, which reflects the person of Jesus Christ, exists due to the relationship between "believing" and "confessing."[43] Creeds exist not just for reciting, as might be the case for a poem, but as an expression of the belief of both an individual and the community of believers of which they are a part. In theo-dramatic terms, they are a means of performing the *Logos*-script to reveal one's character as a *persona* within the theo-drama and, simultaneously, reveal the character of Christ to the world. Further, they set the boundaries of what constitutes fitting performance within the theo-drama. So, the later creeds serve the purpose of enabling performers to confess their belief with clarity, while simultaneously providing a theological boundary against heresy. This is observed in Chal where a dialectical tension exists between the suggestion that "we all with one voice teach the confession of one and the same Son" and the stated opposition to "those who are trying to ruin the proclamation of the truth."[44]

Chal, functioning as a continuation and development of N-CP, clarifies the relationship between the two natures outlining what has become known as the hypostatic union. That is, Christ is

> acknowledged in two natures which undergo no confusion, no change, no division, no separation; at no point was the difference between the natures taken away through the union, but rather the property of both natures is preserved and comes together into a single person and a single subsistent being; he is not parted or divided into two persons, but is one and the same only-begotten Son, God, Word, Lord Jesus Christ, just as the prophets taught from the beginning about him, and as the Lord

---

41. Aquinas, *Summa Theologica* 1a.36.2.
42. Pelikan, *Credo*, 31.
43. Pelikan, *Credo*, 37.
44. Chal, 177–81.

Jesus Christ himself instructed us, and as the creed of the fathers handed it down to us.[45]

It is this measure of orthodox belief regarding the relationship between the two natures of Christ that must be kept in mind when considering the worshiping Jesus. The divine and human natures are not to be divided nor confused. "On the contrary they are brought together in an indissoluble union."[46] This includes in Jesus' own acts of worship.

PERICHORESIS

The concept of *perichoresis* (literally, to dance around) is a theological attempt to describe, first, how the divine and human natures of Jesus Christ interrelate and then, second, the relationship between the three persons of the Trinity and the divine essence. As a Christological term, it seeks to hold in tension the distinction between divinity and humanity in the person of Jesus (the "no confusion" of Chal) and the singularity of his person (the "no division" of Chal). The benefits of this term, connected etymologically to the world of dance, *perichoresis* helped theologians depict the inter-*nature* movement between divine and human (two dancers) that made up the one person of Jesus (one dance). This was then extended to describe the inter-*personal* movement between the three persons of the Trinity: Father, Son, and Mother Spirit. *Perichoresis* reflects the nature of God; "God is love and has his true being in communion, in the mutual indwelling of the Father, Son and Holy Spirit."[47] It is a "ceaseless circulation" of that "love which is himself."[48] Jürgen Moltmann notes that "the doctrine of the perichoresis links together in a brilliant way the threeness and the unity, without reducing the threeness to the unity, or dissolving the unity in the threeness."[49]

More recently the term has been extended to include the church's mystical union with God, in Christ by Mother Spirit. The church, in union with Christ, is drawn into the perichoretic interpersonal relationships of the Trinity such that we are also drawn to "mutual love for one

---

45. Chal, 181.
46. Cyril of Alexandria, *On the Unity of Christ*, 77.
47. Torrance, *Worship*, 38.
48. Bouyer, *Christian Mystery*, 204–5.
49. Moltmann, *Trinity and the Kingdom*, 175.

another."⁵⁰ The church, in communion with the Trinity, experiences communion within itself. The relationships between persons within the church is also described as *perichoretic* in nature.

In theo-dramatic terms, *perichoresis* points to Chal where the relationship between the divine and human natures of Christ is held in dynamic tension: the one performer embodies two natures. Similarly, it also points to the three persons of the Trinity, and then the church, performing together upon the stage. In particular, the inter-*nature* (Christ) and inter-*personal* (Trinity) relationships reveal the "not-not not" quality of this performance.⁵¹ For Christ, his divine nature is "not" his human nature, (the two are not *confused*) and yet there is nothing he performs as a human where his divine nature is "not-not" involved (the two are not *divided*). Every action of Christ is performed by the incarnated *Logos*, the divine and human natures hypostatically united, with both natures *perichoretically* interpenetrating one another. The *persona* is Christ and, as he performs, he simultaneously reveals true humanity and true divinity.

As the definition of *perichoresis* is extended to the inter-*personal* relationships of the Trinity the "not-not not" quality emerges here as well. As Jesus worships, it is "not" the Father or Mother Spirit that worships but at the same time they are "not-not" worshiping. Every action of Christ is an action of the one God, with the three persons of the Trinity *perichoretically* interpenetrating one another. As true divinity is revealed in Christ, we see truly the Father and Mother Spirit; "The Father and I are one" (John 10:30).

Finally, as the church joins the performance, it puts on the character of Christ (Rom 13:14), not in an inauthentic sense, where they pretend to be something that they really are not. Rather, this is the only way the church can authentically and genuinely join the theo-drama, *to, through,* and *with* Christ. So, as the church worships it is "not" Christ worshiping, but it is also "not-not" Christ worshiping (Gal 2:20). Further, as the church is drawn into the *perichoretic* relationships of the Trinity, performing worship *to, through,* and *with* Christ, it is "not" the Trinity that is performing; but it also "not-not" the Trinity. This is seen, for example, in Mother Spirit's union with the groan-filled prayers of the people (Rom 8:26–27); the lines between church and Mother Spirit as the one who performs the prayer are blurred as the two performers become one. As

---

50. Jenson, "Church and the Sacraments," 215.
51. Schechner, *Between Theater and Anthropology*, 123.

Adrienne von Speyr highlights, the very act of prayer itself is the "center of his being... the divine, triune love."[52]

COMMUNICATIO IDIOMATUM

Related to the concepts of the hypostatic union and *perichoresis* is the doctrine of the *communicatio idiomatum* (communication of attributes). This is expressed within the Formula of Concord where the question is raised, "because of the personal union in the person of Christ, do the divine and human natures, together with their properties, really (that is, in deed and truth) share with each other, and how far does this sharing extend?" The response is given that, in the person of Jesus Christ is found "the highest communion which God truly has with man." As such, there is a "sharing of the natures" and a "real and true communion with each other." This union is so profound that "it has become one person with him." So, Christ remains for all eternity, "God and man in one indivisible person."[53]

This doctrine suggests that attributes of the divine and human natures are communicated to the person of Jesus Christ. For example, the divine perfections of love, grace, and humility exist alongside human characteristics, such as mortality, intellectual limitations, emotions, and so on. All attributes of both natures are shared within the one person of Jesus Christ. For example, the divine nature fully participates in the human death of Christ. Luther expressed this when he said, "God in his own nature cannot die; but now that God and man are united in one person, it is called God's death when the man dies who is one substance or one person with God."[54]

The doctrine of *communicatio idiomatum* is a theological consequence of the hypostatic union and is made possible by *perichoresis*. If the two natures were not fully united and did not mutually indwell one another, without confusion or division, then the sharing of attributes from one nature to the other would not be possible. "According to this doctrine, which is affirmed (though with divergent conclusions) also in some Reformed confessions, the attributes of one of the natures of Christ, including the omnipresence or 'ubiquity' of his divine nature, are shared

---

52. Speyr, *World of Prayer*, 13.

53. "Formula of Concord," 190–92.

54. Luther, *VondenKonz.*, WA,L, 590.3–4,19–22; LW XLI, 103, 104, cited in Cross, *Communicatio Idiomatum*, 56.

with the other nature through being communicated to his single divine-human person in the incarnation."[55]

Balthasar highlights that "it is only possible to apply qualities and attributes of the one nature to the other because both are united in the one person or the Logos—not by way of nature, but by way of person; certainly, the natures are 'undivided,' but, however close the union, they are 'unconfused,' 'the properties of each remain unimpaired.'"[56] Cynthia Anderson notes that "anything that is predicated of the divine also can be predicated of the humanity and vice versa because the predication is not at the level of 'nature' but rather all predicates are applied to the one subject, the Word incarnate."[57] In theo-dramatic terms, when an actor enters the role that they are portraying, they take on the personality of the character and, in so doing, the attributes assigned by the *creator* of the character are communicated within the performance of the actor. They become the role that they are portraying and, in many respects, take on the attributes as their own, even though that character is completely distinct from who they are. For Christ, the clear difference in the dramatic analogy at this point lies in the confession that the two natures are both truly and properly his. He is neither "divine and pretending to be human," nor "human and pretending to be divine." Rather, he is fully divine and fully human, hypostatically united in one person. Yet each of those natures bears attributes that, in normal circumstances, cannot be communicated to the other and are even contradictory. They include immortality and mortality, divine knowledge and human intellectual capacities, omnipresence and temporal limitations. For Christ, the difference is the hypostatic union and the *perichoretic* relationship of the two natures. It is based on this union and the mutual indwelling of the two natures that the attributes are communicated between the two.

Further, it is an indissoluble union and so the two natures should not be divided or confused regarding any action of Christ, including his worship. Luther expresses this concern in the following way:

> If you could show me one place where God is and not the man, then the person is already divided and I could at once say truthfully, "Here is God who is not man and has never become man." But no God like that for me! For it would follow from this that space and place had separated the two natures from one another

55. Pelikan, *Credo*, 342–43.
56. Balthasar, *TD*, 3:222.
57. Anderson, *Reclaiming Participation*, 46.

and thus had divided the person.... He has become one person and does not separate the humanity from himself.[58]

This doctrine supports the view that the worshiping Jesus reveals the divine nature. However, it is not that worship is an attribute of his human nature that is communicated to the divine nature but rather the opposite. Worship is a divine attribute that is communicated to the human nature of Christ, in and as Jesus worships. As Fagerberg has suggested, liturgy is an "activity done by God."[59] Fagerberg's definition of liturgy, already stated and critiqued in this book, highlights the divine origin of worship. In the person of Christ, this divine attribute is communicated to humanity most perfectly within himself because of the hypostatic union. As such, in those moments when Jesus is worshiping, humanity joins in the eternal worship taking place within the Godhead. This is the first time a human participates in eternal worship from within. Jesus' worship is a mediatorial act where he, as the prototypical image of God, glorifies God as the God-human on behalf of all humanity.

The importance of this doctrine for the church and its ongoing performance of worship is expressed, tangentially, in two similar stories regarding conversion. James B. Torrance recounts a story told by Karl Barth that is relevant at this point.

> Karl Barth tells the story of an old lady who once went to evangelist Kohlbrügge and asked him, "Tell me, sir, when were you converted?" The evangelist, knowing well that she was interested in the details of his Christian experience, replied, "Madam, I was converted nineteen hundred years ago when Jesus Christ died on a cross for my sins and rose again." He was concerned to point away from himself and his own faith to Jesus Christ.[60]

T. F. Torrance shares a similar story of his own where he was once asked when he had been "born again."

> I still recall his face when I told him that I had been born again when Jesus Christ was born of the Virgin Mary and rose again from the virgin tomb, the first-born of the dead. When he asked me to explain I said: "This Tom Torrance you see is full of

---

58. Luther, *Vom Abendmahl*, WA, XXVI, 332.33–333.1, 333.8–10; LW, XXXVII, 218–19. See too Luther, *Vom Abendmahl*, WA, XXVI, 340.14–21; LW, XXXVII, 228–9 for almost the identical argument, cited in Cross, *Communicatio Idiomatum*, 59.

59. Fagerberg, "Liturgical Theology," 9.

60. Torrance, *Worship*, 75.

corruption, but the real Tom Torrance is hid with Christ in God and will be revealed only when Christ comes again. He took my corrupt humanity in his Incarnation, sanctified, cleansed and redeemed it, giving it new birth, in his death and resurrection .... In a profound and proper sense, therefore, we must speak of Jesus Christ as constituting in himself the very substance of our conversion, so that we must think of him as taking our place even in our acts of repentance and personal decision, for without him all so-called repentance and conversion are empty.[61]

Both authors sought to emphasize the perfection of Jesus' performance in their personal conversion by situating the event in the birth, ministry, death, burial, and resurrection of Jesus. In the stories above, both Barth and T. F. Torrance are united with Christ's person by Mother Spirit. Both authors seek to demonstrate that the effectiveness of their own conversion was not dependent upon their own right performance. Rather, whenever and wherever the event of conversion took place, it had already taken place in the person of Jesus Christ. His conversion is their conversion. His repentance is their repentance. His baptism is their baptism, and so on. This book seeks to demonstrate that the same theological principle is taking place in Christian worship. The church's ongoing worship takes place in union with the worshiping Jesus. Jesus' worship is our worship. The definition of worship is critical here. T. F. Torrance, as will be shown momentarily, suggests that Jesus' worship is a *human* activity, offered on behalf of all humanity, including himself, for the sake of all people. In contrast, what is contended here is that Jesus' worship is *divine* and is communicated to his human nature via the hypostatic union and the *perichoretic* relationship of the two natures. The divine attribute becomes a human one. The glorification of God that is performed by Jesus in his acts of worship is simultaneously for his own benefit and for the benefit of all humanity, and indeed of all creation. Worship as a divine attribute takes place *to*, *through*, and *with* Jesus.

SCENE—IMPROVISING TO EMMAUS AND BACK

Luke transcribes an event that takes place on the day of Jesus' resurrection. Cleopas and his companion are traveling toward Emmaus. While the pericope is often considered from the starting point of Luke 24:13, the

61. Torrance, *Mediation of Christ*, 86.

context that leads up to this dramatic encounter is highly significant. In particular, the role of "the women" in the greater drama is central to Jesus' encounter with the two male disciples. Luke's constant reference to "the women" (23:27–31; 23:49; 23:55; 24:1–12; 24:22) is deliberate and sets up the plot for how, and by whom, the resurrection will be authenticated. It is the women who are the eyewitnesses of the events surrounding Jesus' crucifixion, death, burial, and resurrection. They are the first evangelists. They see Jesus die, see where he was buried, and are the first to testify that the tomb was empty and that Jesus was alive. In contrast, it is the male disciples who don't believe the women and discount their story, because they are women reporting it.

Luke begins to set the scene when Jesus is led away from Jerusalem to the place where he is crucified. The women join others who follow him out to that place (23:27). Significantly, of the limited things that Jesus says from the moment of his arrest until his death, it is to the women that he directs his longest and most compassionate response. Indeed, they are the only long-standing followers of Jesus that he speaks to after Gethsemane. Here, "long-standing" is used in contrast to the brief encounter with the prisoner on the cross (23:43).

Next, the women witness the death of Jesus. Unlike the others, they do not "beat their breasts" as a performance of their grief. Rather, they stand "at a distance, watching these things" (23:49). The descriptive language is important here. For Luke, this establishes the women as eyewitnesses of this event and so it is critical that they watch Jesus die. They see it happen and will testify to this later.

Jesus is buried. At this point, the women follow Joseph and see the tomb and how his body was laid in it. Then they go home and prepare spices and perfumes, since by this time of day the sun was setting and so Sabbath is commencing. They rest on the Sabbath in obedience to the commandment (23:55–56).

Again, the language of "seeing" the tomb and where Jesus was laid is critical. Luke is setting the stage for the women to be the eyewitnesses of the passion. While the faithful men involved change at each given point (Simon of Cyrene, the centurion, Joseph of Arimathea, even the other prisoner), it is the women who are the consistent *personae* linking the plot at this critical point in the drama. Furthermore, their obedience is emphasized in 23:56. They are not rebellious resistance fighters whose testimony could subsequently be called into question. These are faithful Jewish women watching all that takes place. They observe and obey the commandments. They see all that happens. They will testify to it all in the moments to come.

Immediately after the account of the burial, the women shift to become the lead *performers* in the narrative. We follow them as they travel together to the tomb, in order to complete the task they were unable to finish on Friday evening, due to the Sabbath regulations. They find the stone rolled away, enter the tomb, and see the place where they had previously witnessed Joseph laying the body. This time, though, the tomb is empty. "While they were wondering" (24:4) two angels appear before them and say to them that Jesus is not here, for he is risen. They call upon them to "remember" what he had told them in Galilee. When the angels remind the women of Jesus' words they do indeed "remember" them. While it would be nice to include some reference as to whether they "believed" at this point, we are not given the luxury of this information. Given, however, that Luke places a particular emphasis on the male disciples' unbelief at hearing this same news it is fair to suggest that the women's reaction was more positive and immediate. Luke explicitly states that the male disciples "did not believe the women, because their words seemed to them like nonsense" (24:11). The women, though, believe the words of the angels as they recall the words of Jesus in their remembering. He had indeed been raised from the dead, as he previously told them would happen.

The location shifts briefly; however, this is a continuation of the drama, not a new scene. Cleopas and his companion travel on the road out of Jerusalem on their way to Emmaus. Unbeknownst to them, Jesus appears, and they speak with him on the way. They confess that the women "amazed" them. This same word is used by Luke in 8:56 to describe the reaction of the parents when Jesus raised their dead daughter to life. Jesus responds to them with an admonition: "How foolish you are, and how slow to believe all that the prophets have spoken!" (24:25).

Here is where reading this pericope in the broader context aids in interpreting Jesus' words. Disconnecting it from the broader context leads to an interpretation that suggests Jesus spoke these harsh words because the disciples were slow to believe the *message*. However, given Luke's careful and deliberate attempts to incorporate the women as the first eyewitnesses, it is instead that they were slow to believe *the messengers*, that is, "the women." The "prophets" whom they were "slow to believe" were not the "prophets" of old but the "prophets" in their midst: "the women." Luke implicitly suggests that these women are the first to fulfill the prophecy of Joel 2:28, a text he would later explicitly reference in Acts 2:17: "your sons and daughters will *prophesy*." Jesus admonishes these male disciples not only because they failed to believe the message, but more specifically because they failed to believe the message because the messengers were women: Mary Magdalene, Joanna, Mary the mother of James, and the others with them (24:10).

JESUS' IDENTITY IS REVEALED IN PERFORMANCE

D. Brent Laytham highlights how, in the Emmaus pericope, Jesus interprets Scripture in a way that recenters the drama upon himself. He does so within an embodied performance.

> He enacted the divine plan as God had revealed it in Scripture, moving the drama forward toward its conclusion. Having read and understood the script, penetrated to its underlying theme or pattern, and discerned his unique role in the drama, he then performed it with absolute fidelity. Thus Jesus' central interpretive performance is not the text talk on the road, but "these things"—his passion, death, and resurrection. Jesus himself, in his performance (his life, death, and resurrection), is not only the primary interpreter of Scripture; he is its primary interpretation.[62]

This is why, in this book, Jesus has been referred to as the script. It is not Scripture itself that Jesus' life is conformed to and which thereby is authoritative. Rather, it is Jesus himself who is authoritative, and thereby Scripture is interpreted in the light of who he is. For Cleopas and his companion, in the light of the women's testimony about their encounter with the risen Jesus, they see with new light who Jesus is following their interpersonal encounter with him. Throughout the pericope, Jesus improvises his response to their questions and doubts. During the meal, the disciples' "eyes were opened" (24:31) and they finally recognize the one they have been speaking with all along. It is then that the two companions take center stage, improvising their response to their personal encounter with Jesus. Finally, following the lead of the women, having now been convinced of the truth of their story, they proclaim to the other disciples, "the Lord has risen indeed" (24:34).

62. Laytham, "Interpretation on the Way," 104.

Luke highlights the moment in their encounter with Jesus where he was made known to them, "in the breaking of the bread" (24:35). It was not in the talking, not in the walking, not in the physical proximity to the risen Jesus, or even the interpretation of the Scriptures, but in the sensory and embodied experience of eating a meal with Jesus. Indeed, the whole experience was essential to them understanding the significance of the meal and who shared the table with them, but it was the meal itself where the identity of Jesus was revealed to them. "At Emmaus he declares who he is by doing what he always does; his table performance identifies him. As Jesus, the guest-become-host, performs again the familiar fourfold action [he takes bread, blesses, breaks, and gives it to them], the two disciples' eyes are opened to see who he really is—Jesus risen from the dead."[63] The significance of this to this book is that Jesus' identity is revealed in embodied and sensory performances, like meals. This points to why the Lord's Supper is so important to a wide range of Christian traditions. From a theo-dramatic perspective, it extends to the wider narrative of the incarnation as well. Jesus reveals who he is through performances, both his own and then the subsequent and ongoing performances of his disciples. His identity, which is confessed to be fully human and fully divine, is revealed in his life, death, and resurrection. It is also revealed at the meal table, and central to this is the Lord's Supper at the Lord's Table. Focusing upon Jesus' acts of worship, they are his own embodied performances of glorifying God, extending from himself as the incarnated Son, to the Father and Mother Spirit. The question that this now raises is whether these acts of worship extend from his human nature alone or from his person.

---

63. Laytham, "Interpretation on the Way," 111.

4

The Protagonist—Jesus Christ (Part Two)

HAVING OUTLINED THE THEORETICAL foundations of Jesus Christ's identity is revealed in performance generally, attention now turns to the performance of worship by Jesus. Given that the canonical accounts depict Jesus worshiping in a variety of ways, and the creedal confessions affirm that Jesus is fully human and fully divine, this book suggests that worship is a divine act. Jesus' acts of worship extend from his person. In contrast, some authors suggest that Jesus' worship extends from his human nature alone. Their views will be sampled and summarized now.

JESUS WORSHIPING FROM HIS HUMANITY

Kathryn Tanner, in her brief systematic theology, *Jesus, Humanity and the Trinity*, emphasizes a "non-competitive" relationship between God and creation that is founded upon God's "divine transcendence" to "frame . . . the whole God/world relationship."[1] Tanner's framework focuses on the person of Jesus Christ that builds upon these two key principles of non-competitiveness and divine transcendence. Non-competitiveness emphasizes the equality of persons within the Trinity and presents an ideal for the relationships that exist between God and creation and between creation and creation. Such relationships are built upon divine

1. Tanner, *Jesus, Humanity and the Trinity*, 4–5.

THE PROTAGONIST—JESUS CHRIST (PART TWO)   79

transcendence where God is wholly other to creation. Transcendence is the foundation upon which God can incorporate creation into God's self, non-competitively. Were God not transcendent then incorporation would necessarily be competitive.

Tanner suggests that when the *Logos* becomes incarnate in the person of Jesus Christ, "God is not going anywhere when God becomes human; we are being brought to God, assumed into the divine trinitarian life."[2] And so, in the incarnation, "humanity becomes God's own."[3] Elsewhere, Tanner states that the "Christological formula of two natures in one person . . . becomes normative for the church as a model instance of the rule that divine and human predicates are to be attributed to the one subject Jesus Christ."[4]

In considering how the model of two natures in one person is observed within the person of Jesus Christ, Tanner insists that "one should not try here to divvy up the life of Jesus into its divine and human qualities, to figure out where Jesus' humanity ends and his divinity begins, as if human and divine qualities were part of a continuous series or laid out on a continuum."[5] This follows along with the citation from Luther above where he invites the reader to consider the impossibility of finding a single instance where God and human natures act independently.[6]

Tanner, in concert with Luther, suggests that Jesus' life and person are not to be considered in terms of either his humanity or his divinity but rather as a permanent and whole person, wherein the divine nature is the source of the human. The divine and human qualities of Jesus are not set in competition with one another but rather are viewed as a whole, hypostatically united in the one person of Jesus Christ, fully divine and fully human. Viewing Christ in this way applies to all his life, including when he worships.

However, in the follow-up work, *Christ the Key*, Tanner contradicts this important point.[7] In this second work, Tanner suggests that when Jesus worships he does so specifically out of his humanity.

---

2. Tanner, *Jesus, Humanity and the Trinity*, 15.
3. Tanner, *Jesus, Humanity and the Trinity*, 9.
4. Tanner, *God and Creation*, 50.
5. Tanner, *Jesus, Humanity and the Trinity*, 15.
6. Cited in Cross, *Communicatio Idiomatum*, 59.
7. Tanner, *Christ the Key*.

Jesus obeys and worships the Father insofar as he is a man. Obedience and worship are appropriate stances for a human being to take and reflect the disparity of status between a creature and God. Jesus is of course the Word incarnate but divinity and humanity remain distinct in him, and therefore what is appropriately said of him in virtue of his humanity should not be confused with what is said about him in virtue of his divinity. The Word incarnate prays to the Father, but he does so insofar as he is a man and not insofar as he is God.[8]

The result of this is a contradiction where Tanner ends up doing the very thing she insists must not be done. That is, she "divv[ies] up the life of Jesus into its divine and human qualities."[9] Tanner's use of the word "confused" here draws upon Chal that states that the one Christ must be

> acknowledged in two natures which undergo no confusion, no change, no division, no separation; at no point was the difference between the natures taken away through the union, but rather the property of both natures is preserved and comes together into a single subsistent being; he is not parted or divided into two persons, but is one and the same only-begotten Son, God, Word, Lord Jesus Christ, just as the prophets taught from the beginning about him, and as the Lord Jesus Christ himself instructed us, and as the creed of the fathers handed it down to us.[10]

In seeking to avoid confusing the two natures, Tanner suggests that Jesus' worship extends from his humanity alone and, in doing so, depends upon an anthropocentric definition of worship. That definition of worship remains fixed regardless of whether it is Jesus worshiping or someone else. According to Tanner, obedience and worship remain an "appropriate stance" for humanity. It is a distinctively human activity and not an essential characteristic of divinity. The distinction between humanity and divinity, and so creator and creature, is preserved with the actions of obedience and worship remaining solely a human activity. In this regard, Tanner's definition of worship remains unchanged, and this despite Jesus' performance of it. In this schema Tanner avoids confusing the two natures; however, the opposite problem occurs. That is, the two natures are divided.

---

8. Tanner, *Christ the Key*, 182–83.
9. Tanner, *Jesus, Humanity and the Trinity*, 15.
10. Chal, 172–81.

T. F. Torrance places a similar emphasis upon the humanity of the worshiping Jesus. According to Torrance, Jesus "worships for he has assumed the nature that pays worship,"[11] that is, his human nature. Elsewhere, Torrance, like Tanner and Luther above, emphasizes the unity of act between the divine and human natures in Jesus Christ. Like Tanner, he cautions against dividing the human and divine natures in the person of Christ, warning that such a division leads to theological despair.

> Any . . . detachment or disjunction between the being and nature of Jesus and the being and nature of God could only disrupt the message of grace and peace which the Gospel brings, and it would introduce the deepest anxiety into human life born out of a dreadful fear that God may turn out in the end to be utterly different from what we see in Jesus Christ, fear lest there is behind the back of Jesus some dark inscrutable God, some arbitrary Deity of whom we can know nothing but before whom in our guilty conscience as sinners we cannot but quake and shiver in our souls.[12]

In seeking to assure the reader against such theological despair, Torrance affirms that "there is in fact no God behind the back of Jesus, no act of God other than the act of Jesus, no God but the God we see and meet in him."[13] Yet, to suggest that it is Jesus' human nature that performs worship is to portray a God who is different to Jesus, a God who is, in fact, hidden somewhere behind the worshiping Jesus. Even if this is the only part of Jesus' life where such a division exists, nevertheless the warning that Torrance expressed above still applies.

When Torrance suggests that Jesus is worshiping from his humanity, he draws upon the work of Cyril of Alexandria. Cyril, in his commentary upon John 4:22, states that "worship is an act that is most fitting for human beings. It is placed in the category of a debt, and it is offered by us to God. Therefore, he worships as a man since he became human, but he is always worshipped with the Father since he was, is and will be true God by nature."[14] Cyril is seeking to emphasize the equality of the worship offered by Jesus with that offered by humans; "what good, tell me, will it do for the freedom of the only begotten if his worship of the Father is made

---

11. Torrance, *Theology in Reconciliation*, 176.
12. Torrance, "Christ Who Loves Us," 16.
13. Torrance, "Christ Who Loves Us," 17.
14. Cyril of Alexandria, *Commentary on John*, bk. 2, ch. 5.

separate from ours?"[15] That is, worship is offered *with* Jesus. Further, he also acknowledges that worship is rightly offered *to* Jesus. The distinction of the two natures is highlighted when he suggests that the "royal and lordly honor manifests itself in being worshipped, while the status of a servant and a slave is defined by worshipping."[16] This makes it clear that, for Cyril, and those who follow in his theological footsteps, worship is fundamentally a human activity.

In suggesting that Jesus' acts of worship extend from his humanity, each of these authors assign this one action of Christ to one nature over and against the other. The result of this is that the functional definitions of worship they use remain fixed. For these authors, worship remains a human action and not a divine one and, as such, their functional definitions of worship are anthropocentric.

The problem with anthropocentric definitions of worship, particularly as they relate to Jesus the worshiper, is that they come at the expense of the hypostatic union when applied to Jesus Christ. Peterson's assertion that any definition of worship "must apply to Jesus himself" is worth recalling here.[17] More specifically, though, it is essential that the relationship between the divine and human natures within the person of Christ is held in tension when considering Jesus the worshiper. Further, anthropocentric definitions of worship are, in practice, unitarian. Opposing unitarian views of worship is a major task within James Torrance's *Worship, Community and the Triune God of Grace*. There, he suggests that such an understanding of worship has "no doctrine of the mediator or sole priesthood of Christ, is human-centered, has no proper doctrine of the Holy Spirit, is too often non-sacramental, and can engender weariness."[18]

Kevin Navarro's *Trinitarian Doxology* thoroughly examines the theologies of James Torrance and T. F. Torrance.[19] Navarro has similarly identified, and seeks to respond to, the issue of anthropocentric definitions of worship. "Most approaches to liturgical theology are anthropocentric: the study of liturgy is primarily focused on what we, the worshippers, do. While some have attempted to offer a more theological approach to the subject of worship, they still have not gone far enough."[20] Navarro then

15. Cyril of Alexandria, *Commentary on John*, bk. 2, ch. 5.
16. Cyril of Alexandria, *Commentary on John*, bk. 2, ch. 5.
17. Peterson, *Engaging with God*, 17.
18. Torrance, *Worship*, 20.
19. Navarro, *Trinitarian Doxology*.
20. Navarro, *Trinitarian Doxology*, 9.

suggests that Christian worship is "not something we primarily do at all but rather it is something that has been done and is being done on our behalf and that whatever we are doing in worship, it is participation by the Spirit in the Son's communion with the Father."[21]

For Navarro, anthropocentric worship is that which is "both initiated *and* responsive worship when it does not factor in the mediation of Christ."[22] The problem in this regard is that worship can become a series of human activities (prayer, preaching, singing, etc.) that attempt to glorify, or even appease, the divine out of human strength and ability alone. Ashley Cocksworth and John C. McDowell point out that this exhibits "something of an exercising of power."[23] Worship, in an anthropocentric model, flows from humanity to the divine yet often neglects the role of the mediator within the worship act itself. Ironically, while such worship seeks to glorify the divine it ends up doing the opposite. Given its emphasis on what *humans* do in worship, the efficacy of worship is determined by the quality of its performance *by the human*. At its worst, all reference to the divine could be purely functional, or indeed disappear entirely, and no one would notice.

It is essential to a Christian understanding of worship to give primacy to Jesus Christ as the central figure of Christian worship. It is the faithfulness of Jesus that purifies and perfects the worship of "all humanity."[24] It is Jesus Christ, performing the role of Great High Priest (e.g., Heb 6:20) who is the true worshiper. T. F. Torrance and James Torrance both suggest that authentic Christian worship is participation in the worship of Jesus Christ. James Torrance's well-known definition of worship is critical at this point; "worship is the gift of participating in the incarnate Son's communion with the Father, and in so worshipping we worship and glorify the Father, the Son and the Holy Spirit."[25] In this understanding of worship, humanity is enabled to share in the Son's communion with the Father, by Mother Spirit. This, it is suggested, is the foundation of trinitarian worship. Alan Torrance, summarizing his father James's theology, expresses this point.

---

21. Navarro, *Trinitarian Doxology*, 11–12.
22. Navarro, *Trinitarian Doxology*, 37.
23. Cocksworth and McDowell, "Introduction," 1.
24. Navarro, *Trinitarian Doxology*, 12.
25. Torrance, "Christ in Our Place," 42; See also Torrance, *Worship*, 9; Similarities in this definition can be observed in Torrance, *Theology in Reconciliation*, 82–88.

> In Jesus Christ each and every one of us finds our worship, prayers, and intercessions lifted up, sanctified and presented by the one who is the sole Priest and Representative of each of us. The very nature of our ongoing life of worship and, indeed, ethics (worth-ship) is to be conceived, therefore, in terms of this very concrete participation, by the Spirit, in our sole priest, intercessor and *leitourgos*. In worship we are not "turned back upon ourselves" to try and generate what God requires of us. Worship and, indeed, every facet of our response (all that is required of us by the torah) is to be conceived as participation, by grace, in Christ's fulfillment of these *dikaiomata*, in his Amen, in his "Yes" to the Father, and in his worship. In the Eucharist and in prayer and, indeed, in every facet of the Christian life the Spirit seeks to lift us up to share in his perfect response and ongoing worship offered on our behalf.[26]

While this points in the direction of addressing the problem, ultimately it still fails to address anthropocentricity in worship. The authors, above all, focus on the human nature of Jesus Christ in his worship. He perfectly performs worship, but what he is doing, by definition, is a human task. And so, as Christians worship, their worship is joined by Mother Spirit to the worship of the human nature of Jesus Christ. It is perfected and offered by him, but it ultimately remains a human activity.

What is missing from this perspective is any acknowledgment of the glimpses of the worshiping Father and Mother Spirit depicted in the Scriptures. Worship, in an anthropocentric model, is something *only* the Son does, and specifically *only* from the incarnation onward. Critically, the examples of the Father and Mother Spirit engaged in worship are not acknowledged as evidence of worship taking place within the Trinity (such examples will be examined further below). The definition of worship as participation in the Son's communion with the Father by the Spirit remains a *human* activity. It remains fundamentally anthropocentric as it centers upon the human nature of Jesus Christ.

The problem is with anthropocentric definitions of worship and their failure to revisit such definitions in the light of the incarnation. Anthropocentric models of worship can only apply to Jesus the worshiper if worship is seen to extend from Jesus' human nature *alone*. That is the path that Tanner and T. F. Torrance have taken above. In James Torrance's definition, the use of the word "participating" contributes to the problem. This word suggests that the worshiping Jesus is doing something *new*. If

---

26. Torrance, "Introduction," 9–10.

Jesus is *participating* in worship, then it can be said that there was a time, specifically, before the incarnation, when he was *not participating*. This can only make sense if worship is something *human* taken up by Jesus in the incarnation. Thus, worship remains a human activity, and functionally unitarian; it is "what *we* [humans] do before God."[27] So, while these definitions are framed in trinitarian terms, they have failed to view Jesus' acts of worship as a part of the performance of the eternal glorification of God that is taking place within the Trinity. When Jesus worships he reveals God worshiping.

SCENE—JOHN 17

In John 17, the *liturgia Dei* is most definitively on display. Jesus prays to the Father in front of the disciples; Jesus and Father are both *personae*, the Son is the primary *performer*, with the Father and the disciples the primary *audience*. In a grand soliloquy Jesus, whom John has already shown to be the primary *personae* of the theo-drama up to this point, is center stage; all eyes are upon him. Prayer is offered in one particular moment in time, but this is also one part of a conversation that has been ongoing for eternity.

The theme of glorification is paramount. In an unexpected twist to the plot to this point, the Son invites the Father to glorify him so that the Son may glorify the Father (17:1). Until now, the Son has been glorifying the Father. Now it is revealed that the Son and the Father together worship and glorify one another and have been doing so "before the world existed" (17:5). Reading this text through the lens of N-CP reveals how a theocentric understanding of worship is needed to make sense of what is taking place. Specifically, the creed states that Mother Spirit is "co-worshipped and co-glorified with Father and Son." This prayer reveals that Jesus' prayer is not just temporal but eternal. So too the worshiping and glorifying of God is eternal. Glorifying God does not have a human origin but a divine one.

Worship takes place within the divine presence with a glory that is shared between Father and Son. Even though the focus in this pericope is upon the *personae* of Father and Son, we know that Mother Spirit is present at this moment as well, an ever-present *persona* throughout the entire theo-drama. Throughout this performance, the Father and Son

27. Torrance, *Worship*, 20.

make known their glory to the disciples and, through them, to those who will come after them, to those who will believe even though they have not seen.[28] Even more so, Father and Son continue to make their glory known to each other. On display is a glimpse, in time and space, of the eternal glorification that the three persons of the Trinity give one to another throughout eternity.[29] This is the ongoing, theo-dramatic performance of glorifying God extending from, and returning to, the eternal relations of Father, Son and Mother Spirit. This is the *liturgia Dei*.

Alongside the giving of glory from Father to Son and Son to Father, the disciples are a part of the gift. As *audience*, they behold God and, in so doing, they become the glory of God; "For the glory of God is a living man; and the life of man consists in beholding God."[30] Jesus is "glorified in them" (17:10). Despite beginning as *audience*, here they are united with the primary *performer*; they become one with Christ. The stage is expanded and the company of *performers* increases and another *audience* is revealed: the readers of the text, who are acknowledged as present and invited into the theo-drama. In speaking out his prayer, Jesus "breaks the fourth wall" and includes this audience in the act of glorification. "The glory that you have given me I have given them" (17:22). This secondary *audience* then make the same transition to become *personae* and yet another *audience* is revealed, the world. Throughout this performance, the primary aim of the theo-drama is named: that the Father, the disciples, the readers, and the world may all "see" the glory of Jesus Christ and in seeing him come to believe in him and become one with him.

Vanhoozer names Jesus as the "primary illocutionary act" of God and the "principal actor in the theo-drama's climax."[31] Further, as Gundry suggests, in the fourth Gospel "the proclaimer and the proclaimed" have "become one in the same."[32] That is, Jesus the *performer* is, at one and the same time, the *script*. He performs the words that the Father gives him to perform, while at the same time being that very Word-Act that is embodied

---

28. Vanhoozer, *Faith Speaking Understanding*, 76.
29. Speyr, *World of Prayer*, 28.
30. Irenaeus, "Against Heresies" 4.20.7.
31. Vanhoozer, *Drama of Doctrine*, 192-93.
32. Gundry, *Jesus the Word According to John the Sectarian*, 49.

in performance, the *Logos*-script. He performs his character upon the stage of the world and, as he performs, he reveals his true identity.

SCENE—THE LAST SUPPER AS A PERFORMANCE OF THE PASSOVER

The Last Supper, according to the Synoptic Gospels, was Jesus' performance of the Passover meal (Matt 26:17–29; Mark 14:12–25; Luke 22:7–38). This meal is "Israel's quintessential performance of its own scriptures."[33] Laytham notes that the "Bible is a text meant to be performed" and that, therefore, "the heart of scriptural interpretation is the Christian life itself."[34] Jesus' performance of Passover is both a single performance among many ongoing performances of this Jewish memorial and the institution of a new memorial that Christians perform in liturgical celebrations.

The Passover was, from the outset, a form of performed theology, an all-encompassing, embodied expression of trust in the saving activity of the God of Israel. It is both a "day of remembrance" and a "perpetual ordinance" (Exod 12:14). It is a meal that involves the whole community, with questions asked by the children, and responses given by the adults, and so all of the people are both *performers* and *audience*. The meal engaged all of the senses and, although repeated, was new with every annual performance. Further, God is an active *persona* in the performance; "For the Lord will pass through" (12:23). In perpetuity, the people of Israel celebrate this annual meal to remember God's saving acts in the past, perform their responses in the present, and express their hope of future salvation.

Jesus and his disciples gathered in the upper room to celebrate the Passover. It was not the first time either Jesus or the disciples celebrated the meal, neither would they have thought, at the time, that it would be the last. Despite John's account of the gospel situating the Last Supper on the night before Passover, still his account of the gospel records two other occasions when the festival occurred (John 2:23; John 6:4).

Throughout the meal, Jesus improvises on the theme of Passover. In doing so, he recenters the meaning of the meal upon himself. Where previously Passover told the story of God's saving acts in the exodus from Egypt, now the meal tells this story of Jesus and the salvation that

33. Laytham, "Interpretation on the Way," 112.
34. Laytham, "Interpretation on the Way," 101.

would come through him. The unleavened bread previously served as a reminder of "what the Lord did for me when I came out of Egypt" (Exod 13:8). Now, Jesus takes that bread and transforms its significance as he tells the disciples "this is my body" (Matt 26:26; Mark 14:22; Luke 22:19; see also 1 Cor 11:24). Similarly, the wine, which doesn't appear in the Passover institution text and so serves only a functional purpose at that meal, is now invested with Christocentric meaning: "this is my blood of the covenant" (Matt 24:28; Mark 14:24; Luke 22:20; see also 1 Cor 11:25).

Jesus' improvisation upon the theme of salvation in the Passover meal is a "yes, and" to the offer that is handed down through generations. By instilling new meaning to a meal that was familiar to his disciples, he simultaneously created a new meal that became an ongoing and improvised performance by the company of believers; "for as often as you eat this bread and drink the cup, you proclaim the Lord's death until he comes" (1 Cor 11:26). The Passover improvised at the Last Supper becomes the Lord's Supper which becomes the improvised and eschatological meal of the kingdom.

JESUS WORSHIPING FROM HIS PERSON

Drawing upon these scenes from John 17, the Last Supper, and Emmaus, it is necessary to suggest an alternative to the suggestion that Jesus worships only from his humanity. In its place, it is suggested that he worships from his person. To do this, the emphasis is placed upon the Son's pre-existent communion with the Father. When Jesus prays to "My Father" he does so from his one person; the human and divine natures remain united. In contrast to James Torrance's definition above, it is not that Jesus is "participating" in something new, a human activity that he joins in via the incarnation.[35] Rather, he is *performing* a pre-existent eternal communion, living out his divine character in front of the world and upon the stage of creation in an incarnated, embodied performance. This is to suggest, with Speyr, that worship is a divine activity that is eternal, "because Father, Son and Spirit have been in conversation from all eternity, united in an eternal expectation and an eternal decision."[36]

---

35. Torrance, *Worship*, 9.
36. Speyr, *World of Prayer*, 28.

So, in consideration of Jesus' own worship, and specifically the prayer of John 17, it is necessary to rework James Torrance's definition in theo-dramatic terms. Namely, Jesus' own worship is an embodied performance of the eternal communion of Father, Son, and Mother Spirit, upon the stage of the world. This eternal communion exists in the giving and receiving of glory from person to person and the accompanying response of faithful obedience. This giving and receiving of glory, and responses of faithful obedience one to another are what constitutes the *liturgia Dei*, worship that is taking place within the Trinity.

What can be suggested at this point, based upon these initial observations of Jesus worshiping, is that, in Jesus Christ, the *Logos* is observed giving glory to the Father in theo-dramatic performance, and this glorification has been taking place from "before the world existed" (John 17:5). God is worshiping God. From a theo-dramatic viewpoint, the glory of God that we see in Jesus is not just a kind of static, motionless photograph of the inherent worth and splendor of the divine, but rather a dynamic, dramatic, audience-engaging glory that reflects in his person the eternal, ongoing, and inherent glory of God (see, for example, Heb 1:3). This is the *liturgia Dei*.

It is important, also, to keep in mind the brief glimpses we have of the Father and Mother Spirit performing the *liturgia Dei* upon the stage of the world. In the scene from John 17 above, the Father glorifies the Son. Similarly, Mother Spirit joins in the groan-filled prayers of creation and God's people when words cannot be found (Rom 8:22–26). The giving of glory from one person to another is attributed to the incarnated *Logos*, and to the Father and Mother Spirit as well. It is a trinitarian act performed on both the stage that is God and the stage of the world.

God is revealed as one who worships. So, a theocentric and trinitarian alternative definition of worship is proposed as follows: the ongoing, theo-dramatic performance of glorifying God that extends from, and returns to, the eternal relations of Father, Son, and Mother Spirit. The church joins in this *to, through,* and *with* Jesus. This is the *liturgia Dei*. In considering Jesus' own worship it is possible to apply this definition without confusing the two natures, while preserving the hypostatic union.

SCENE—GETHSEMANE IN PERFORMANCE

The synoptic Gospels all transcribe Jesus' prayer in the garden. The praying Jesus is depicted "throwing himself to the ground" (Matt 26:39), crying out in a prayer that is filled with grief and agitation. From a position on the ground, either prostrated or kneeling, he prays, "Father, if you are willing, remove this cup from me; yet, not my will but yours be done" (Luke 22:42). Matthew and Mark both record that Jesus prayed three times.

In Mark's account of the prayer in the garden Jesus prays initially, "Abba, Father, everything is possible for you. Take this cup from me. Yet not what I will, but what you will" (14:26). He returns to his disciples and finds them sleeping. "Simon, are you asleep? Couldn't you keep watch for one hour? Watch and pray so that you will not fall into temptation. The spirit is willing, but the flesh is weak."

Once more he went away and prayed "the same thing" (14:39). The assumption may be that Jesus prayed his *first* prayer a second time ("take this cup from me"). However, "the same thing" may not be in reference to his *first* prayer but rather his *second* prayer; the one he instructed Simon to pray—"Watch and pray so that you will not fall into temptation. The spirit is willing, but the flesh is weak" (14:38).

If it is this second prayer, then the assumption can be made that Jesus immediately receives a direct response to the first prayer. There is no other way; he must drink this cup. Upon returning to the disciples, he sees enacted before him the "temptation" to give in to not drinking the cup, symbolized by the disciples sleeping when they should be watching. He sees before him failing humanity.

If, when Jesus returns to pray this second time, he is seeking not to be relieved of the cup of suffering (having already accepted it) but rather praying for his disciples (and perhaps additionally himself) that their flesh would be strengthened in a time of temptation, then there is a different focal point of the performance on each return. The first return may indeed depict Jesus resolved, having received confirmation that the cup of suffering must be drunk. The second return may depict Jesus' compassionate concern for his disciples' weakness. Now they need him more than ever. The final return may depict Jesus upright and resolved, facing toward his destination (much like Luke 9:51). The disciples, despite their weariness, must respond to Jesus' call to "Rise! Let us go!" This is a firm instruction to get up, to resist temptation, and to join Jesus on the journey toward the cross. Each time Jesus prays, there is a different motivation and therefore a different result.

It is in Matthew's account where the prayer of Jesus is most clearly his own: "*My* Father" (26:39). But it also here that the recipient of his prayer is most clearly known: "My *Father*." Jesus has referred to his Father on many occasions (7:21; 8:21; 10:32; etc.). Here, though, the intensity and the deeply personal nature of the relationship are fully on display. Matthew suggests that, on each occasion, Jesus' prayer is focused upon the cross, albeit with some variation between the first (v. 39) and second (v. 42) accounts of it. The third account is not given; rather, Matthew states that Jesus prayed "the same thing" (v. 44). Accompanying this focus on Jesus' personal prayer is a downplaying of the disciples' inability to remain alert. When Jesus first returns, he only speaks to Peter and, between the second and third prayers, there is no indication that the disciples are woken by Jesus at all, nor do they acknowledge his return (as occurs in Mark's account). Instead, the struggle in the garden is Jesus' and Jesus' alone.

From a performance perspective, the emotional intensity increases. He begins by being "overwhelmed with sorrow to the point of death" (26:38) and falls with his face to the ground to pray. When he returns the first time, he finds them sleeping. The loneliness intensifies as Jesus speaks only to Peter, giving him alone the instruction to watch and pray. On the second return, the disciples continue to sleep. There is no interaction with them; he simply turns and prays his prayer again—alone, without even his closest friends able to support him in his time of need. In contrast to the Markan account, the Matthean Jesus is depicted with increasing introspection and burden as he faces intense suffering and does so on his own.

Luke's account suggests another perspective on this prayer. Only one account of the prayer is provided here. The response from heaven is depicted with angels appearing to strengthen him. Despite the heavenly support, the emotional display of Jesus' anguish is on display through embodied prayer. His sweat is "like drops of blood falling to the ground" (Luke 22:44). The focus of Luke's account is upon the intensity of the prayer. Not even angelic support can help Jesus in this moment.

In contrast to Mark and Matthew, there is only one return to the disciples in Luke's account. The instruction to "get up" is combined with the instruction to "pray so that you won't fall into temptation" (v. 46). Whereas, in Mark's account, the "Rise" and "Go" are performed in such a way that the disciples meet the betrayer and his accompanying crowd on the way, in Luke the disciples rise to pray but are interrupted by the approaching crowd.

Reviewing the synoptic accounts of this prayer of Jesus, the texts are first recognized as a *transcript* of Jesus' performance; the record of a prayer of an individual in a garden just outside Jerusalem some two thousand years ago. It was prayed by Jesus on the night before his crucifixion and is included by the evangelists as a part of each of their greater narratives of his life, death, and resurrection. It is Jesus' individual prayer to the Father. The prayer he uses adopts the language of the prayer he gave to his disciples but is applied subjectively to himself. That is, the corporate prayer of "your will be done" (Matt 6:10) becomes the individual prayer of "not my will but yours be done" (Luke 22:42). He turns away from himself toward the salvific will of the Father, regardless of the cost. At this first level of a *transcript*, we recognize the enormous cost to Jesus personally, if only based on the historicity of the event.

Viewing the passage through the lens of N-CP and Chal the prayer is offered "for us humans and for our salvation."[37] The *Logos* bows before the Father and mediates on behalf of humanity for the cause of their salvation. His prayer is effective because it is offered from his person, a fully human and fully divine prayer. Although the disciples are incapable of remaining awake to pray for themselves, nevertheless Jesus prays for them, and ultimately all people, that the will of the Father may be fulfilled. Here is the Great High Priest interceding on behalf of humanity for their salvation.

Considering the text as an opportunity to pray the *Logos*-script, the prayer of Jesus can become the prayer of the penitent, *the* sinner's prayer. The church joins in the prayer of Jesus through contemporary, embodied performances in accordance with the *Logos*-script. This prayer is not meant to be just recited verbatim or only studied in a classroom, with priority given to the original meaning of the text to its first recipients, as important as those things are. Rather it is meant to be performed, embodied, translated into new and emerging contexts, and even improvised upon. The fitting performance of the text provides the context where the recitation of the text, and the careful consideration of the original meaning, make ultimate sense. An example of this will be considered later in this book of the use of the Mercy Seat in The Salvation Army as a place of embodied performances of the *Logos*-script of this prayer.

---

37. Chal, 181.

TOWARD A THEOCENTRIC DEFINITION OF WORSHIP

In drawing this chapter to a close, the preliminary definition of worship that has been offered so far needs to be considered. Speyr first suggests that, "when the incarnate Son manifests his love to the Father in the form of worship, he is doing nothing new. He is doing what he has done from all eternity."[38] Later, though, she states that "the Son's adoration is human. It is not simply the corollary and the continuation of the divine vision."[39] What appears to be a contradiction is resolved, however, since it is the old covenant that conditions the Son's worship. In becoming fully human, he must experience the fullness of the human condition, and this includes learning what it means to worship as a human.

Through his acts of worship, the Son is fulfilling the old covenant as human at the same time he is inaugurating the new covenant as the *Logos*, as a part of his divine mission. Such a mission cannot be carried out by a human person but only by God's self. Here is where the apparent contradiction is resolved and where, in contrast to those who have suggested that Jesus worships out of his humanity, Speyr emphasizes the person of Jesus.

> Thus it is expressly and necessarily as *God*-Man that the Son on earth adores the Father. The first part of this task is that he must translate the vision which he possessed in heaven as God and which remains natural to him on earth as the God-Man. But, secondly, this vision becomes in him an imparted vision, which must be in him the origin and harbinger of the vision of many who are to come after him.[40]

What is taking place in and as Jesus worships is the fulfillment of the old and the inauguration of the new within his person.

This draws upon the theology expressed by the author of the book of Hebrews. There, it is suggested that Christ "did not glorify himself" but was appointed high priest by the one who said to him, "You are my Son" (Heb 5:5). Perhaps unexpectedly, though, all of this takes place through suffering. "He gives thanks for his suffering and as a sufferer he worships."[41] As he worships through suffering, Jesus experiences the fullness of humanity and simultaneously reveals the vastness of divine

---

38. Speyr, *World of Prayer*, 52.
39. Speyr, *World of Prayer*, 85.
40. Speyr, *World of Prayer*, 85.
41. Speyr, *World of Prayer*, 220.

love. The author of Hebrews suggests that, when Jesus offered up prayers "with loud cries and tears," he "learned obedience through what he suffered" and "became the source of eternal salvation for all who obey him" (5:8-9). So, when he prayed in the garden, "not my will but yours be done" (Luke 22:42), the earthly prayer of suffering and the heavenly vision of worship are revealed.

Furthermore, the worshiping Jesus is taken to the cross and there he gathers "all the sins of humanity, in order to bear them in himself."[42] While this vision of the atonement is nothing new, Speyr also suggests that Jesus "gathers together all the goodness of which men are capable, all their love of the Father and hope and faith in him, in order to concentrate their radiance as intensely as possible."[43] In this way, the best of heaven and earth are on display. Divinity and humanity are united in the person of Jesus Christ. His worship is offered by God the Son. "On the Cross the Lord gives his spirit back to the Father, to suffer finally as a naked human being. Yet this does not mean that he ceases to be God-Man and becomes merely human, for the Father accepts what has been commended to him so that it will be efficacious in the spirit of the Son as the Son would wish."[44]

Drawing upon Speyr's theology, this book suggests that there is a need for a thoroughly theocentric and trinitarian definition of worship. The following is offered in this regard; worship is the ongoing, theodramatic performance of glorifying God that extends from, and returns to, the eternal relations of Father, Son, and Mother Spirit, the *liturgia Dei*. The church joins in the performance of the *liturgia Dei* as it glorifies God *to*, *through*, and *with* Jesus Christ.

All of Jesus' life is a performance out of his person. There are no acts that are performed solely from either his divinity or his humanity. There are acts that are performed because he is human, for example, eating, drinking and sleeping. There are also acts that are performed because he is divine, for example, healing the sick, forgiving sins, and raising the dead. On no occasion, though, is any one act of the incarnate Jesus *only* human or *only* divine. This is made even more important when considering those acts of worship performed by the Father (e.g., John 17) and Mother Spirit (e.g., Rom 8:26).

Once again, the writer of Hebrews captures this when it is suggested that Jesus is a "minister [λειτουργὸς—*leitourgos*] in the sanctuary and the

42. Speyr, *World of Prayer*, 254-55.
43. Speyr, *World of Prayer*, 255.
44. Speyr, *World of Prayer*, 223.

true tent that the Lord... has set up" (8:2). Prior high priests offered worship solely from an earthly temple, for what other option did they have? In contrast, Christ has offered worship from a unique position. As the God-human his worship is offered from his person to the divine. Given his immediate and eternal access to the Father, by nature of their shared essence, his worship is perfect. That is, it is a "more excellent ministry" (διαφορωτέρας τέτυχεν λειτουργίας—*diaphoroteras tetuchen leitourgias* Heb 8:6).

On the other hand, the qualitative distinction between humanity and the divine is a central tenet of theology. God is God and creation is not. The uniqueness of the incarnation is such that the divine and human natures, and therefore God and creation, are united in the person of Jesus Christ. As such, we see in the person of Jesus Christ true divinity and true humanity displayed in perfect performance. It is not necessary to distinguish "divine" acts from "human" acts in the person of Jesus Christ for in his person they are united and so are one and the same. There is no debate that worship can be a human act performed for the divine. What this book suggests is that it is also a divine act performed for the divine. Indeed, it is *primarily* a divine act. This is made evident through the worshiping Jesus. Jesus the worshiper reveals that worship is an eternal theo-dramatic performance of glorifying God that extends from, and returns to, the eternal relations of Father, Son, and Mother Spirit.

The language of performance theory is helpful at this point. There are human actions performed by Christ that are "not" divine. But these human actions, because they are performed by Christ, are also "not-not" divine. Similarly, there are divine actions performed by Christ that are "not" human. But these divine actions, because they are performed by Christ, are "not-not" human. This apophatic approach to the problem helps to hold the tension between confusing and dividing the two natures in Christ and, by extension, the persons of the Trinity. What the next chapter will seek to do is take a kataphatic approach to the problem to show that worship is primarily a divine act.

CONCLUSION

What has been argued in this chapter is that when Jesus worships he does so out of his person, not just his human nature. Chal affirms the perfection of the two natures of Christ, "perfect in divinity and perfect in humanity." Further, it holds in tension the relationship between the two natures; the two natures "undergo no confusion, no change, no division, no separation; at no point was the difference between the natures taken away through the union, but rather the property of both natures is preserved and comes together into a single person and a single subsistent being."[45] It is from this "single person" and "single subsistent being" that Jesus' worship extends. So, any definition of worship needs to account for Jesus' active performance of it and do so from his person. It must include his humanity and his divinity. This highlights the inadequacy of anthropocentric definitions of worship and, therefore, the need for a theocentric one. Further, the glimpses that are provided of the Father and Mother Spirit performing acts of worship need to similarly be kept in view. As such, any theocentric definition of worship needs to be trinitarian. This is where attention now turns in the following chapter.

---

45. Chal, 181.

5

The Protagonist(s)—The Trinity

IN THE LAST CHAPTER, it was shown that Jesus worships from his person, not from his humanity alone. Focus turns now to what can be said about worship within the Trinity. It has been shown to this point that viewing Jesus at worship through the lens of the creeds demonstrates that Jesus worships as the God-human. When Jesus worships, he does so as the incarnated *Logos*, revealing that worship is a divine action. In this chapter, consideration is given in more detail to the divine foundation of worship. Specifically, the research question being addressed is, "What is revealed about intra-trinitarian relations when Jesus performs worship?" It will be demonstrated how God is *creator*, *personae*, *performer*, and *audience* within the theo-drama. The theology of Adrienne von Speyr and David Fagerberg will be considered in detail to support this task.

ADRIENNE VON SPEYR

Speyr's *The World of Prayer* grounds prayer in the inner life of the Trinity. Rather than a conversation between creation and the divine, prayer is first and foremost an eternal communion taking place within the Godhead.

> Prayer has no beginning because Father, Son and Spirit have been in conversation from all eternity, united in an eternal expectation and an eternal decision. The Father possesses one Word—the Son. The Son is his Word, and the Father is continually bringing forth this one Word, who is always being fulfilled

in him and in the Spirit. All that the Father intends, thinks and utters is always expressed in the Son as Word, intelligible and understood. And the Word of the Father is prayer, since he is simultaneously a conversation with the Father and the Spirit.[1]

Speyr considers worship to be an aspect of prayer. It is "fellowship with God," and is one way that fellowship is enacted.[2] She emphasizes that this fellowship is eternally taking place within the Godhead. She depicts an "overwhelming vision of the gate of heaven cast open, revealing the dynamic inner life of the Trinity."[3] Worship is eternally present in the Trinity and subsequently made available for creation to join in via the Incarnation of the *Logos* and the ongoing work of Mother Spirit.

The foundation of Speyr's vision of worship is the doctrine of the Trinity, specifically, the perichoretic fellowship of love between the three persons and the unity of essence in their divinity. "The love which joins Father and Son in the Spirit reveals to the Father the greatness of the Son, to the Son the greatness of the Father, to the Spirit the greatness of both, and to both the greatness of the Spirit. Love is the basis for this discovery, and love unites with each of the divine attributes."[4]

When one of the persons gazes upon another, they see there the fullness of divinity; "God discovers anew . . . what God is."[5] Worship flows out of this discovery. Herein lies Speyr's unique vision of worship, "the expression of God's encounter with God in love" and "the loving recognition of God."[6] Here, Speyr offers a theocentric understanding of worship that is centered upon God's being. This vision of worship relies upon the full equality of persons within the Trinity as it is described in N-CP; all three persons are "co-worshipped and co-glorified."[7] Any hint of subordinationism would mean that it would crumble. Matthew Sutton suggests that Speyr "presents a dynamic interaction of the triune Persons while holding on to the essential oneness of God."[8] Given the equality of persons, Speyr boldly suggests that:

---

1. Speyr, *World of Prayer*, 28. Elements of this section have been published in Couchman, "Performing in the Theodrama."
2. Speyr, *World of Prayer*, 21.
3. Sutton, *Heaven Opens*, 11.
4. Speyr, *World of Prayer*, 51.
5. Speyr, *World of Prayer*, 51.
6. Speyr, *World of Prayer*, 51–52, 53.
7. N-CP, 163.
8. Sutton, *Heaven Opens*, 5.

Because [the Son] is God, [the Father] perceives . . . God everywhere in the Son; the Father "sees, hears, smells, tastes" God in the Son. All his "senses" react to the manifestation of the Son's divinity. And this impression both results from and extends uniformly to all particulars in such a unity that the whole divine perception, in every respect and direction, is absorbed in discovering and worshipping love. The discovery of the full nature of God in the beloved is the highest experience possible; therefore it continually calls forth worship.[9]

The worship that is taking place within the Trinity is called "first worship" by Speyr, and it is "like a great silence between Father and Son."[10] First worship is the full contemplation of the divinity seen in the other. It is a "relation to a Thou, a relation so strong and pure that only the Thou is of any account."[11] Since Father, Son, and Mother Spirit share in divinity equally it results in the fullest expression of love for another that is possible. Love is eternally given and received from person to person and back again. Worship consists of "nothing other than the love of the Three, actively loving and passively being loved, where the core of every action and every contemplation is always love."[12] The giving and receiving of love here opens the way for worship in the church to be framed in theodramatic terms, with performance at the heart of such an understanding.

Earlier, it was demonstrated how Balthasar and Speyr speak with *una voce*.[13] The following quote was used as a key example of this writing style and part of it is shared again to focus attention upon its content. "When God stands before God we can say 'that God shows honor to God' 'in a reciprocal glorifying,' 'in an eternal, reciprocal worship.' 'Worship as we know it is a grace that comes from the triune worship. Nothing is more rooted in God than worship.'"[14] This view of worship summarizes Speyr's vision of worship as it is expressed across a number of her works. It flows from the foundational assumption that the eternal conversation taking place within the Trinity is the realization of divine love given and received by the three persons to and from each other, and beyond to

9. Speyr, *World of Prayer*, 53.
10. Speyr, *World of Prayer*, 54.
11. Speyr, *World of Prayer*, 209.
12. Speyr, *World of Prayer*, 53.
13. See "The Working Relationship of Balthasar and Speyr" above.
14. Balthasar, *TD*, 5:96. In this quote Balthasar cites from multiple texts from Adrienne von Speyr. Respectively, these are *Kath. Briefe*, 1:319; *Philipper (Dient der Freude)*, 20; *Objektive Mystik*, 82; and *Welt des Gebetz* [*World of Prayer*], 56.

creation. "Each person of the Trinity enjoys the one divine will in divine freedom."[15] The Son lives out this divine love in obedience to the Father's will, even "when the Father's will appears 'alien and unintelligible' to him, he will carry it out to perfection."[16] In contemplating the Son we are given access to the inner life of God. This access is more than just an approximation of divine love, but a genuine encounter and opportunity to join in loving and being loved; a genuine performance of love.

> In faith—and not in open sight—we are drawn into this threefold nature as a result of our meeting and fellowship with the Son on earth. From a strictly theological point of view, therefore, our "seeing, hearing and touching" of Jesus Christ, the "Word of life," mediates to us a knowledge (veiled, no doubt, but absolutely true and objective) of the triune life of God. Grace is our mode of sharing in this life; it therefore endows us with the appropriate subjective faculty so that, with the certainty of faith, we can see the trinitarian side of the phenomenon of Christ as the object of our contemplation.[17]

Here, Balthasar contradicts those who suggest worship flows from the human nature of Christ alone, for it is not theologically appropriate to divide Christ's actions into those he "performs 'as God' and those 'as man'; instead, it will see all that he does, and says, and is, as the translation of the nature of God in human terms." Balthasar suggests that "every concrete event of Jesus' human life at this 'opening' to the divine, which consists in the mystery of the two natures in unity; there, in the 'opening,' each event can tell us something of God's inner life."[18] So, in seeing Jesus worship we see God worship. In him "faith's trinitarian background becomes completely visible."[19]

Speyr and Balthasar together suggest that the inner life of God is a life of worship for "nothing is more rooted in God than worship."[20] Worship is grounded in the divine life and takes place between the three persons of the Trinity. It is eternal, reciprocal, and essential to the divine

---

15. Balthasar, *TD*, 5:95.
16. Speyr, *Kath. Briefe*, 2:206, cited in Balthasar, *TD*, 5:95.
17. Balthasar, *Prayer*, 178–79.
18. Balthasar, *Prayer*, 164–65.
19. Balthasar, *Prayer*, 61.
20. Speyr, *Philipper (Dient der Freude)*, 20, cited in Balthasar, *TD*, 5:96.

nature. This "trinitarian conversation" is, for both authors, the "prototype of all prayer."[21]

DAVID FAGERBERG

David Fagerberg has expressed a consistent definition of liturgy across many of his publications as "the Trinity's perichoresis kenotically extended to invite our synergistic ascent into deification."[22] This definition emphasizes that liturgy is an "activity done by God" and so is thoroughly theocentric in its focus.[23] The key theological terms of *perichoresis*, kenosis, synergy, and deification are drawn together to provide a "thick definition" that emphasizes the centrality of divine activity in liturgy.[24] Indeed, according to Fagerberg, the inner life of God is itself liturgical. God, in God's self, is a "community of love. The mutual indwelling of Father and Son and Holy Spirit turns outward toward other creatures and invites them to participate in divine, eternal life."[25] As a result, any liturgical acts of the church or of individual Christians are a "synergistic ascent into deification."[26] Further, the church's liturgy is a joining in of a liturgy already in progress.[27] In theo-dramatic terms, the drama is eternally being performed with ever-changing and inter-changing *audiences*, *personae*, and *performers*. It is God, the *creator* of the theo-drama, who is the eternal foundation, but also *performer*, of worship. The church moves from first being *audience* to then joining in as *performers*. It does this *to*, *through*, and *with* Jesus.

Fagerberg notes that this does not mean there are two different liturgies, the divine and the human, or the heavenly and the earthly. Rather, there is only one liturgy since it is an action of "the whole Christ."[28] In emphasizing this, Fagerberg seeks to ensure a theocentric understanding of what is taking place in liturgy. He seeks to move beyond simplistic

21. Balthasar, *TD*, 5:96.
22. Fagerberg, "Liturgical Theology," 12; Fagerberg, "Liturgy, Signs, and Sacraments," 455; Fagerberg, *Liturgical Mysticism*, 12.
23. Fagerberg, "Liturgical Theology," 9.
24. Fagerberg, "Liturgical Theology," 9.
25. Fagerberg, "Liturgy, Signs, and Sacraments," 456.
26. Fagerberg, "Liturgical Theology," 12; Fagerberg, "Liturgy, Signs, and Sacraments," 455; Fagerberg, *Liturgical Mysticism*, 12.
27. Fagerberg, "Liturgy, Signs, and Sacraments," 457.
28. Fagerberg, "Liturgy, Signs, and Sacraments," 458.

understandings of worship that rely upon a "thin, horizontal, and natural definition" of worship to a "definition that is theological in nature, biblical in foundation, cosmic in function, eschatological in orientation, and ecclesiological in depth."[29]

So, Fagerberg offers a definition of worship that draws together key doctrines (*perichoresis*, kenosis, deification, etc.) into a succinct statement. It also places emphasis upon the divine foundation of worship, which is then "extended" to invite "our" performance of it. Unlike most other definitions of worship, Fagerberg's is theocentric in nature. What is lacking, however, is a direct application to the worshiping Jesus. Here we recall David Peterson's criteria, highlighted throughout this book, that any definition of worship "must apply to Jesus himself, since he is a worshipper."[30] Fagerberg's definition retains a distinction between divine and human worship; a distinction that does not apply to the person of Jesus Christ in whom the divine and human natures are united. In terms that this book has been using, it remains unclear from this definition how worship takes place *to*, *through*, and *with* Jesus. Where both Speyr and Fagerberg agree is upon the divine origin and centrality in worship. It is first and foremost a divine activity and, so, a thoroughly theocentric definition of worship is required.

SCENE: BASIL'S *ON THE HOLY SPIRIT*

St. Basil the Great (ca. 330–379) wrote *On the Holy Spirit* in response to questions on the faith he had received from Amphilochius of Iconium. At the commencement of the treatise he recounts a story regarding prayer.

> Lately when I pray with the people, some of those present observed that I render the glory due to God in both ways, namely, to the Father, with the Son together with the Holy Spirit, and to the Father, through the Son, in the Holy Spirit. They said that we used foreign and contradictory words. But, for the sake of helping these people, or—if they are completely incorrigible—for the sake of strengthening anybody who encounters them, you think it an exceedingly good idea to articulate some clear teaching on the power contained in these words. We must, then,

---

29. Fagerberg, "Liturgy, Signs, and Sacraments," 456.
30. Peterson, *Engaging with God*, 17.

speak briefly so that we are able to give a suitable starting-point for our explanation.[31]

It is the comparison between praying "with the Son together with the Holy Spirit" to praying "through the Son, in the Holy Spirit," that is the focus of Basil's text. What is of first significance, from a methodological point of view, is how Basil uses liturgical forms of prayer and baptismal rites as authoritative theological source material. This text is an excellent example of *lex orandi, lex credendi* in use.

Basil criticizes the "hair-splitting reasoning" of those who would concern themselves with the syllables and words; "for they love to win an argument and to point out the different expressions of the Father, Son, and Holy Spirit, as if from this they will have an easy proof of their difference in nature."[32] Instead, Basil suggests that the argument that "from whom" and "through whom" suggests "things of different natures" is taken from pagan wisdom. This, he suggests, contains "foolish, empty, and deceptive observations" that "make God the Word inferior" and abolishes the Holy Spirit.[33]

Instead, Basil provides a large selection of proof texts that demonstrate that both liturgical forms of prayer are appropriate. Further, he shows that neither form of prayer demonstrates that there is a distinction between the natures of Father, Son, and Mother Spirit. Rather, "we perform the doxology to the Only-begotten with the Father, and we do not separate the Holy Spirit from the Son."[34] Basil offers an apologetic for trinitarian prayer in both liturgical forms and demonstrates how Father, Son, and Mother Spirit are all equal and share the same essence.

> Let them listen to the Lord himself, as he plainly shows that his own glory is equal in honor to the Father's, when he says, "He who has seen me has seen the Father" (Jn 14:9). And again, "When the Son comes in the glory of the Father" (Mk 8:38). And, "So that they may honor the Son just as they honor the Father" (Jn 5:23). And, "We beheld his glory, the glory of the Only-begotten of the Father" (Jn 1:14). And, "the Only-begotten God, who is in the bosom of the Father" (Jn 1:18). They do not take into account any of these texts, and they relegate the Son to the place set aside for his enemies. The footstool is for those who

---

31. Basil the Great, *On the Holy Spirit*, 29–30.
32. Basil the Great, *On the Holy Spirit*, 30.
33. Basil the Great, *On the Holy Spirit*, 31–32.
34. Basil the Great, *On the Holy Spirit*, 39.

need to fall down in submission, but the bosom of the Father is the proper seat of the Son.[35]

Further, since there is a fundamental equality between all three persons of the Trinity, and they share the same essence, this negates any suggestion that the naming of only one in prayer or baptism does not include the others; "for the invocation of Christ is the confession of the whole."[36] Therefore, prayer that is offered *to* Christ is considered just as trinitarian as one that is offered using the formula "to the Father, with the Son together with the Holy Spirit," or one offered using the formula "to the Father, through the Son, in the Holy Spirit."[37]

In the midst of his argument in support of this claim, Basil highlights how the three persons of the Trinity glorify each other.

> As he said about himself, "If I have glorified you on the earth, I have finished the work which you gave to me to do" (Jn 17:4). He also speaks in this way about the Paraclete: "he will glorify me because he will take from me what is mine and proclaim it to you" (Jn 16:14). And just as the Son will be glorified by the Father who says, "I have glorified you, I will glorify you again" (Jn 12:28), thus also the Spirit is glorified through the communion that he has with the Father and the Son as well as through the witness of the Only-begotten who says, "Every sin and blasphemy will be forgiven you by men, but the blasphemy against the Spirit will not be forgiven" (Mt 12:31).[38]

This scene from Basil depicts a vision of the three persons glorifying the others that is consistent with Speyr and Balthasar, who emphasized that "when God stands before God we can say 'that God shows honor to God' 'in a reciprocal glorifying,' 'in an eternal, reciprocal worship.'"[39] Similarly, it supports the suggestion by Fagerberg that liturgy is an "activity done by God."[40] That is, worship is eternally taking place within the divine nature. It is an eternal glorification of God taking place between Father, Son, and

35. Basil the Great, *On the Holy Spirit*, 41–42.
36. Basil the Great, *On the Holy Spirit*, 59.
37. Basil the Great, *On the Holy Spirit*, 29–30.
38. Basil the Great, *On the Holy Spirit*, 82.
39. Balthasar, *TD*, 5:96. In this quote Balthasar cites from multiple texts from Adrienne von Speyr. Respectively, these are *Kath. Briefe*, 1:319; *Philipper (Dient der Freude)*, 20; and *Objektive Mystik*, 82.
40. Fagerberg, "Liturgical Theology," 9.

Mother Spirit. This is the *liturgia Dei*. From this theocentric foundation, this book moves to consider how the performance categories of *creator, personae, performer,* and *audience* apply to God. This will demonstrate how God exists in, behind, and within the church's liturgy.

GOD AS CREATOR

Foundational to N-CP is the belief that God is creator of all, the "maker of heaven and earth, of all things both seen and unseen."[41] Creation flows from God's being out of a "superabundance of love,"[42] *creatio ex amore*. This is "truly a hymn of the glory of the inaccessible and inexpressible God," a "musical harmony which produces a blended and marvelous hymn of the power which controls the universe."[43] This love is essential to who God is and, in trinitarian terms, is given from person to person, within the one divine nature, in an eternal glorification. Each person loving and each person being loved, each person glorifying the other, and each person being glorified. Gregory of Nyssa describes this movement taking place within the Trinity.

> You observe the circular course traced by glory, always going through things that are like. The Son is glorified by the Spirit; again the Son has glory from the Father and the Only Begotten becomes the glory of the Spirit. For by what else will the Father be glorified save by the true glory of the Only Begotten? Again, in what else shall the Son be glorified, save in the greatness of the Spirit? And so again the argument goes round in a circle, glorifying the Son through the Spirit and the Father through the Son.[44]

This performance is taking place eternally within God's self. That is, the stage is God. Then, in a moment of divine improvisation and extravagance, God makes room upon the stage for something that is not God—creation. God acts and creation is formed (Gen 1:3). In this divine performance, the divine audience looks and sees that it is very good (Gen 1:31); God applauds the drama that has both concluded and just begun.

---

41. N-CP, 163.
42. Gregory of Nyssa, "Great Catechism," 478.
43. Gregory of Nyssa, *Treatise on the Inscriptions of the Psalms*, 89–90.
44. Gregory of Nyssa, "Against the Macedonians" (GNO III.1.108.33), cited in Meredith, *Gregory of Nyssa*, 42. Meredith's translation.

At the conclusion of this "work," the first act of the theo-drama, God rests (Gen 2:2).

The Son and Mother Spirit function as *creators* in the performance as well, "beginning from the Father, advancing through the Son, and completed in the Holy Spirit."[45] The Son as the *Logos* enacts the performative action (John 1). The Son "is the triune God's primary illocutionary act (Heb 1:1)."[46] As such he is the Word-Act. Mother Spirit hovers over the waters of chaos (Gen 1:2), over that which is without narrative, without a place within the drama, improvising life upon a stage that, until this moment, has no form or function. Together Father, Son, and Mother Spirit create space within themselves for something that is not God, for creation. They create a stage upon the stage.

On this new stage, that which is not God performs *to* God. As creator God gives life to creation, inhabiting the actors through their very breath (Gen 2:7); therefore the actors perform *through* God. The actors, made in the image of the creator, are invited to perform wholeheartedly and freely, within the confines of love for God and the rest of creation; therefore they perform *to*, *through*, and *with* God upon the stage of creation. The freedom to perform, to improvise and to say "yes, and" to God, is central to what it means to be a creature and a reflection of God's superabundant love. The ongoing performance of the theo-drama depends upon this freedom. "[God] must love his characters but for that very reason he must also cherish their autonomy. He owes it to himself, however involved he may be in the fate of his characters, to stand above them, so that in the very last analysis he can embody their destiny."[47]

There are, however, limits to this freedom. If the actors respond with a "yes, and" to God then they choose to respond within the same theo-drama. They join in its eternal performance. They take that which is offered, love—God's very self—and offer it back to God. This is worship. It is to love God and neighbor with all of oneself, joining in the eternal glorification of God by giving back to God what belongs to God. To respond to the offer with a "no" is to go beyond the bounds of love for God and neighbor. This blocks the drama and prevents it from moving forward. Instead of the actors responding to the invitation to love God, they turn in toward themselves, toward sin. Divine love given for the sake of the other becomes selfish love (which is not really love at all) kept for the

---

45. Gregory of Nyssa, "On the Holy Spirit," 320.
46. Vanhoozer, *Drama of Doctrine*, 191.
47. Balthasar, *TD*, 1:280.

sake of the self. Sin leads to the death of the human actor's performance in the narrative and, ultimately, the death of the actors themselves. That which was created in the image of the creator, to perform that image on the stage of creation for the divine audience, departs from the beauty and likeness of the divine.[48] This enacts what Shannon Craigo-Snell has called Deadly Church. "The deadly church is not really church at all. It is what we do, creating our visible No-God."[49]

Despite the introduction of evil, sin, and death into creation, the theo-drama continues. By his understanding of a twofold process of creation, Gregory of Nyssa recognizes the hope built into the drama.[50] Interpreting the parallelism of Gen 1:26–27 as two stages of the creative process, he sees the image of God first as the idea or original plan of the creator. This image is seen in all of humanity and "extends equally to all the race," for "they equally bear in themselves the Divine image."[51] He then suggests that Gen 1:27 represents a "resumption of the account of creation,"[52] specifically in the designation of humanity as being created male and female. Significantly, Gregory interprets this as a "departure from the Prototype."[53] Gregory makes it explicit that by "Prototype" he means Christ, not the first humans. Gregory interprets Gen 1:26–27 through the lens of Gal 3:28 when he says, "in Christ Jesus . . . there is neither male nor female."[54]

The distinction within a twofold creation, Gregory suggests, extends from the graciousness of God. In foreseeing the fall and realizing that death would follow sin's entry onto the stage, God benevolently equipped humanity with the capacity to reproduce, something that Gregory assumes would not be needed had the fall not occurred. Procreation, while not part of the image of God, is still a gracious capacity given to humanity. It is that which enables humanity to delay the extinction of the race until the incarnation of Christ, and thus recreation. So, procreation bears some salvific significance, albeit in a limited sense, in Gregory's theological anthropology. "The immortality of humanity is secured, so that death,

---

48. Gregory of Nyssa, "On the Making of Man," 399.

49. Craigo-Snell, *Empty Church*, 139. At this point, and throughout the book, Craigo-Snell is adapting the term "Deadly Theatre" from Brook, *Empty Space*, 7–48.

50. For more on this see my earlier book, Couchman, *In the Image of the Image*.

51. Gregory of Nyssa, "On the Making of Man," 406.

52. Gregory of Nyssa, "On the Making of Man," 405.

53. Gregory of Nyssa, "On the Making of Man," 405.

54. Gregory of Nyssa, "On the Making of Man," 405.

though ever operating against us, thus in a certain measure becomes powerless and ineffectual."[55] As a result, the theo-drama continues with the hope of redemption written into the narrative.

GOD AS PERSONAE

The action of the theo-drama reveals who the characters are within it. Importantly, while God is *creator*, and therefore the author of the theo-drama, the stage upon which the stage is built, she is also actively performing within it. This "tells us who the Author is by telling us what he has done."[56] Balthasar emphasizes that God "has the chief role,"[57] and so is the primary *persona*, in the theo-drama. God is revealed within the theo-drama because God acts. God is revealed within the theo-drama through those acts.

God is called upon by name: YHWH, a name that is given to the people for the express purpose of communication with God (Exod 3:14). Furthermore, the people improvise other names for God that are generated in response to God's acts within the theo-drama: the God who sees (Gen 16:13); the God who shepherds (Gen 48:15); the God who is among the people (Deut 7:21); the God who does no wrong, is upright and just (Deut 32:4); the God who fights (Josh 23:3); the God who rescues (Judg 8:34); and so on. These names reflect encounters with the divine as one who acts within the theo-drama; "the completely 'other' partakes of the here and now."[58]

The distinction that is important in naming God as *personae* is to acknowledge that God is more than just *audience*. Speyr's vision of worship taking place within the Trinity reveals how God is both *personae* and *audience* at the same time. Each person actively loving and passively being loved throughout eternity is now being performed upon the stage of creation, alongside the created *performers*, who also become *audience*. As God improvises, revealing God's self, and fulfilling God's desires, humans are invited to "perceive it" (Isa 43:19). For example, at the dedication of Solomon's temple, God's glory fills the temple. God is present so fully

---

55. Gregory of Nyssa, "Great Catechism," 497.
56. Balthasar, *TD*, 2:11.
57. Balthasar, *TD*, 2:17.
58. Smith, "Like Deities, Like Temples," 12.

that the priests are overwhelmed and unable to perform (1 Kgs 8:11). As Balthasar questions, "who else *can* act, if God is on stage?"[59]

The problem of God's overwhelming presence within the theo-drama is also evident in Isaiah's vision of the heavenly temple from within the earthly temple (Isa 6). On that occasion, God towers above Isaiah, God's position is "high and lofty" (Isa 6:1), and "God's *šûlāyw* alone filled the sanctuary."[60] H. G. M. Williamson suggests the word *šûlāyw* is not the "train," as some English translations suggest (e.g., NIV, KJV) but rather the bottom edge of the garment ("hem of his robe" NRSVUE). This suggests that God's presence so overwhelms the physical space of the temple that *only* this part of God's garment can be seen in the temple. More importantly, in both the dedication scene and Isaiah's vision, God is *present* in the space and that presence impacts upon everyone else in the scene. In theo-dramatic terms, God is *personae*, active and present within the performance. Here, the "complex web of interdependence" that Olkinuora describes is observed in a liturgical setting. God's presence upon the stage of creation impacts upon others.[61] In those moments where God overwhelms the stage, other performers become *audience*, unable to do anything other than watch and observe. Where they would want to respond with a "yes, and" all they can muster is silence; a dramatic pause envelops the narrative and all that is seen, heard, and observed is the glory of God.

GOD AS PERFORMER

God is a *performer* within the theo-drama. God is actively engaged in the action, reacting to the offers made by God's people and calling on them to respond in kind. While God performs upon the stage that God created, God nevertheless remains transcendent above it. The stage of creation is set within the stage of God, but it is also not God. It is only because of God's transcendence that the theo-drama can exist and not be consumed within the fullness of God. Rather, since God is over and above the stage of creation, God can enter and withdraw as God pleases. Kathryn Tanner refers to this as the "non-competitive relation between creatures and God."[62]

59. Balthasar, *TD*, 2:17.
60. Williamson, "Temple and Worship in Isaiah 6," 124.
61. Olkinuora, "Performance Theory," 26.
62. Tanner, *Jesus, Humanity and the Trinity*, 2.

There are various entries of God as *performer* that can be observed within Scripture. God follows the humans out of the garden when they are excluded from its perfection (Gen 4). God encounters Moses through the burning bush (Exod 3), within the cloud (Exod 19:9), and in the cleft of the rock (Exod 33:22). Sometimes God's entries are veiled behind other actors when another *performer* speaks, and God speaks through them; for example, when a prophet declares "thus says the Lord" (e.g., Jer 2:2 and others). Consider also how N-CP includes reference to this when it says that Mother Spirit has "spoken through the prophets."[63]

God's withdrawals from the stage are also theo-dramatically significant. The repeated cries of the psalmist experiencing one of God's withdrawals are heard in the cry "how long, O Lord?" (e.g., Ps 35:17). The dramatic expression of emotion as the psalmist senses God's exit from the stage serves to emphasize the freedom to improvise that is given to the human performers in the theo-drama. It also emphasizes the point, made above, that God is actively engaged in the performance. While the psalmist experiences the withdrawal of God, there is also an underlying hope that the God who acted before will act once again. God's character has been revealed through performance. The psalmist confidently calls upon the God who has seen, spoken, and acted in the past in the hope that God will see, speak, and act once again.

> You have seen, O Lord; do not be silent!
>   O Lord, do not be far from me!
> Wake up! Bestir yourself for my defense,
>   for my cause, my God and my Lord!
> Vindicate me, O Lord, my God,
>   according to your righteousness,
>   and do not let them rejoice over me. (Ps 35:22–24)

GOD AS AUDIENCE

This is arguably the most familiar of the four theo-dramatic roles in this schema since anthropocentric definitions of worship emphasize this role for God above all others. These definitions tend to primarily depict God functioning as the spectator of human liturgical activities. Worship, in this view, is unidirectional, from humanity toward God. God is the

---

63. N-CP.

audience, who follows the flow of the drama but, ultimately, has very little, if any, role within the action.

However, in both performance theory and theo-dramatic theology, the audience is more than an observer. The audience is active in the performance. In some theatres, the proscenium emphasizes a divide between stage and seating that creates a functional delineation between *performers* and *audience*. The performance happens on the stage, by the *personae*, and the *audience* remains off stage and is there to be entertained; it is performed for them. Even the one action that the audience is expected to engage in—reacting to the performance (applause, laughter, shock, and so on)—serves to emphasize the perceived distinction between those in the drama and those observing. For anthropocentric definitions of worship, this is akin to the infinite qualitative distinction between God and creation that is associated with the doctrine of *creatio ex nihilo*. Consider again Tanner's suggestion that "obedience and worship are appropriate stances for a human being to take and reflect the disparity of status between a creature and God."[64] However, as Vanhoozer invites us to recognize, "where the doctrine of creation trains us to draw a God/humankind *distinction*, the doctrine of the *imago Dei* trains us to make a God-humankind *connection*."[65] This is why the order of moving from the performance of worship by the person of Christ to the performance of worship within the Trinity has been employed in this book. Since Christ is the "image of the invisible God" (Col 1:15), in Christ, the connection between God and humankind is on display. The connectedness of the two natures of Christ in the hypostatic union has demonstrated how both the divine and human natures of Christ, not just his humanity, are engaged in his performance of worship. The infinite qualitative distinction between God and creation is bridged within the person of Christ.

Craigo-Snell describes the "doubleness" of performance whereby there is an "undifferentiated unity between the performer and the role or action she is performing."[66] When Christ worships, the unity of person and act is beyond undifferentiated; it is hypostatic. As Cyril of Alexandria states, "in the case of Christ [the two natures] came together in a mysterious and incomprehensible union without confusion or change."[67] His acts of worship, therefore, reveal the unity of human and divine as it is

64. Tanner, *Christ the Key*, 182–83.
65. Vanhoozer, *Drama of Doctrine*, 379.
66. Craigo-Snell, *Empty Church*, 14.
67. Cyril of Alexandria, *Unity of Christ*, 77.

performed from his person. Further, worship is not unique to the incarnated *Logos*, but an action performed by all three persons of the Trinity.

In contrast to the perceived distinction between performers and audience above, Schechner highlights the connection between performers and audience when he suggests that the "audience is the dominant element of any performance."[68] A performance is an event where actors and audience "co-create."[69] In contrast to traditional theatres that use a proscenium, other designs encourage greater levels of interaction between actors and audience. Consider Peter Brook's opening line to his *The Empty Space*: "I can take any empty space and call it a stage."[70] Regardless of the design of the physical space, Schechner suggests that all performances create a single event, a single performance, that is unique, genuine, and everyone present is affected in some way. The design of the theatre serves to facilitate the performance, including the active interaction between actors and the audience.

In worship, God is the *audience* when God is the one to whom worship is addressed, e.g., "Our Father." But such prayers assume an audience who will respond and act. This is why the prayers, and the Lord's Prayer in particular, include requests for God to act; to "give," "forgive," "save," and "deliver."[71] While the pray-er prays this prayer upon the creation stage, the prayer itself functions as an offer to God to perform an improvised response, to say "yes, and" to the prayer. The request itself, despite its regular use and repeated words, will always be different as it is always prayed by new performers in new contexts. So, every response by God to each new context will also always be different. God, as *audience*, then responds. The shift is made from *audience* to *performer* in the theo-drama and, by God's response, the theo-drama is taken into new and emerging contexts. God and the pray-er become *co-creators* of theo-drama in that moment. They worship together. That is, the prayer and the response from God are together a part of the ongoing, theo-dramatic performance of glorifying God that extends from, and returns to, the eternal relations of Father, Son and Mother Spirit. As the church prays, it joins in the performance of worship *to*, *through*, and *with* Jesus.

---

68. Schechner, *Performance Theory*, loc 1635.
69. Schechner, *Performance Theory*, loc 3815.
70. Brook, *Empty Space*, 7.
71. English Language Liturgical Consultation, "Lord's Prayer."

GOD AS CREATOR, PERSONAE, PERFORMER, AND AUDIENCE

In worship, as in theatre, the roles of *creator, personae, performer,* and *audience* overlap, intersect, and blend into one another. The relationship between the roles, especially regarding God's role in worship, is dynamic and fluid. As God creates the stage upon which the theo-drama is performed, God is identified as one who is *in* the theo-drama. God performs and offers invitations for creation to improvise performances as well and, as creation does so, God becomes the *audience*. Then, as God responds to the invitations offered from creation to God the roles change from *audience* to *performer* and back again, with God and creation moving freely between roles, upon the theo-dramatic stage, in ways that offer and receive glory to and from God. This takes place *to, through,* and *with* Jesus Christ. In the person of Christ, this interchange of roles is seen most clearly. He reveals all four of these roles as the protagonist in the theo-drama.

Anthropocentric definitions of worship do not allow for the performance of worship by any of the persons of the Trinity. For those definitions, worship is a human activity. In this book, Jesus is the *Logos*-script that is performed. The speaking of Jesus into the world is not just by words alone. Rather, he is *Word-Act*. The *Logos*-script is revealed through an embodied performance of his divine character, united with his human nature, in the one person of Jesus Christ upon the stage of creation. Balthasar and Speyr express this idea in this way.

> What is not difficult is the idea that the Son, as man, continues the eternal dialogue of prayer of the Divine Persons in heaven; it is not difficult to think of the eternal Word clothing himself in human words. And since Christ gives us a share in his own prayer, every word of the Lord is a prayer to the Father and a gift and a task for the Church. And just as God's prayer causes each Divine Person to do the will of the Others, so on earth the Father always does the will of the Son, who is obedient to him in all things (Jn 11:42). Anyone who asks in the Spirit of Christ, that is, in a trinitarian context, will infallibly be heard. Such a person has power over God; he has the "key to heaven."[72]

The *Logos* that proceeds from the divine nature is a gift of God the Father to creation. Jesus is that gift and the giver at the same time. So, as

---

72. Balthasar, *TD*, 5:122–23.

Robert H. Gundry suggests, in the unity of the person of Jesus, who is fully God and fully human, "Jesus is what *is* spoken even as he *does* the speaking."[73] Here it is also suggested that Jesus *is* what is worshiped even as he *does* the worshiping. *Performer* and *audience* intersect in his person. Jesus offers the worship that God the Father gives him to offer. The "distinction" between the two natures of Christ confessed within the creeds is just enough to ensure that this act cannot be considered any form of narcissistic self-gratification. Rather it is an offer of genuine glorification from one divine person to another. Yet the sameness of the essence confessed within the creeds is what transforms that worship from a human activity toward the divine into a revelation of the divine life. This is the *liturgia Dei* in performative action.

PHILIPPIANS 2—THE FATHER AND SON REVEAL THE *LITURGIA DEI*

Attention turns now to the Christ hymn in Phil 2:6–11 as an example of the *liturgia Dei* in performative action. Some key assumptions can be made about this well-known passage. It is a preexisting text or oral saying Paul is citing and so, logically, it predates the letter itself. Paul cites this text or oral saying because it was something his recipients, or at least some of them, were familiar with. It bears the literary structure of poetry and so is likely to have been an early Christian hymn. Given these assumptions, it can be said that this passage is "the earliest extant example of a Christian hymnic composition."[74] It is one of the earliest passages of the New Testament. It is, in general, one of the earliest pieces of Christian theology, and, more specifically, one of the earliest forms of liturgical theology. As such, it is important that this passage be considered within this book.

Paul draws upon this early Christian hymn because it was a common text to both author and recipients. The church in Philippi used the hymn as a way for them to offer worship *to* Jesus. Further, Jesus is depicted as offering himself in the hymn itself; that is, it depicts Jesus offering worship. Therefore, as the Philippians offer worship *to* Jesus they also offer worship *with* Jesus. Following on from the theoretical work above, though, the hymn provides a glimpse into the worship that is taking place

---

73. Gundry, *Jesus the Word*, 49. Emphasis in original.
74. Hurtado, *How on Earth Did Jesus Become a God?*, 84.

within the Trinity, specifically, the Father and Son glorifying one another. In this hymn, the Son worships the Father and the Father worships the Son. This is the *liturgia Dei* in performative action.

Paul's intent at this point in the letter is to encourage the readers to "be of the same mind" (2:2). This is not just the same mind as each other but the "same mind... that was in Christ Jesus" (2:5). He makes the same request specifically to Euodia and Syntyche later in the letter (4:2). This will be returned to later in the book. For now, it is enough to note that it is in this context that the hymn is brought into the letter.

Viewed from a theo-dramatic perspective the hymn reveals how both Jesus *and* the Father are *performers* of worship. Jesus is the primary *performer* in the first half of the hymn; he empties himself, takes on the form of a slave, humbles himself, and becomes obedient to death on a cross. The Father is the primary *performer* in the second half of the hymn; he exalts Jesus "even more highly," and "gave him the name that is above every other name." Larry Hurtado notes that it is "astonishing" that this hymn is "claiming that in some way God has given to Jesus (to share?) the divine name that was represented in Greek by *Kyrios* and represented in Hebrew by the tetragrammaton."[75] Here, it is suggested that the astonishment goes even further. These acts are much more than an expression of the resurrection, or an acknowledgment by the Father of the divinity of the Son. Instead, this is a liturgical act performed by the Father toward the Son. The Father is worshiping the Son. The glorification of the Son by Father performed in John 17 is performed again in the Father's exaltation of the Son.

The Father extends an offer to all creation to join in this performance. God invites creation to embody the glorification of the Son that the Father has first offered, as every knee bends and every tongue confesses that Jesus Christ is Lord. Given this is an early Christian hymn, the singing of the hymn, and indeed the subsequent and ongoing reading of the text as Christian Scripture, constitute ongoing performances by new *personae* in the theo-drama.[76] The singing and re-singing of this hymn is an example of "twice-behaved" performances.[77] The performances within the text itself, though, reveal the *personae* of Father and Son engaged as *performers* of liturgical acts, acts that all creation subsequently join in as

---

75. Hurtado, *How on Earth Did Jesus Become a God?*, 93–94.

76. Bauckham, "Worship of Jesus," 128.

77. Schechner, *Performance Theory*, loc. 5195; Schechner, *Between Theater and Anthropology*, 35–116.

performers as well. These liturgical acts are "non-competitive,"[78] since the Father and Son are "co-worshipped and co-glorified."[79]

> [Jesus] is worshipped because he participates in the unique divine sovereignty and bears the name YHWH, which names the unique divine identity. Since he does so as the Son of the Father, sharing—not rivalling or usurping—his Father's sovereignty, worship of Jesus is also worship of the Father.[80]

Michael Gorman notes the importance of the word ὑπάρχων (*hyparchōn*) in the phrase "though he existed in the form of God" (Phil 2:6). This word could be translated "concessively" ("though" or "although"), "causally" ("because" or "since"), or "temporally" ("being") with a temporal translation constituting an attempt at a middle ground between the concessive and causal options.[81] The NRSVUE, along with most translations, chooses to translate this word concessively as "though." The NIV opts for the temporal translation by using the word "being." Theologically, the choice is significant. If the choice is concessive then Jesus is performing *out of his divine character* as he embodies the acts that follow. He is doing something other than in his divine character. Gorman paraphrases the meaning here as follows: "Although Messiah Jesus was in the form of God, a status that means the exercise of power, he acted out of character—in a shockingly ungodlike manner, contrary in fact to true (Imperial) divinity—when he emptied and humbled himself."[82]

If, on the other hand, the choice is causally then Jesus is performing *in his divine character*. Again, Gorman paraphrases the meaning here as follows: "Although Messiah Jesus was in the form of God, a status people assume means the exercise of power, he acted in character—in a shockingly ungodlike manner according to normal but misguided human perceptions of divinity, contrary to what we would expect but, in fact, in accord with true divinity—when he emptied and humbled himself."[83]

Gorman notes that a "both/and" approach to the text is important. He suggests that the Christology of this passage is "essentially Chalcedonian in affirming that Christ embodied both true divinity and . . . true

---

78. Tanner, *Jesus, Humanity and the Trinity*, 4–5.
79. N-CP, 163.
80. Bauckham, "Worship of Jesus," 134.
81. Gorman, *Inhabiting the Cruciform God*, 20.
82. Gorman, *Inhabiting the Cruciform God*, 26.
83. Gorman, *Inhabiting the Cruciform God*, 27.

humanity, with both 'natures' manifested in the story of incarnation and cross."[84] In recognizing Christ's humanity and divinity on display it is possible to see that the "servant-like, kenotic activities attributed to Christ . . . are in fact divine in character."[85] Balthasar summarizes this, in his assessment of this passage with the word "obedience," noting that "an act of obedience is not necessarily foreign to God himself."[86] Karl Barth, whom Balthasar is summarizing at this point, is even more direct when he states that "the true God—if the man Jesus is the true God—is obedient."[87]

In short, Gorman, Balthasar, and Barth all recognize that the passage under investigation reveals something important about the nature of divinity. It is servant-like, kenotic, and obedient. Where this book extends this line of thinking is to suggest that the same is true for worship. Worship, too, is servant-like, kenotic, and obedient. More importantly, this passage demonstrates that it is essential to the divine nature. Christ's self-humbling is an act of worship toward the Father, and this reveals something of the nature of divinity. Equally, the Father's exalting of the Son and giving him the name that is above all names is an act of worship that also reveals something of the nature of divinity.

Viewed from a broader canonical perspective, the actions of Father and Son in the hymn of Phil 2 mirror the content of the prayer in John 17. When the Son calls upon the Father to glorify him, the Father exalts the Son and glorifies him by giving him the name that is above all names. "The Son glorifies the Father through his obedience. The Father glorifies the Son through his resurrection and exaltation."[88] The glorification of Father and Son is an eternal performance that is revealed in the incarnated *Logos*, and in his interactions with the Father transcribed in Scripture, such as the hymn in Phil 2. It is the eternal glorification of God revealed in both the Father and the Son. It is the *liturgia Dei* revealed.

Further, the Father's eternal glorification of the Son is what enables all of creation to join in. It is the stage upon which all earthly glorification of the divine takes place. The Father's exaltation is both creative and performative, yet also an open offer to all creation to join in the improvised glorification of the Son. In a similar way, when the Son gives his glory to

---

84. Gorman, *Inhabiting the Cruciform God*, 11.
85. Gorman, *Inhabiting the Cruciform God*, 31.
86. Balthasar, *Mysterium Paschale*, 82.
87. Barth, *Church Dogmatics* 4/1:164.
88. Moltmann, *Church in the Power of the Spirit*, 59.

his disciples, he enables them to join the Father in exalting him as they call upon him with the name that is above all names. For, "in Christ's pre-existent and incarnate kenosis we see truly what God is truly like, and we simultaneously see truly what Adam/humanity truly should have been, truly was not, and now truly can be in Christ."[89] So, creation joins in with Christ's kenotic self-humbling when it gives glory away from self towards the Father. Gorman summarizes this succinctly when he says, "kenosis is theosis."[90]

In this book, this is extended into the realm of worship. Christ's incarnate kenosis reveals that the *Logos* gives glory away toward the Father. The Father, in return, receives that glory and gives it away in exaltation of the Son. If kenosis is theosis then worship is a joining in the giving away of glory toward the divine, a performance that joins in the theo-dramatic and kenotic self-humbling that takes any glory received and simultaneously gives it away to the one worthy of receiving it. For the Father, that is *to* the Son and Mother Spirit. For the Son, it is *to* the Father and Mother Spirit. For Mother Spirit, it is *to* the Father and the Son. Father, Son, and Mother Spirit give glory *to* and *with* each other. This is what Speyr pointed toward when she described the perception of the other taking place within the Trinity: "the discovery of the full nature of God in the beloved is the highest experience possible; therefore it continually calls forth worship."[91]

ROMAN 8—MOTHER SPIRIT REVEALS THE *LITURGIA DEI*

The final step necessary in demonstrating worship in the Trinity is to account for the role of Mother Spirit. The Spirit is an active participant in the *liturgia Dei*, one who also performs the glorification of God. We get a glimpse of this in Rom 8, firstly in the "Spirit bearing witness with our spirit" as disciples join in Jesus' own prayer to "Abba! Father!" (Rom 8:15; Mark 14:36). Secondly, it is observed in the Spirit's own groaning prayer (Rom 8:26), which is reflected in the groans of creation and the disciples (Rom 8:22–23).

---

89. Gorman, *Inhabiting the Cruciform God*, 37.
90. Gorman, *Inhabiting the Cruciform God*, 37.
91. Speyr, *World of Prayer*, 53.

Romans 8 represents the culmination of a larger section of the letter that commences at chapter 5. Paul builds an antithetical comparison between Adam and Christ, sin and righteousness, and life and death, that culminates in Christ rescuing the "I" of chapter 7, an act that echoes the rescuing of Israel from slavery. Thus, disciples are called not to live with a "spirit of slavery" but with a "spirit of adoption" (Rom 8:15). As disciples follow the Spirit as children of God, they are empowered to call upon God as "Abba! Father!" This prayer is the same prayer that Jesus prayed in the garden as it was transcribed by Mark (14:36). And so, the Spirit unites disciples to Jesus and joins their prayer with his. "The Spirit of the Son enables us to pray like the Son . . . . Indeed the distinctive intimacy with which Jesus prayed to the Father . . . becomes our privilege because the same Spirit that animates his life of communion with the Father animates our own."[92]

Further, it can be said that Mother Spirit also empowers the prayer of Jesus himself. It is Mother Spirit who descends upon Jesus at his baptism, a moment where his identity as "Son" is confirmed to him; "You are my Son, the Beloved; with you I am well pleased" (Mark 1:11). Jesus knew God as Father, and called upon him as Father, and this revealed his identity to his disciples. His prayer life also reveals this relationship.[93] In a similar way, the Father also reveals this relationship on the Mount of Transfiguration where the words spoken at Jesus' baptism are repeated, but this time the audience has changed to become the disciples: "This is my Son, the Beloved; listen to him!" (Mark 9:6).

Mother Spirit's descent upon Jesus at his baptism is significant here. She affirms Jesus' sonship at the moment the Father declares it from heaven. So, it can be suggested that the words of Paul regarding the Spirit in Romans first applied to Jesus before they applied to the disciples; "When we cry, 'Abba! Father!' it is that very Spirit bearing witness with our spirit that we are children of God" (Rom 8:15–16). At Jesus' baptism, Mother Spirit bore witness to Jesus that he was God's Son.

As Mother Spirit bears witness in disciples, it is "deeply felt and intensely experienced."[94] As N. T. Wright suggests, "here it is the Spirit's task to enable genuine humanness."[95] That humanness is seen in the person of Jesus Christ. In joining the disciples' prayer to the prayer of Jesus,

---

92. Cole, *He Who Gives Life*, 235.
93. Pinnock, *Flame of Love*, 27.
94. Moo, *Romans*, 502.
95. Wright, *Romans*, 599.

the disciples are also given "a status comparable to that of Jesus himself," namely, children of God.[96] That status includes joining Jesus in suffering and being "glorified with him" (Rom 8:17). Here we recall Speyr's assertion regarding the connection between suffering and worship in the life of Jesus; "He gives thanks for his suffering and as a sufferer he worships."[97] And so, as the disciples join with Jesus in his worship, crying "Abba! Father!" they join with him in both suffering and glorification.

Mother Spirit is doing more than just joining the disciples to the prayers of Jesus. She also prays as well, "with groanings too deep for words" (Rom 8:26). Douglas Moo asks an important question regarding Mother Spirit's prayer: "What . . . is the nature of this intercession? Specifically, is it an intercession that comes about through our praying, aided by the Spirit? Or is it an intercession that is accomplished solely by the Holy Spirit on our behalf?"[98] The same term, στεναγμός (*stenagmōs*), is used in reference to creation, disciples, and finally the Spirit (Rom 8:22, 23, 26). It is an expressive term that demonstrates how all three performers—creation, disciples, and Mother Spirit—all enter the suffering-worship that Jesus performs most definitively in his passion. Moo, in answering his own question above, suggests that it is not that the groans of the Spirit are really the believer's prayer aided by the Spirit. This would suggest that in some way Mother Spirit is dependent upon the believer to perform her prayer for her. Rather, Moo suggests that it is the Spirit's own "language of prayer."[99] Barth notes that we don't possess the Spirit, rather the Spirit possesses us; "the action of the Spirit is independent."[100] So, when Mother Spirit prays, she does so independently. Viewed from a broader canonical perspective, the groaning-prayer of Mother Spirit is the glorification of the Son referred to in John 16:14; "[Mother Spirit] will glorify me."

Regarding Mother Spirit praying, Cole suggests that "both Son and Spirit pray according to the Father's will."[101] Cole's suggestion is important, but there is a simpler reality that is foundational here. Namely, *both* the Son and Mother Spirit pray. This reality, having been performed in the incarnation by the Son, is also performed by Mother Spirit in her

---

96. Moo, *Romans*, 502.
97. Speyr, *World of Prayer*, 220.
98. Moo, *Romans*, 524.
99. Moo, *Romans*, 525.
100. Barth, *Epistle to the Romans*, 315.
101. Cole, *He Who Gives Life*, 236.

groaning-prayer. Both reveal that God is eternally praying. Mother Spirit intercedes with all humanity (Rom 8:26) and this includes the one who unites with humanity in order to save it, the *Logos*. Both the Son and Mother Spirit pray. The prayer of the Spirit "come[s] before God as true prayer, true intercession" and so it is that "the groaning of the church, in the midst of a groaning world, is sustained and even inspired by the groaning of the Spirit."[102]

CONCLUSION

In concluding this chapter, attention returns to where it began, with the suggestion from Speyr that "prayer has no beginning because Father, Son and Spirit have been in conversation from all eternity, united in an eternal expectation and an eternal decision."[103] It has been demonstrated that, in theo-dramatic terms, God is *creator*, *personae*, *performer* and *audience*. Further, following on from the previous chapters' analysis of the Son at worship, it has been shown how glimpses of Father and Mother Spirit also joining worship can be observed in specific passages: John 16 and 17, Phil 2, and Rom 8. Jürgen Moltmann has suggested that "the relations between the discernible and visible history of Jesus and the God whom he called 'my Father' corresponds to the relation of the Son to the Father in eternity. The *missio ad extra* reveals the *missio ad intra*. The *missio ad intra* is the foundation for the *missio ad extra*."[104] Moltmann's principle can be extended with reference to worship. The *liturgia ad extra* reveals the *liturgia ad intra*. The *liturgia ad intra* is the foundation for the *liturgia ad extra*.

All three persons of the Trinity share an essential equality, which is observed in how they give glory from one to another (*ad extra*). The kenotic character of the divine nature (*ad intra*) is revealed in the way each person gives glory away from themself to the other persons. So, within the divine nature, there is an eternal glorification of God taking place between Father, Son, and Mother Spirit, the *liturgia Dei*. The Son, in the incarnation, joins with humanity bringing them into this eternal worship. The church joins in the *liturgia Dei* by offering worship *to*, *through*, and *with* Jesus. Mother Spirit is the means by which the church is united

---

102. Wright, *Romans*, 598.
103. Speyr, *World of Prayer*, 28.
104. Moltmann, *Church in the Power of the Spirit*, 54.

with Jesus so they can worship *through him*, and they can join in this eternal glorification *to* God. From here we turn to considering worship in the believers and humanity, as the *imago Dei* reflects the *liturgia Dei* in their being.

6

The Company of Worshipers

To this point, it has been argued that Father, Son, and Mother Spirit are revealed as eternally glorifying one another and so worship is a characteristic of the divine essence. This point has been made through an investigation of Jesus the worshiper and, using creedal statements made about his person as an interpretive lens, followed by consideration of accounts of the Trinity at worship. From this, it has been argued that a theocentric and trinitarian definition of worship is required. That is, the ongoing glorification of God that extends from, and returns to, the eternal relations of Father, Son, and Mother Spirit, herein summarized as the *liturgia Dei*. In this chapter, consideration will be given to how the *liturgia Dei* is observed within humanity. The focus turns now to the company of worshipers and, indeed, worship is the characteristic that defines humanity. Drawing upon James K. A. Smith's suggestion that humans are fundamentally worshipers (*homo liturgicus*), it will be argued that this characteristic of humanity is a reflection (*imago Dei*) of the worship that is essential to the divine nature (*liturgia Dei*). That is, humans join in the performance of the eternal glorification of God that takes place *to*, *through*, and *with* Jesus Christ.

LITURGICAL ANTHROPOLOGY

Humans are ritualistic animals. From the everyday mundane activities of life—eating, sleeping, brushing one's teeth—to the matters of greater social significance—cultural standards, family traditions, narratives that enable communities to function—rituals shape the identity of humanity. Further, these identity-shaping ritualized behaviors are socially constructed through performance; "there is no ritual if it is not performed."[1] Even the mundane activity of brushing teeth before bed is regularly taught to children as a function of what it means to be a part of a given family; "this is what we do here." The activity is performed and re-performed, within the context of a social unit, joined with many other similarly mundane activities to create meaning. Together they define what it means to be *this* kind of person, a part of *this* family, in *this* community. In this regard, rituals function as a means of personal and communal identity formation. They create and express meaning, identity, and the desire to be a human that contributes positively to family and community. As Tobias Tanton states, summarizing the theology of Tertullian, "rituals do not merely symbolize certain . . . ideas, rather they are performative, bringing about a new reality."[2]

Rituals can also be used negatively—to enforce control, define political boundaries by excluding others, or maintain the status quo. Take, for example, the pejorative term "unAustralian" which is used in political and social contexts as a means of defining boundaries on the acceptability of a group of activities or beliefs. An example of this may be the celebration of Halloween in Australia, regularly described as "unAustralian."[3] This description has been used by persons in positions of power (perceived or real) to try to exclude this activity and therefore regulate how Australian society should behave and function, according to the script of the one applying the label. There, anyone who chooses to participate in the rituals of Halloween is subsequently forced to decide what they will do in response to the label of "unAustralian" that comes with its performance. The need to control the performance of rituals that historically lie outside of a given community's norms, such as Halloween in Australia, demonstrates that there is a perception that the ritual's ongoing performance will somehow influence the identity of that community. If the ritual is allowed to take hold, then the status quo, the definition of what it means to be "Australian," and the culture of the community, will all change. Despite its negative use here, the fact

1. Stephenson, "Ritual as Action, Performance, and Practice," 51.

2. Tanton, *Corporeal Theology*, 228.

3. Lavelle, "Shock, Horror, Treat." See Smith and Phillips, "Popular Understandings of 'Unaustralian,'" 331.

that the term "unAustralian" exists and is applied in this way serves to confirm that rituals function to express and mold something of a person's, a family's, or a community's identity and that, therefore, humans are ritualistic by nature. Humans "are shaped cognitively (implicitly and explicitly), affectively, and bodily through participation in liturgical practices that are social in origin."[4]

Dru Johnson contends that "ritual participation forms us to recognize and then discern as one of its central functions. Because humans are ritualized creatures, we will always have an embodied understanding of the world even where our understanding appears to be solely verbal."[5] Yet, beyond the rituals of life, both sacred and mundane, formal and informal, individual and communal, there is a deeper essence to humanity that is the driving force behind this behavior. In short, all humans desire something and rituals are the way that desire is expressed. Even the mundane example of teaching a child to brush their teeth every night is effective because the child desires to show that they are part of *this* family; "if this is what *we* do, then this is what *I* do."

In *Desiring the Kingdom*, James K. A. Smith suggests that humans are primarily "liturgical animals" because they are "embodied, practicing creatures whose love/desire is aimed at something ultimate." He argues against a view of humanity as primarily "*homo rationale* or *homo faber* or *homo economicus*."[6] Instead, he suggests that humans are *homo liturgicus*; that is, they are "fundamentally and primordially lovers."[7] The term *homo liturgicus* is not invented by Smith, but it has become influential since the 2009 publication of his *Desiring the Kingdom*. Before considering more thoroughly Smith's use of the term, it is beneficial to consider how several authors also used the term before him. So, a brief survey of its use is helpful in preparation for considering its usefulness in this book.

HOMO LITURGICUS BEFORE JAMES K. A. SMITH

Alexander Schmemann uses a term that is conceptually similar to *homo liturgicus* when he suggests that humans are *homo adorans*. "The first and

---

4. Cockayne and Salter, "Liturgical Anthropology," 73–74.
5. Johnson, *Knowledge by Ritual*, 5.
6. Smith, *Desiring the Kingdom*, 40.
7. Smith, *Desiring the Kingdom*, 41.

basic definition of man is that he is *the priest*. He stands in the center of the world and unifies it in his act of blessing God, of both receiving the world from God and offering it to God—and by filling the world with this Eucharist, he transforms his life, the one he receives from the world, into life in God, into communion with Him."[8] Smith acknowledges his dependence upon, and subsequent departure from, Schmemann when he adapts Schmemann's term *homo adorans* into *homo liturgicus*. The contrast between the two terms lies primarily in the author's respective definitions of worship. For Schmemann, the term "worship" is reserved for specifically Christian usage since secularism is the "negation of worship."[9] In contrast, Smith does not see secularism as the opposite of worship but rather an alternate form of worship where the focus of human desires is directed away from God. Worship, as Smith defines it, is a "formal, ineradicable structure of human being-in-the-world, and the particular *direction* that can take (which can be authentic or inauthentic)."[10] Despite these differences, there is still agreement between the two authors, where Schmemann suggests that "man remains essentially a 'worshipping being,' forever nostalgic for rites and rituals no matter how empty and artificial is the ersatz offered to him."[11] This echoes more closely Smith's assertion that humans are liturgical animals.

Godfried Cardinal Danneels used *homo liturgicus* in an address given in 1995. There, Danneels stated that liturgy is "first 'God's work in us' before being our work on God."[12] This is a similar contention made by Fagerberg earlier, and to that being suggested with the *liturgia Dei*. However, as an example of what he means by the preexistence of the liturgy, Danneels points to the Eucharist as a "making present of a particular meal: that of Christ with his disciples on the night before he suffered."[13] In this sense, there is a difference between Danneels's understanding of the preexistence of the liturgy as compared to how it is understood by Fagerberg and in this book. Namely, for Danneels, there is an historical starting point for liturgy, a moment in time and space where it was created by God and given over to humanity to perform. It therefore remains a human activity, albeit with a divine origin. In contrast, in this book it

8. Schmemann, *For the Life of the World*, 15.
9. Schmemann, *For the Life of the World*, 125.
10. Smith, *Desiring the Kingdom*, 90n1. Emphasis in original.
11. Schmemann, *For the Life of the World*, 125.
12. Danneels, "Liturgy Thirty Years After," 10.
13. Danneels, "Liturgy Thirty Years After," 11.

is contended that liturgy is much more than a human activity. It is an eternal characteristic of the divine being. Danneels uses the term *homo liturgicus* in a manner consistent with his view of liturgy as participation in a preexistent rite. It is an "attitude of prayer, of handing ourselves over and letting God's will be done in us."[14] Participation in this preexistent liturgy stems from a contemplative attitude. Given that this is an attitude of being human and not the defining characteristic of what it means to be human, Danneels's application of *homo liturgicus* differs from Smith's use of the term.

The term *homo liturgicus* was used by Antje Jackelén in a 2002 article entitled "The Image of God as *Techno Sapiens*." There, in considering the implications of technology upon the doctrine of the *imago Dei*, *homo liturgicus* is used by Jackelén to summarize an Eastern theological anthropology.

> *Homo liturgicus* comes close to the ideal person in Eastern Orthodox tradition. He or she is surrounded by a certain mystification: the priest prays beyond the iconostasis, concealed from the laity; there are symbols that are not easily understood, and there is a sacred language that nowadays is far from everyday language. In regard to the aim of *Homo liturgicus*, Eastern anthropology is firmly embedded in the concept of *theosis* (divinization).[15]

Jackelén's use of the term focuses upon its liturgical application and destination. That is, how humans who are created in the image of the creator are sanctified through enacting symbolic liturgical forms. The ongoing, ritualized performance of liturgy serves the purposes of Christian holiness (*theosis*).

Scott Hahn has identified the liturgical origins of the Scriptural text with regard to both its composition and canonization. Hahn notes that:

> There is a liturgical reason and purpose for the creation of the world and the human person, and there is a liturgical destiny toward which creation and the human person journey in the pages of the canonical text. At each decisive stage in God's covenant relations with humanity, the divine-human relationship is expressed liturgically and sacrificially. The mighty acts of God in Scripture at every point climax in the liturgy, from the sacrificial offering of Noah following the flood to the institution of the Eucharist at the Last Supper. From the first page to the

---

14. Danneels, "Liturgy Thirty Years After," 12.
15. Jackelén, "Image of God as *Techno Sapiens*," 300.

last, the canonical text presents us with a liturgical anthropology—the human person is *homo liturgicus*, created to glorify God through service, expressed as a sacrifice of praise.[16]

It is significant that Hahn suggests that God's covenant relations are expressed "liturgically and sacrificially." This echoes the argument that the *liturgia Dei* is the foundation of human liturgical activity. Further, Hahn points to the Christological hymn of Phil 2, noting that "life itself is here seen as liturgy."[17] In a similar manner to this book, Hahn highlights that Jesus the worshiper is the central focus of liturgy. With language that echoes the theo-dramatic framework employed in this book, Hahn also notes how the reading of Scripture within liturgy is intended for behavioral change: "When proclaimed in the church's liturgy, Scripture is intended to 'actualize' what is proclaimed—to bring the believer into living contact with the *mirabilia Dei*, the mighty saving works of God in the Old and New Testament."[18] While Hahn recognizes the performative elements of the reading of Scripture in liturgy, there is a deeper purpose to this ritualized behavior. It is not for living contact with the saving works of God, but rather living contact with the God who performs saving works. That is, it is an activity that enacts and expresses the love that exists within the divine-human covenantal relationship.

One final example of the use of *homo liturgicus* prior to Smith is found in Ken Parry's publication from 1996, *Depicting the Word*. This is presented here out of chronological order due to its contrasting use by Parry in comparison to Smith and the other authors above. In a chapter describing the use of written and unwritten traditions for the Scriptural text he suggests that "for Maximos [sic], the Christian is primarily *homo liturgicus*, and therefore it is in praise and worship of God that the true meaning of salvation is found. As we have seen, it was in the area of liturgical practices that the appeal to unwritten tradition was often made."[19] Parry's source for the term *homo liturgicus*, which he attributes to Maximus the Confessor, is Pelikan's *The Spirit of Eastern Christendom*.[20] In that work, Pelikan cites Maximus as saying, "For this is the true worship [αληθης λατρεία—*alethes latreia*], genuinely pleasing to God, the strict

---

16. Hahn, "Canon, Cult and Covenant," 213.
17. Hahn, "Canon, Cult and Covenant," 224.
18. Hahn, "Canon, Cult and Covenant," 228.
19. Parry, *Depicting the Word*, 157.
20. Pelikan, *Spirit of Eastern Christendom*, 137.

discipline of the soul by means of the virtues."²¹ In all three authors, Maximus, Pelikan, and Parry, the focus is on the sources and authority of Scripture. Yet, Parry's use of the term *homo liturgicus*, and specifically his attribution of it to Maximus, is misleading. Instead, Maximus suggests that moral living is the ultimate act of true worship [αληθης λατρεία— *alethes latreia*], not that worship is the true meaning of salvation. It is significant that Maximus' term translated "worship" is *latreia* and not *leitourgia*. As a result, Parry's use of the term *homo liturgicus*, given its misattributed patristic source, is more likely a summary term he drew from an alternative source or thought of himself. Parry has used the term to describe the relationship between written and unwritten tradition in the formation of the Scriptural text. It is not, as in Smith and the other authors who have used it before him, an anthropological description of the nature of humanity. As such, Parry's use of the term needs to be discounted.

The term *homo liturgicus* has a history prior to Smith's influential use of it in *Desiring the Kingdom* and onward. Apart from Parry's use, the term has been broadly used as a summary term to describe humans as liturgical animals, that is, in liturgical anthropology. The term is useful for this purpose but, as it will be shown below, it will provide a means of demonstrating that the *liturgia Dei* is reflected in humanity. From here, attention turns to Smith's use of *homo liturgicus* before that demonstration is made.

HOMO LITURGICUS ACCORDING TO JAMES K. A. SMITH

All humans ultimately desire something even if they do not realize or recognize that desire themselves. For some the desire is toward their work, others their favorite sports team, others the accumulation of wealth. Regardless of what the desire is aimed toward humans are "fundamentally and primordially—lovers."²² Humans express this love as they exist within the world; in theo-dramatic terminology, they perform this love on the stage of the world. The way people perform their lives is shaped by what they love. Smith draws this idea from Augustine:

---

21. Maximus the Confessor, "Questions to Thalassius on Scripture" (PG 90:260), cited in Pelikan, *Spirit of Eastern Christendom*, 137.

22. Smith, *Desiring the Kingdom*, 41.

Great are you, O Lord, and surpassingly worthy of praise. Great is your goodness, and your wisdom is incalculable. And humanity, which is but a part of your creation, wants to praise you; even though humanity bears everywhere its own mortality, and bears everywhere the evidence of its own sin and the evidence that you resist the proud. And even so humanity, which is but a part of your creation, longs to praise you. You inspire us to take delight in praising you, for you have made us for yourself, and our hearts are restless until they rest in you.[23]

Smith takes Augustine's assertion that all humanity "longs to praise" God and universalizes it to describe human behavior; "we are liturgical animals—embodied, practicing creatures whose love/desire is aimed at something ultimate."[24] While humans are created to worship God, this love/desire can be aimed at something other than God. Human behavior both shapes and stems from the liturgical desire within people. So, the things that humans spend their money on or invest their time into, all is shaped and determined by what they love. This is synonymous with saying that "you are what you worship."[25] Regardless of whether or not they direct their worship to God or not, *all* humans are worshipers; they are *homo liturgicus*.

Smith demonstrates this through an illustration he entitles "making the familiar strange." He takes the reader on an imaginary journey through a suburban shopping mall but, in doing so, substitutes the familiar terms of "mall," "advertisement," and "cashier," etc. with the strange categories of "sanctuary," "icon," and "altar."[26] The strange categories are substituted from the realm of the Christian liturgy to demonstrate that "the mall is a religious institution because it is a liturgical institution."[27] Smith even suggests that the marketing industry, with its emotional, erotic, and persuasive modes of communication, understands this philosophical anthropology better than much of the church given its ability to connect with "our heart and our imagination."[28] Marketers understand that humans do not commit to purchasing something just because they

23. Augustine, *Confessions* 1.1.1; Smith, *Desiring the Kingdom*, 47; Smith, *You Are What You Love*, 7–10.
24. Smith, *Desiring the Kingdom*, 40.
25. Smith, *You Are What You Love*, 23.
26. Smith, *Desiring the Kingdom*, 19–23.
27. Smith, *Desiring the Kingdom*, 23.
28. Smith, *Desiring the Kingdom*, 76.

understand its functionality or can describe its mechanics, as important as these things may be to a consumer. Rather, humans purchase something because they are *homo liturgicus* and thus desire things. Effective marketing, understanding this principle, seeks to persuade people to *love* their product, not just purchase them. Smith even suggests that, given its effectiveness in shaping and appealing to the desires of consumers, the marketing industry is "operating within a better, more creational, more incarnational, more holistic anthropology than much of the evangelical church."[29]

Smith points out, though, that the desire at the heart of humanity cannot ultimately be satisfied by any product, service, or consumer experience. The latest mobile phone will eventually be superseded and left unused in the third drawer of the kitchen, the service provided will conclude, and the experience will eventually come to an end. Thus, despite all the effective marketing that suggests that these things will satisfy the desires of the human heart, in the end what they are offering is *nothingness*.[30]

Also of significance here is that Smith's philosophical anthropology describes humans as "liturgical animals" who live in the world as "characters in a drama." "We are acting out a script, improvising in an unfolding drama."[31] Since humans are always loving something they are directing worship toward something. They give glory away to some *thing* external to or, alternatively, toward themselves—they *worship*. "Lived worship is the fount from which a worldview springs, rather than being the expression or application of some cognitive set of beliefs already in place."[32] In all of this, humans participate in the roles of *creators, personae, performers*, and *audience* in a drama. In this book, it is argued that this drama is the divine theo-drama, the only drama where what is offered, in contrast to the nothingness above, is life itself through participation in the divine nature (2 Pet 1:4). Humans are always worshiping because they are *homo liturgicus*. This is a reflection of the theological concept of the *imago Dei*. The role of Christian liturgies is to point these desires in the direction of God, to join in the eternal glorification of God that is taking place between Father, Son, and Mother Spirit, *to, through*, and *with* Jesus Christ. This is expressed in Augustine's prayer, "So let me seek you, Lord, while

29. Smith, *Desiring the Kingdom*, 76.
30. Smith, *Desiring the Kingdom*, 100.
31. Smith, *Imagining the Kingdom*, 126–27.
32. Smith, *Desiring the Kingdom*, 136.

I invoke you in prayer; and let me invoke you while I believe in you. You have been preached to me. That faith of mine, Lord, which you have given to me, which you breathed into me by the incarnation of your Son, invokes you in prayer through the ministry of your preacher."[33]

HUMANS AS THE *IMAGO DEI*

The doctrine of the *imago Dei* is a distinguishing feature of theological anthropology. Drawn primarily from the first creation narrative in Gen 1:26–28, it is important not only because it enables theologians to speak of humans in the light of God but also since it performs "the double function of referring both to human beings and to God."[34] As such, any consideration of the *imago Dei* needs to take into account both humanity and divinity. It is broadly accepted across the theological spectrum that humans are created to reflect their creator, albeit with differing views on what exactly constitutes the image. Michael Pomazansky suggests that humans are the "crown of creation" and that, since every image reflects something of the archetype, the *imago Dei* "testifies to a reflection of the very attributes of God in man's spiritual nature."[35]

The concept of the *imago Dei* summarizes "all things that characterize Deity."[36] Gregory of Nyssa suggests that Christ is the prototypical *imago Dei*. He explains that Christ, out of love for humanity, became the "image of the invisible God" and took on human form, thus restoring humanity to its original state as an "image of the Image."[37] This idea is echoed by John Calvin, who describes Christ as the "perfect image of God,"[38] drawing on Paul's emphasis that Christ is the "image of the invisible God" (Col 1:15). This centers the *imago Dei* upon Christ, who images the invisible God through his acts of worship and love (1 John 4:8). Gregory further suggests that God created out of a "superabundance of love,"[39] which spills over into creation. In creating humanity, God made them to share in the divine nature—to love God and neighbor, by sharing

---

33. Augustine, *Confessions* 1.1.1.
34. Fulkerson, "*Imago Dei*," 95.
35. Pomazansky, *Orthodox Dogmatic Theology*, 124.
36. Gregory of Nyssa, "Great Catechism," 479.
37. Gregory of Nyssa, "On Perfection," 111.
38. Calvin, *Institutes* 1.15.4.
39. Gregory of Nyssa, "Great Catechism," 478.

in God's very self. "For He who made man for the participation of His own peculiar good, and incorporated in him the instincts for all that was excellent, in order that his desire might be carried forward by a corresponding movement in each case to its like."[40]

Humanity has been created with an inner desire to move toward that which it images. Balthasar expresses this same thought this way: "And as the Son in God is the eternal icon of the Father, he can without contradiction assume in himself the image that is the creation, purify it, and make it enter into the communion of the divine life without dissolving it (in a false mysticism)."[41] This is where *homo liturgicus* and the *imago Dei* intersect. Smith suggests that all people desire some *thing*, and Gregory suggests that this desire draws them toward the God who created them in the divine image. It is in God alone where this desire is fulfilled.

The "participation" and "corresponding movement" Gregory refers to can be summed up with the word "performance." Such performance carries human desire forward toward wherever love is directed. Ideally, this is directed toward God, but as Smith has demonstrated this is not always the case. Sin causes humans to love that which is not God, to direct their desires, intentionally or unintentionally, toward things that do not satisfy—toward *nothingness*. Smith suggests that "secular liturgies capture our hearts by capturing our imaginations and drawing us into ritual practices that 'teach' us to love something very different from the kingdom of God."[42] As a result, it is necessary that Christian liturgies serve to restore the "original, creational desire for God."[43] Not only do liturgies, secular or Christian, *reflect* what matters to their performers, they *shape* what matters to their performers.[44] In this way Christian liturgy has the important function of continually redirecting the desires of people toward the one whom humans image, the divine.

This ongoing performance is what the author of 2 Peter describes as participation in the divine nature (2 Pet 1:4). Through ongoing performance, humanity *enacts* what it was created to be and it also *becomes* what it was created to become—what Balthasar describes as "a 'second God,' an *imago exemplaris omnium*."[45] Further, as they grow and de-

---

40. Gregory of Nyssa, "Great Catechism," 479.
41. Balthasar, "Resume of My Thought," 473.
42. Smith, *Desiring the Kingdom*, 88.
43. Smith, *Desiring the Kingdom*, 88.
44. Smith, *Desiring the Kingdom*, 93.
45. Balthasar, *TD*, 1:268.

velop, they reflect more and more their likeness to the Divine nature. This is the dynamic quality of the *imago Dei*. It is an ongoing "growth in goodness."[46] The *imago Dei* is the ground that enables this performance upon the stage of the world within the theo-drama. The Divine Nature, which is love, is the *creator, personae, performer*, and *audience*. *Gaudium et Spes* states that all people "are called to one and the same goal, namely God Himself."[47] Speyr states that this happens through prayer; "we are in the presence of the Father, the Son and the Holy Spirit, and in and through them we strive to become what the Father created us to be—his children."[48] The dynamic quality calls forth performance with an expectation that humans will accept the responsibility to continuously live out the *imago Dei* upon the stage of the world.

THE INTERSECTION OF *HOMO LITURGICUS*, THE *IMAGO DEI*, AND THE *LITURGIA DEI*

The concept of the *liturgia Dei* suggests that this same love is also directed to and received by all three persons of the Trinity. The Father loves the Son and Mother Spirit. The Son loves Mother Spirit and the Father. Mother Spirit loves the Father and the Son. Each person loves and is loved, for God is love. "God the Father stands before God the Son and God the Spirit, perceiving God in each of them. But what the Father adores in them is not the nature which is his but that which is distinctively theirs. And the Son and Spirit adore the Father in the same way."[49]

This love expresses itself in the created world through the giving and receiving of glory, one to another. Furthermore, humanity is incorporated into the giving and receiving of glory through Christ, by the Spirit. Speyr demonstrates this through the example of Mary's prayer of Luke 1:38.

> As she says the words: *Be it done to me according to your word*, Mary receives this mystery from the Trinity, handing it on to her Son. The son gives it back to the Trinity, because he gives everything he has to the Father in the Spirit. And then, when it is once

---

46. Gregory of Nyssa, *Life of Moses*, 6.
47. Paul VI, *Gaudium et Spes* 2.24.
48. Speyr, *World of Prayer*, 21.
49. Speyr, *World of Prayer*, 31.

again in the Father's hands, it is distributed to mankind in the overflowing generosity of the Eucharist and of the Holy Spirit.[50]

Mary's improvised performance is an example of a "yes, and" response to the offer given to her; "let it be with me according to your word" (Luke 1:38). She then, as exemplified in the story of the wedding in Cana, passes the offer to the Son who, eventually, responds with "yes, and" as well; "Do whatever he tells you" (John 2:5). Jesus' improvised response on that occasion becomes a performative revelation of his glory upon the stage of the world, causing those who follow him to "believe in him" (John 2:11). "With his open Yes, a person invited to be a disciple receives a place within infinity already while on earth."[51]

All of this is centered on the person of Jesus Christ. "Christ . . . is the one who integrates and unveils the true, the good, and the beautiful so that he can communicate to us God's life of love found within the eternal processions of the Godhead. God's giving of himself, then, becomes the focal point of the divine being since his self-showing and self-saying culminate in his self-giving."[52] The ongoing performance of worship by the church is a joining in the eternal worship that is taking place within the *liturgia Dei*. "In praying, man will not be calling something new into being. His prayer will be a participation in the eternal conversation between Father, Son and Spirit."[53] Further, it is in Christ that humanity attains perfection in this performance:

> Rather than the isolated human person, it is the divine person of Christ who is ultimately responsible for the human being's perfection, for Christ is both the instrumental and final cause of this perfection. He is the instrumental cause of our perfection because it is through him and in him, the one mediator between God and man (cf. 1 Tim 2:5), that the latter is accorded the grace of redemption and sanctification whereby the image of God is perfected in him (or her). Likewise, Christ is the final cause of our perfection, because it is to Christ, the Omega, that we tend as to our perfection: we are sons and daughters in the Son, in whose image we were created (the Alpha and predecessor of Adam).[54]

---

50. Speyr, *Handmaid of the Lord*, 18.
51. Speyr, *Boundless God*, 7.
52. Garrett, "Dazzling Darkness of God's Triune Love," 423.
53. Speyr, *World of Prayer*, 76.
54. Schumacher, *Trinitarian Anthropology*, 105.

Christ is the prototypical *imago Dei*, who unites the *liturgia Dei* and *homo liturgicus* within himself. Through his performance as the incarnated Word-Act all three concepts are drawn together within one embodied *persona*. The superabundant love of God is the source of the incarnation wherein glory is given to the Son from the Father and returned by the Son to the Father and Mother Spirit. Furthermore, the desire of humanity within the person of Jesus Christ is perfectly directed toward the divine. That is, he is the perfect embodiment of *homo liturgicus*, the *imago Dei*, and the *liturgia Dei* at the same time.

Christ demonstrates through his death on the cross the full extent of his love for the Father.

> Here the God-man drama reaches its acme: perverse finite freedom casts all its guilt onto God, making him the sole accused, the scapegoat, while God allows himself to be thoroughly affected by this, not only in the humanity of Christ but also in Christ's trinitarian mission. The omnipotent powerlessness of God's love shines forth in the mystery of darkness and alienation between God and the sin-bearing Son; this is where Christ "represents" us, takes our place: what is "experienced" is the opposite of what the facts indicate.[55]

Balthasar and Speyr together suggest that the Son's descent into hell goes even further to reach that which has been cast furthest from God. "This descent can take place in obedience (the uttermost, absolute obedience, of which only this Son is capable) because absolute obedience can become the economic form of the Son's absolute response to the Father."[56]

Also of significance is that, in the descent into hell, Christ does not change his character. He remains fully human and fully divine.

> As the one descending from heaven to earth, from the earth to the Cross, from the Cross to hell, he was always the same person he has been from eternity in heaven. He does not need to expropriate himself of his essence and character in order to live for a while in time. As man, [Christ] is not a modified God, and, as God, he is no altered man. He is fullness in person: God and man, and both in a perfect, immutable manner.[57]

In this way, Jesus "expresses in the *oikonomia* what he has always expressed anew in the eternal, triune life: his complete readiness to carry

---

55. Balthasar, *TD*, 4:335.
56. Balthasar, *TD*, 3:530.
57. Balthasar, *TD*, 5:513.

out every one of the Father's wishes."[58] The *liturgia Dei* is fully observed in the person of Jesus Christ. The God-human is the prototypical *imago Dei* who lived out *homo liturgicus* and the *liturgia Dei* as he worshiped. The "double function"[59] of the *imago Dei* intersects in the person of Christ. These doctrines intertwine via the hypostatic union. Christ as the prototypical *imago Dei*, performs *homo liturgicus* and the *liturgia Dei* simultaneously in his person. This performance is seen in the worshiping Christ. It is also performed in the worshiping church. Balthasar and Speyr together express this as follows:

> The Son, as man, continues the eternal dialogue of prayer of the Divine Persons in heaven; it is not difficult to think of the eternal Word clothing himself in human words. And since Christ gives us a share in his own prayer, every word of the Lord is a prayer to the Father and a gift and a task for the Church. And just as God's prayer causes each Divine Person to do the will of the Others, so on earth the Father always does the will of the Son, who is obedient to him in all things (Jn 11:42). Anyone who asks in the Spirit of Christ, that is, in a trinitarian context, will infallibly be heard. Such a person has power over God; he has the "key to heaven."[60]

THE HUMAN PERFORMANCE OF ETERNAL GLORIFICATION

Irenaeus famously stated that "the glory of God is a living man; and the life of man consists in beholding God."[61] Earlier in the same text, though, Irenaeus ensures that this action is tied inseparably to Christ:

> But as regards His love, He is always known through Him by whose means He ordained all things. Now this is his Word, our Lord Jesus Christ, who in the last times was made a man among men, that He might join the end to the beginning, that is, man to God . . . and causing us to serve Him in holiness and righteousness all our days, in order that man, having embraced the Spirit of God, might pass into the glory of the Father.[62]

58. Balthasar, *TD*, 5:513.
59. Fulkerson, "*Imago Dei*," 95.
60. Balthasar, *TD*, 5:122–23.
61. Irenaeus, "Against Heresies" 4.20.7.
62. Irenaeus, "Against Heresies" 4.20.4.

In this way, humanity enters the glory of God through Christ. In being made fully alive in Christ, by Mother Spirit, humans glorify God. That life consists in being united with God. Regarding worship, and the assertion that humans are *homo liturgicus*, the "beholding God" that Irenaeus describes above is a joining in the performance of the eternal glorification of God that is taking place between Father, Son, and Mother Spirit. This occurs *to*, *through*, and *with* Jesus Christ. This constitutes the fitting performance of worship by humans.

God's glory appears "supremely in Christ."[63] With lives that image Christ, who is the supreme *imago Dei*, and with the desires of the human heart directed toward their divine focal point, humans reflect the eternal glorification of God between Father, Son, and Mother Spirit. Furthermore, in performing the giving of glory to God, humans become receivers of glory from God. As they are "conformed to the image of his Son," they are "glorified" (Rom 8:29–30). The distinction between the divine eternal glorification and the joining in by humans remains in constant eschatological tension. For the divine nature, the glorifying is perfect, constant, and dynamic. For humans, it requires constant conformity to the person of Christ, with the constant risk that desires may be distracted away from their divine focal point to something or someone else, or toward the self. Despite the risk of the fragility and distractibility of human free will, nevertheless, Christ enables his followers to join in the giving and receiving of glory, at his initiation. "The glory that you have given me I have given them, so that they may be one, as we are one, I in them and you in me, that they may become completely one, so that the world may know that you have sent me and have loved them even as you have loved me" (John 17:22–23). Believers are given this glory, not so that they may hold onto it, but that they will give it back to God, becoming performers on the stage of creation of the eternal glorification of God, *to*, *through*, and *with* Christ. "For the Son of God, Jesus Christ, whom we proclaimed among you, Silvanus and Timothy and I, was not 'Yes and No,' but in him it has always been 'Yes.' For in him every one of God's promises is a 'Yes.' For this reason, it is through him that we say the 'Amen,' to the glory of God" (2 Cor 1:19–20). The believers' glorification of God constitutes their "Amen" response to the Father's "Yes" in Christ (2 Cor 1:20). This becomes their improvised "yes, and" response to God's glorification of them.

---

63. Balthasar, *TD*, 4:12.

This view of human performance of the *liturgia Dei* can also be expressed negatively at this point. If, as anthropocentric definitions suggest, worship is fundamentally a human activity, then it must be, by definition, something that is *not* divine. More specifically, it is something that lies *outside* of the *imago Dei*, for how can something that is not divine simultaneously reflect divinity? Worship, according to these definitions, is something humans do that does *not* reflect the divine and stems from human initiation alone. By logical extension, when Jesus worships, he must also be doing something that is *not* divine; putting aside his divinity in order to perform what is a human activity. So, anthropocentric definitions fail to take account of the divinity of Christ and, therefore, divide his human and divine natures. The consequence of this is that anthropocentric definitions of worship contradict Chal when they are applied to Jesus and, in the moments when he worships, he ceases to be the image of the invisible God.

CONCLUSION

Given this, if humans are *homo liturgicus* and are created in the *imago Dei*, and this reflects the *liturgia Dei*, then anthropocentric definitions of worship fail when applied to Christ. In contrast, following on from Irenaeus above, the human fully alive is the glory of God; they join the eternal performance of the glorification of God that extends from, and returns to, the three persons of the Trinity. Putting on Christ, and bearing his *persona* as the prototypical *imago Dei*, humans *perform* worship just as Christ did, *to, through*, and *with* him. They give glory to God and are themselves glorified by God. This is their fitting performance of the *liturgia Dei*. Therefore, in Christ, *homo liturgicus* reflects the *liturgia Dei* through the *imago Dei*. This is true both for Christ and for humankind, thus satisfying Peterson's criteria that any definition of worship must apply to Jesus as well as humanity.[64] Having demonstrated this, attention turns now to how the *liturgia Dei* should be performed within the church, with attention given to past failures, critiques, and suggestions for the future.

---

64. Peterson, *Engaging with God*, 17.

7

The Characterization of the Company

THE LAST CHAPTER SHOWED that humans are ritualized animals who are created to love and express that love toward the divine, to worship. This has been summarized with the term *homo liturgicus*. *Homo liturgicus* reflects the *liturgia Dei* through the *imago Dei*. Jesus Christ, as the prototypical image of God, is the one in whom the connection between the *liturgia Dei* and *homo liturgicus* is seen most definitively. Moving from this claim, the *liturgia Dei* is brought to bear upon the liturgical practices of the church. Consideration needs to be given to how the church worships and, specifically, in what way those practices do or do not reflect the eternal glorification of God taking place between the Father, Son, and Mother Spirit. Attention now turns to calls for liturgical renewal, focusing firstly upon the liturgical misapplication of "unworthy" reception of the Eucharist, followed by feminist critiques of liturgical practices. Consideration is given to how the *liturgia Dei* offers theological ground to respond to these critiques. Finally, consideration is given to John Wesley's open Table as a solution to these two issues.

THE CALL FOR LITURGICAL RENEWAL

Liturgical renewal is necessary, not because the church is united, but because it is divided. Divisions based upon theological and liturgical differences have resulted in the "other" being pushed to the margins while those who wield power occupy the center. Nicholas Cochand, Isaïa

Gazzola, and Job Getcha have highlighted that "any training in liturgy and through liturgy which adopts an ecumenical scope demands hard work and availability, insofar as it is a reflection of the way in which we consider ecumenical commitment to be urgent and essential in our own Churches."[1] This hard work exists because unity has constantly eluded the church. Yet, this is not for lack of effort. The church continues to "make every effort to maintain the unity of the Spirit" (Eph 4:3). Yet, Sara Ahmed's observation regarding equality in universities applies equally well to the church; "feminist centers and feminist programs [exist] because we do not have feminist universities: that is to say, because sexism, gender inequality, and sexual harassment continue to structure university environments."[2] Following the pattern of Ahmed's argument that such programs exist because of the problem, the hard work of ongoing ecumenical efforts continues because unity is not yet reality.

Baptism, Eucharist, and Ministry claimed that, "If the divided churches are to achieve the visible unity they seek, one of the essential prerequisites is that they should be in basic agreement on baptism, eucharist and ministry."[3] In contrast to this requirement for doctrinal agreement, here it will be shown that, for unity to be visible and central, it is necessary to listen to voices that have been marginalized. Those who wield the most power must actively displace themselves from the center and move to the margins to stand in solidarity with the oppressed. This is one way the church can join the kenotic performance of the *liturgia Dei* as exampled by the prototypical worshiper, Jesus Christ. The Eucharist is a performance given by the inaugurator of the *liturgia Dei*. It was given to the church to be its great symbol of unity. Sadly, it has become a means of creating and reinforcing divisions. The following scene serves as an illustration of such divisions.

SCENE—*SOCIETAS LITURGICA* AND THE TENSION OF THE FINAL EUCHARIST

In 2019 I attended, for the first time, the biennial *Societas Liturgica* Congress which, on that occasion, was being held in Durham, UK. I had been accepted to present a paper, content from which was later published in

---

1. Cochand, Gazzola, and Getcha, "Formed Ecumenically Through Liturgy."
2. Ahmed, *Living a Feminist Life*, 110.
3. *Baptism, Eucharist and Ministry*, v.

Studia Liturgica and has also formed a part of this book.[4] It was the first time that I had met the majority of the people in attendance, but we each shared a common interest in all things worship, so I immediately felt at home with like-minded people. It was incredible to attend the opening worship that took place in Durham Cathedral. Having traveled from Australia which, in colonial terms, has juxtaposed a young history of Christian worship with an ancient history of Indigenous spirituality, I now found myself in a location that had been the site of Christian worship and pilgrimage for almost one thousand years, four times the age of colonial Australia yet less than 1 percent of the age its Indigenous history.

The congress is an opportunity for liturgical scholars to gather and share in academic conference over five days, with both paper presentations and mealtime conversations. Something that was no surprise to me was that each day commenced with a shared time of worship. Different leaders from various parts of the world, and a variety of Christian traditions, led prayer, singing, and scripture reading together on behalf of the gathered people. The highlight, though, was the final Eucharist together. This event was held in the magnificent chapel of Ushaw College.

At the time I was a Salvation Army Officer living within the tension of its neo-sacramental theology.[5] The Salvation Army (TSA) has, since 1883, not included the dominical sacraments as a part of its sacramental identity. Instead, it has, I had contended for several years, replaced the historic sacraments of baptism and the Lord's Supper with sacraments of its own making, *neo*-sacraments. In a manner that has always appeared to be out of character for the autocratic first General, and co-founder of TSA, William Booth, the decision to discontinue practicing the sacraments was not framed as a *ban* on their administration but rather a *postponement*. He asked, "Is it not wise for us to postpone any settlement of the question, to leave it over to some future day, when we shall have more light, and see more clearly our way before us?"[6] Any thoughts of seeing "more light" were put to bed, though, when a similarly autocratic General, Shaw Clifton, clarified that the sacraments had no place in TSA worship. In 2007 he stated, "No Officer or local Officer is at liberty to introduce into an Army meeting, event or gathering any

---

4. Couchman, "'Not My Will but Yours Be Done.'"
5. Couchman, "Neo-Sacramental Theology of the Salvation Army."
6. Booth, "General's New Year Address to Officers," 135–37.

ceremony or action of a sacramental nature or that could be mistaken for a sacrament."[7]

This was the first time, at least in writing, that the ban on the sacraments had been made explicit. The final closing of the curtain, which would block out any possibility of a change in position, occurred when, under the leadership of the same General Shaw Clifton, the 2010 publication of the *Handbook of Doctrine* edited the previous edition of this official theological text of TSA. The 1998 version, printed under the title *Salvation Story*, suggested that "early in our history, The Salvation Army chose not to observe specific sacraments as prescribed rituals."[8] The later version was edited to become "early in our history, The Salvation Army was led of God not to observe specific sacraments, that is baptism and the Lord's Supper, or Holy Communion, as prescribed rituals.[9] This deliberate editorial revision boldly claims that the source of the original change was not TSA itself, but rather God. The result of this revision of history was much more political than theological, yet its theological consequences were immense. Anyone who would disagree with the position must now reason why it is that God's decision in 1883, not TSA's, was now somehow wrong, an unnecessary but oft-repeated argument Clifton had previously put forward.[10]

While the ban on practicing the sacraments within TSA prevented me from presiding over the Lord's Supper in any setting, it has also been a long-standing and accepted convention that any Salvationist may partake of the sacraments wherever they are welcomed. And so it was that I approached the final Eucharist of the Congress with great anticipation and enthusiasm. I was going to share in communion with new friends; Christian sisters and brothers from all over the world and from many different traditions.

For many years I had pushed back against William Booth's suggestion, reiterated in many conversations with similarly minded, anti-sacramentalist Salvationists, that "a general division of opinion" existed between the churches regarding the sacraments.[11] I had hoped that this

---

7. Clifton, "Our God-Given Position on Sacraments," 3; see also Clifton, "Salvationism," 30.

8. Salvation Army, *Salvation Story*, 114.

9. Salvation Army, *Salvation Army Handbook of Doctrine*, 271.

10. Clifton elsewhere argued that any proposal for change must outline "the reasons for supposing that God has now spoken plainly by his Spirit to the Army and has told us he is releasing us from our calling to be a witness to the truths set down clearly by Army writers and leaders through the years." Clifton, "Thinking Aloud and Candidly," 124.

11. Booth, "General's New Year Address to Officers."

Eucharist would be a moment when the church, represented here by so many different traditions, nationalities, and cultures, at a congress of eminent liturgical scholars, would prove the detractors to be incorrect. Sadly, I was wrong. The tension in the room was palpable. The divisions were evident, visible, and painful to watch.

The tradition of *Societas Liturgica* is that the Eucharist at congress uses the denominational tradition of the president of that year. If the president is Catholic, then the *Roman Missal* is used. If they are Anglican, then it is the *Book of Common Prayer*, and so on. Attempts are made to reconcile differences where it is possible but, in the end, on every occasion someone is left unable to participate due to personal conviction, Canon law, theological difference, or historical precedent.

As I looked around the room some stood, some wept, including many who participated. I was one of them. In conversation with friends afterward, some expressed a desire to participate but recognized that they were prevented from doing so by their own tradition's rules, rules that felt eerily like the ban I was subject to in my own tradition. One who stood but did not partake suggested to me that his actions were intended to express some solidarity with those who were prevented from participating due to denominational restrictions, while reaching forward with eschatological hope to the time when all people can gather at the Table of the Lord without fear of reprisal.

I had to wonder why, among this group of liturgical scholars of all settings, we could not find unity at the Lord's Table. The pain of this disunity was expressed and felt by many, including myself. I was left wondering why we had to wait for the return of Jesus for all to be welcomed at his Table. If he wanted us all to gather together at that time, then why not now?

In the Anglican Church of Australia, the right to receive Holy Communion is restricted to those who have been baptized.[12] Further, the administration of the sacrament is a responsibility given only to those people who are duly authorized by the church to perform it.[13] While practice and policy are likely to diverge, such divergence would be an interesting research project in its own right. Still, these are policies that remain official, despite any divergence, or even contradictory practices.

---

12. Anglican Church of Australia, *Admission to Holy Communion Canon 1973*.
13. *APBA*, article 23.

Given this, the focus will only be upon the official liturgical texts of the Anglican Church of Australia.

The restrictions on who can receive and who can preside over Holy Communion exist, in the main, in response to concerns over receiving the sacrament in an "unworthy manner" (1 Cor 11:27). The fear is that if someone receives this sacrament in such a way they will "purchase to themselves damnation."[14] The restrictions are motivated by pastoral concerns for the eternal well-being of recipients; "the danger is great, if we receive the bread and cup unworthily."[15] These restrictions are based upon a misreading of the scriptural source and so starting with this text is important. Despite good intentions, there are unintended consequences that come from the restrictions themselves and these must be considered. So, attention turns to the scriptural text, 1 Cor 11:27, that is the foundation for these practices.

PAUL'S CONCERNS REGARDING THE LORD'S SUPPER IN CORINTH

Paul's first letter to the Corinthians includes Jesus' words of institution. Paul states that these words are something that he received from the Lord, and he then passed them onto the church in Corinth (1 Cor 11:23). Jaroslav Pelikan notes that, given this letter likely predates the Gospels, this constitutes the earliest written form of Jesus' words.[16] The significance of this text and its ongoing use within liturgy therefore cannot be overstated.

Acting as bookends around the words of institution, Paul expresses concerns over the way the church has been celebrating the Lord's Supper (1 Cor 11:17–22) and warns against eating the bread and drinking the cup in an "unworthy manner" (1 Cor 11:27). Those who eat in an unworthy manner "will be answerable for the body and blood of the Lord" and "drink judgment upon themselves" (1 Cor 11:27–28).

The problem Paul is addressing is centered upon inequality at the meal table as the church gathers. Some are eating more than their share and getting drunk on wine, while others are going without either bread

14. *APBA*, article 25.

15. *APBA*, 108, 74. The second order does not include any reference to receiving in an "unworthy manner" within the variants available. It does, however, include a corporate confession prior to the reception of the sacrament.

16. Pelikan, *Credo*, 393.

or wine (1 Cor 11:21). The problem is selfishness, and it is the poor, in particular, who miss out the most. The Lord's Supper is meant to differ from the hierarchical meals hosted outside of the church. It is intended for all to share, to be a unifying meal where the barriers that separate persons are overcome, as the people of God gather as one at the table. The church, the body, is to be unified, and the meal is to both symbolize and actualize that unity. As a result, given the problem of selfishness leading to disunity, Paul declares that the meal they are partaking in is not the Lord's Supper at all (1 Cor 11:20). Rather, they are receiving in an unworthy manner.

In response, he issues a warning against those who eat in an unworthy manner. Gordon Fee notes that problematic English translations of the text, commencing with the King James Version's "unworthily," have led to linking unworthiness to the righteousness of an individual participating rather than the collective way the meal is being shared. The result is that these words have been, and remain, a "dire threat for generations of English-speaking Christians."[17] In a similar manner to the KJV, article 23 of the Anglican Articles of Religion[18] also includes the language of "unworthy manner." This doctrinal statement is also reflected liturgically as a stern warning within the *BCP*.

> My duty is to exhort you in the mean season to consider the dignity of that holy mystery, and the great peril of the unworthy receiving thereof; and so to search and examine your own consciences, (and that nor lightly, and after the manner of dissemblers with God; but so) that ye may come holy and clean to such a heavenly Feast, in the marriage-garment required by God in holy Scripture, and be received as worthy partakers of that holy Table.[19]

The warning is also expressed in the liturgy of *APBA*, specifically, in the prayer of preparation in the first order of Holy Communion.

> Brothers and sisters in Christ, we who would come to the Holy Communion of the body and blood of our Savior Christ must consider how St. Paul exhorts us to examine ourselves before presuming to eat of that bread and drink of that cup.
> For the benefit is great, if with a penitent heart and lively faith we receive that holy sacrament. We then spiritually eat the flesh

---

17. Fee, *Corinthians*, 560.
18. *APBA*, article 23.
19. *BCP* (1662), 147.

of Christ and drink his blood; we dwell in Christ and he in us;
we are one with Christ and Christ with us.

Yet also the danger is great, if we receive the bread and cup unworthily. Judge yourselves therefore, that you be not judged of the Lord. Repent truly of your sins, having a steadfast faith in Christ our savior. Amend your lives and love your neighbor.[20]

Brian Douglas has summarized a large number of examples that highlight the ongoing historical concern for receiving in an "unworthy manner." These include two pamphlets written to aid communicants to prepare themselves to receive, throughout the week, between Sunday services. *The Old Week's Preparation towards a Worthy Receiving of the Lord's Supper* was first published in 1679. It became a standard text and was reprinted fifty-one times up until 1751. The follow-on text, *The New Week's Preparation for a Worthy Receiving of the Lord's Supper*, first published in 1739, also went through many editions and continued to be in use into the nineteenth century. Both texts were "aimed at assisting those preparing for Holy Communion to do so worthily and thereby obtaining the benefits of the life and death of Christ and the spiritual presence of his body and blood."[21] Douglas's historical survey of Anglican eucharistic theology demonstrates a long-standing tradition of applying this individualistic interpretation of the text into liturgical settings. Since the *BCP*, and the Articles of Religion's first publication, individuals have been called to examine themselves, confess their sins, and become right with God *before* receiving the Lord's Supper. As such, it is considered normative and incumbent upon each person to examine themselves to ensure that they are ready to receive Holy Communion.

Fee shows how this is based upon a misinterpretation of the original text. Rather than being a call for individuals to interrogate themselves to determine whether they are ready to receive, "unworthy manner" should be understood in the light of the problem Paul names previously in the text: namely, selfishness at the meal table. As such, receiving in an "unworthy manner" is a corporate rather than an individual problem. An individualized interpretation of "unworthy manner" only serves to reinforce an individualized, and therefore selfish approach to the Table; "if I am right with God then I can approach the Table." The presence, or lack thereof, of others at the meal becomes irrelevant as examination and discernment are a matter for the individual. The flow-on effect of this is that receiving

20. *APBA*, 108.
21. Douglas, *Companion to Anglican Eucharistic Theology*, 306, 84.

Holy Communion, once the individual is made right with God through confession, becomes about the individual's relationship with God. The fellowship of believers, the unity of the church, and particularly the needs of others become secondary, or even irrelevant matters, in this schema.

The hermeneutical problem is complicated by the multifaceted meaning of the term "body." It can mean the literal body of Christ, the bread, or the church, and in this passage all three meanings are present. The individualized interpretation of "unworthy manner" above follows to Paul's instruction to "discern the body" (1 Cor 11:29), understanding "body" to refer to the bread of the Eucharist. In applying this interpretation, participants need to seek to know and understand the bread's symbolic meaning and thus prepare themselves to receive it. Fee suggests that the result of this is that "the point of the whole argument is . . . missed altogether."[22] In contrast, Hans Conzelmann interprets "body" here communally. That is, it is referring to both the bread and the church, not the bread alone. These two meanings (bread and church) are interconnected in this verse and the wider context of the passage, and so it is that "we offend against the Lord because we offend against his body, the community."[23]

The wider context of the letter adds strength to favoring this communal interpretation of the text. Earlier in the letter, Paul connects the "bread" with the unity of the church; "Because there is one bread, we who are many are one body, for we all partake of the one bread" (1 Cor 10:17). Later, in 1 Cor 12:12–27, the body is the church. So, "discerning the body" (1 Cor 11:29), which falls between these two passages, constitutes a call for the Corinthians to keep the needs of others in mind as they gather to share at the table. The needs and concerns of all are placed above the needs of the individual as together the gathered church considers how everyone's needs are met. They discern the body—the church. In particular, they are to join with those that they, through their own selfishness, have previously marginalized, listening to and sitting with them at the table, for the sake of the whole body.

This interpretation calls into question the liturgical wording and ordering of *APBA*, *BCP*, and article 23, where the ongoing use of "unworthy manner" reinforces this misinterpretation of the scriptural text. It is necessary for revision of the liturgies so that they emphasize the communal nature of the Lord's Supper, given that an "unworthy manner" is

---

22. Fee, *Corinthians*, 559.
23. Conzelmann, *First Epistle to the Corinthians*, 202n104.

that which places the needs of individuals over and against the needs of the whole. Further, the need for individual confession before receiving the sacrament, the pattern which is evident in all three orders of *APBA*, may be helpful but should not be seen as essential for right practice.

To affirm this communal interpretation of 1 Cor 11 it is helpful to consider the performance of the instituting meal itself, since this is the meal that was "received from the Lord," and "handed on to you" (1 Cor 11:23). In that original setting, Judas's betrayal of Jesus did not preclude him from being invited to share in the original meal. In between receiving the thirty pieces of silver and the kiss of betrayal in the garden, Judas's hand was "on the table" (Luke 22:21; see also Matt 26:25–29; Mark 14:1–25).[24] The liturgical progression toward the Table should therefore stress the call to unity within the church, even among its brokenness, disunity, and sinfulness. Liturgical invitations should be opened to all people to share in the sacrament, regardless of their status in the world, their sinfulness, and even their baptismal status. As the Lord's Supper is served at the Lord's Table it remains open to all, a place where all know that Jesus "welcomes sinners and eats with them" (Luke 15:2). Following this examination of the text from 1 Cor 11, it is important to now listen to critiques of current liturgical practices from feminist authors. While not representing all marginalized voices, they are historically the largest.

THE *LITURGIA DEI* AND FEMINIST LITURGICAL CRITIQUE

The theological concept of the *liturgia Dei* suggests that worship is essential to the divine nature. This worship does not detract from the equality of the persons within the Trinity but rather affirms it. The selflessness of this equality leads to the glorification of the other among the persons. This becomes an invitation for the church to reflect that equality through selflessness within its liturgical performances. Such performances need to be examined to ensure that they reflect the *liturgia Dei*. This includes much more than just the words of liturgical texts but the performative aspects as well for, as Nicola Slee highlights,

---

24. Judas's reception is contested. Here, it is argued that the pattern of the text, with the betrayal bookending the institution narrative, suggests that Judas's reception is meant to be assumed and arguing for his either being refused or abstaining are not supported by the text. See Winner, *Dangers of Christian Practice*, 52.

> Words may be underlined or undone by the visual clues and dominant spatial arrangements in the liturgy.... In some settings, words may be of limited interest to those who pray: to young children or adults with profound learning needs, for example, but also to many adults for whom the cognitive function of words may be far less important than their affective or aural functions. None of this implies that words do not matter—only that they are not the whole story.[25]

Lavinia Byrne's important critique of liturgical practices also needs careful consideration. "The faith development of women is undermined where the saving action of God is appropriated by half the human race and not the other half. The personal faith response of praying women cannot but be influenced by sexism, however hard we try to resist this."[26] The gendered bias highlighted by Byrne is antithetical to the doctrine of the Trinity where the fundamental equality of persons is paramount. Elizabeth A. Johnson shows how such gendered bias is theologically suspect:

> Feminist theological analysis makes clear that exclusive, literal, patriarchal speech about God has a twofold negative effect. It fails both human beings and divine mystery. In stereotyping and then banning female reality as suitable metaphor for God, such speech justifies the dominance of men while denigrating the human dignity of women. Simultaneously this discourse so reduces divine mystery to the single, reified metaphor of the ruling man that the symbol itself loses its religious significance and ability to point to ultimate truth. It becomes, in a word, an idol. These two effects are inseparable for damage to the *imago Dei* in the creature inevitably shortchanges knowledge of the Creator in whose image she is made. Inauthentic ways of treating other human beings go hand-in-glove with falsifications of the idea of God.[27]

In some settings, it is only men who preside at the Eucharist, preach and teach, and lead the procession of the liturgy. Women and children are expected to remain silent wherever men are present. In these examples, men are the only *personae* while women and children remain the *audience*, without any interchange of these roles. Slee highlights how this kind of liturgical performance serves to reinforce, and indeed authorize, forms of oppression that marginalize others based upon race, gender, sexuality,

---

25. Slee, "Prayer, Gender and the Body," 651.
26. Byrne, *Women Before God*, 10.
27. Johnson, *She Who Is*, 36.

culture, physical and intellectual ability, attributes that have been used by the powerful to oppress others.[28]

Similarly, the spaces in which liturgical acts take place need reexamination. Spaces where the laity is physically separated from clergy, with the president and preacher physically raised above others, reinforce a distinction between persons within the church. With limited movement from the elevated positions or restricting such movement to authorized persons (i.e., clergy) the result is that this distinction between clergy and laity reflects something other than the equality of persons in the Trinity. This is important since "speech about God in the exclusive and literal terms of the patriarch is a tool of subtle conditioning that operates to debilitate women's sense of dignity, power, and self-esteem."[29]

Leanne Van Dyk has suggested that "the strongest and thickest walls against women's leadership in the church have traditionally been raised between the sacraments and women."[30] Lauren Winner suggests that the practices themselves are subject to deformation, since "nothing apart from God (not church, not sacraments, not saints) is exempt from the damage produced by the Fall."[31] Therefore, a constant reevaluation of the practices themselves is necessary.

In response, feminist liturgies insist upon spaces that emphasize the equality of the persons participating with a "fully embodied, face-to-face gaze and encounter."[32] For Letty Russell, this means church in the round which "emphasizes connection, for when we gather around we are connected, in an association or relationship with one another."[33] Slee suggests that such approaches do not remove differences among people, whitewashing over them to leave a bland sameness in its place. Rather the divine Other is encountered in difference, in encountering the *otherness* of another person before me "in all their strangeness, challenge and difference as a brother or sister with whom I am intimately joined."[34]

Ashley Cocksworth recounts the scene of the "Pussy Riot Prayer" where the rules of liturgical practice were subverted when prayer was performed in a way that was simultaneously "liturgically literate" and

28. Slee, "Prayer, Gender and the Body," 652.
29. Johnson, *She Who Is*, 38.
30. Van Dyk, "Gifts of God for the People of God," 208.
31. Winner, *Dangers of Christian Practice*, 16.
32. Slee, "Prayer, Gender and the Body," 657.
33. Russell, *Church in the Round*, 18.
34. Slee, "Prayer, Gender and the Body," 657.

"rebellious."³⁵ In reacting against the church's political alignment with Vladimir Putin, the women entered the sanctuary and prayed. However, "they did not kneel, but stood; they did not close their eyes, but kept them open; they did not clasp their hands, but waved them high; they were not ordained, but lay; they were not men, but women. This was a prayer of protest."³⁶ As such, the act of praying became a means of revolting against the power structures and those they had aligned with politically.

Marjorie Procter-Smith's "mourning meal" offers a similar disruptive approach where the forms of the Eucharist are used but the language is changed to bring attention to issues of abuse, power imbalance, and exclusion. In performing her version of the meal, the bread is to be stale, and the cup filled with bitter wine, vinegar, or salt water.³⁷

Both the Pussy Riot Prayer and the Mourning Meal use the liturgical form with altered content in order to disrupt the status quo. Such disruptions serve to smash the idols of patriarchal perceptions of God. "Normative imaging and conceptualization of God on the model of ruling men alone is theologically the equivalent of the graven image, a finite representation set up and worshiped as if it were the whole of divine reality."³⁸ The following scene is a further demonstration of applied response to feminist critiques, the result of which is disruption of the status quo. While not a liturgical example it does represent a theo-dramatic performance of one such disruption.

SCENE—FEMINIST PROTEST HIDING IN PLAIN SIGHT

In 2023 I attended, once again, the Congress of *Societas Liturgica* in Maynooth, Ireland. My wife and I attended together and, having enjoyed the conference, we now turned our attention to being tourists. On the recommendation of a friend, we visited Chester Beatty Library in Dublin. The library has an extensive collection of biblical papyri donated by the founding benefactor, and many of them were on display in an exhibition entitled "First Fragments: Biblical Papyrus from Roman Egypt." The marketing for the exhibition promotes that the papyrus fragments have "much to tell us about the material histories of writing and bookbinding,

---

35. Cocksworth, "When Prayer Goes Wrong," 15–16.
36. Cocksworth, "When Prayer Goes Wrong," 15.
37. Procter-Smith, *Praying with Our Eyes Open*, 137.
38. Johnson, *She Who Is*, 40.

textual histories of translation and transmission, and later object histories of ownership, publication and display."[39] Indeed, this was observable throughout the exhibition as each group of papyri were displayed in groups around this scribal theme: book makers, scribes, authors, readers, scholars, collectors.[40] The curation of the collection was, on the surface, pragmatic, historical, and informative. It was designed to take the visitor through an educational journey focused upon authors, editors, scribes, collectors, and readers. Historically, these were positions filled by men. Hiding in plain sight, though, were many, many women and, once they were seen, their presence was undeniable.

An example of this was the section on "Authors." In a single display cabinet were five papyri and an ancient water bottle. Each of these historic items was most likely the result of the labor of a man, or several men: the authors of the texts, the potter who sculpted the bottle, and so on. Yet the content of the text, and more so the object labels that guided the visitor along way, pointed to the many women and the roles they have played within the theo-drama: Sarah and Hagar (Gen 21), Tamar (Gen 38), Dina (Gen 34), Woman in labor (Jer 4), and God as a woman (Isa 42). In a similar way, the object label for the water bottle did not point to the construction methods or materials but rather became a visual metaphor of a scene from the biblical text:

> A vital source of life, water is also used as a metaphor for faith. When Sarah demanded that Abraham cast out Hagar and Ishmael, he sent them away with a single skin of water. When the water was gone an "angel of the Lord' . . . called to Hagar and provided a well of "living water" . . . Hagar filled the skin and their thirsts were quenched. Neither Abraham nor Sarah called Hagar by her name; only the messenger spoke Hagar's name, granting her full personhood.[41]

The curator of the exhibition, Jill Unkel, deliberately constructed the exhibition to tell the story of women alongside, and at times in place of, men. "This interchange of ideas and diverse sources is presented here, through the biblical works selected and discussed. In particular, this allows readings of how the lives of women are interpreted, and employed as

---

39. "First Fragments."
40. Unkel, *First Fragments*.
41. Unkel, *First Fragments*, 64.

evocative metaphors."[42] Without shame, women whose stories are often excluded from public worship were brought into the light and given the dignity of visibility. Dina (Gen 34), for example, was raped by Shechem, an act of violence that was met with more violence when her brothers deceived, and ultimately murdered, her rapist. Throughout her story, Dina is a silenced character. Her story is told by men, avenged by men, and then ultimately silenced by men when her story is excluded from liturgy when, for example, it is not a part of the *Revised Common Lectionary*. Yet, in this exhibition, her story is on display. She is named and included among other women who form a part of the theo-drama. Even though "the fate of . . . Dina herself, is not further elucidated."[43]

Unkel's curation of the exhibition is itself a performance within the theo-drama. Unkel takes on the role of narrator in the theo-drama, pointing the *audience* in the direction of the *actors*, telling their story, and constructing the drama in such a way that brings light to parts of the stage that have historically been darkened and raises the profile of *personae* who previously found their name much further down the list of credits. This narration uses the traditional forms common to most museum exhibitions—display cabinets, lighting, object labels, educational framework—but subverts them with an underlying feminist narrative that confronts patriarchal power structures and empowers women.

Returning to feminist critiques of liturgical practices, Lavinia Byrne states that:

> When the language offered for our use in church fails to name women it excludes me and most of what I do . . . . The presence of women in the community of the faithful is denied by the prayers used in formal liturgical contexts. The service of women in the community of the faithful, and notably in the base community of our own domestic setting, is denied by coupling those particular nouns, pronouns and verbs.[44]

Similarly, Procter-Smith has suggested that "traditional Christian public prayer (and, by extension, private and personal prayer) is based on problematic assumptions about the nature of God, about the nature of human life and need, about the necessary rituals which surround the act

---

42. Unkel, *First Fragments*, 59.
43. Unkel, *First Fragments*, 68.
44. Byrne, *Women Before God*, 10.

of prayer."[45] Further, Bonikowsky notes that "when the experience of men is normalized, God is imagined as male, arranging women into the subordinate role in the spiritual world as well as the physical."[46]

This emphasizes the problem with anthropocentric definitions of worship. They are built upon assumptions about the nature of God and hierarchical assumptions about the relations between the persons of the Trinity that lead to liturgical practices that empower one group of people over and against others. The *liturgia Dei* emphasizes the theocentric nature of worship which highlights the essential equality of the divine persons of the Trinity, Father, Son and Mother Spirit. Further, humanity is created and called to reflect that equality of persons, and so liturgical practices need to be revised regularly to ensure this occurs effectively. This challenges the power imbalance inherent in some liturgical practices.

Within God, an eternal glorification of the other is taking place between Father, Son, and Mother Spirit. As *homo liturgicus*, created in the image of God, humans are both a performance of this eternal glorification and are also invited to become actors in the theo-drama. "The creation of the world is . . . an expansion of his fatherly attribute, and yet—as accords with God's essence—not at the expense of the other Persons, but in such a way that the Son and the Spirit, and even man, are included in the glorification."[47]

This brief sample of feminist critiques of liturgical practices demonstrates problems with the inequality of male-only presidency, the gendered and sacrificial language that is employed in the liturgy, and the imbalance of power within the liturgy. In response to this sample of feminist critiques and the ongoing misinterpretation of 1 Cor 11, attention turns to John Wesley's open Table to consider how this theology may offer a way forward.

JOHN WESLEY'S OPEN TABLE

Paul Wesley Chilcote has noted that the revival sparked by John and Charles Wesley was both evangelical and eucharistic.[48] This highlights

---

45. Procter-Smith, *Praying with Our Eyes Open*, 9 cited in Slee, "Prayer, Gender and the Body," 652.
46. Bonikowsky, "Also a Mother," 20.
47. Speyr, *Countenance of the Father*, 19–20.
48. Chilcote, *Recapturing the Wesleys' Vision*, 81.

the importance of the Lord's Supper to the Christian life. Indeed, Wesley partook of the sacrament frequently himself, at least weekly, and encouraged others to follow this practice.[49] Wesley's sacramental theology is expressed in his sermon "The Means of Grace." Foundational is his assertion that "there is no inherent power in the . . . bread and wine received in the Lord's Supper." For Wesley, it is God who gives grace through any means, or even none at all.[50] However, there are specific means of grace given for use within the church and, given these are instituted by Christ, it is incumbent upon Christians to participate in them faithfully and frequently.

Further to faithful and frequent participation, Wesley also considered the Lord's Supper to be open to anyone who faithfully sought after God, even those who might be considered "unworthy" in other settings. In his journal entry from June 27 and 28, 1740 he argues against the suggestion that the Lord's Supper is only a *confirming* ordinance. Instead, he suggests that it can be *converting* as well. The sacrament was "ordained by God, to be a means of conveying . . . either preventing, or justifying, or sanctifying grace."[51] As such, in order to receive the sacrament there is "no previous preparation indispensably necessary, but a desire to receive whatsoever [God] pleases to give."[52] This openness to all who would receive grace regardless of their current status is also echoed in Wesleyan hymns.

> Come to the supper come;
>   Sinners there still is room;
>   Every soul may be his guest,
>   Jesus gives the general word;
>   Share the monumental feast,
>   Eat the supper of your Lord.[53]

Here, he discounts the need for someone to be "worthy" *before* receiving. In fact, he encourages the "sinner" to keep "partaking of the Lord's Supper, till God, in the manner that pleases [God], speaks to his heart, 'Thy faith hath saved thee. Go in peace.'"[54] Everyone is welcome to come to the Table.

---

49. Collins, *Theology of John Wesley*, 262.
50. Wesley, "Means of Grace," 382.
51. Wesley, "Journal Entry—June 28, 1740."
52. Wesley, "Journal Entry—June 28, 1740."
53. Wesley and Wesley, *Hymns on the Lord's Supper*, hymn 8.
54. Wesley, "Means of Grace."

In assessing the history of the application of this theology, Karen B. Westerfield Tucker has shown that there has never been a consensus regarding "conditions necessary for admission to the Lord's Supper."[55] Tucker notes examples of Methodists practicing forms of "open" communion that were restricted to "Christians in good standing from other congregations and churches" and others offering it to "any individual who could answer the Invitation."[56] Tucker has outlined history of these different practices and has noted that, in American Methodism,

> The only official standard for admission remained the invitation to Communion within the eucharistic rite. Efforts to mandate a baptismal prerequisite continue to fail, because the broad definition of open Communion was deemed normative by many. Much depended upon local custom and pastoral discretion to determine which, if any, preconditions existed for admission to the table.[57]

Here, the broader and open interpretation of Wesley's theology will be considered as a praxis that both reflects the *liturgia Dei* and provides theological ground to respond to the feminist critiques above.

Wesley's broad and open sacramental theology provides an avenue for conversations regarding the revision of liturgical texts, such as *APBA*, that place an unnecessary emphasis on the need for self-examination and individual confession *before* receiving the sacrament. Instead, Wesley opened the Table for all to come and receive the grace of God through the sacramental means of grace.

Furthermore, Collins notes that Wesley, in some sense, calls into question the need for priestly mediation of the sacrament.[58] It is God, not the priest, who gives Christ to those who receive the sacrament; "Draw near ye blood-besprinkled Race; And take what God vouchsafes to give."[59] Despite Collins' suggestion, it is unlikely that Wesley himself would have had anyone other than an ordained priest administer the sacrament. However, an open reception at the Table does bring with it questions regarding the possibility of open presidency.

---

55. Tucker, *American Methodist Worship*, 143.
56. Tucker, *American Methodist Worship*, 147.
57. Tucker, *American Methodist Worship*, 148.
58. Collins, *Theology of John Wesley*, 261.
59. Wesley and Wesley, *Hymns on the Lord's Supper*, hymn 71.

It has been argued that the individualized interpretation of an "unworthy manner" of reception of the Lord's Supper is founded upon a misinterpretation of the text from 1 Cor 11. Further, this misinterpretation influenced the construction of the Anglican Articles of Religion and, as a result, the *BCP*. As a text that flows out of the *BCP*, *APBA* continues to perpetuate this individualized interpretation of the text. The result of this are liturgical practices that exclude and continue to cause harm, as exampled by the critiques offered by feminist authors. Knowing that this harm is being caused and then continuing to perpetuate it is more than just a problem; it is abusive.

In contrast to these eucharistic practices that are exclusively reserved for those who are considered "worthy," an open Table welcomes all to come and receive grace. This theology welcomes revisions of the liturgical texts, and indeed the Articles of Religion, to lead to a place where, for example, when the liturgical invitation is extended to "all of you" to participate in the sacrament, this "all" really does mean "all."[60] Any such conversations, though, must be led by the marginalized, not by those in power. They are the ones who have been excluded and therefore been caused the most harm by that exclusion in the past. Listening to and welcoming their voices is the first step to healing for them and for liturgical renewal in the church. It is suggested that these conversations, and the liturgical outcomes that will emerge from them, better reflect the essential unity of the Trinity. The fundamental equality as *creators, personae, performers,* and *audience* within the theo-drama will be reflected in the church as it joins in the performance, *to, through,* and *with* Jesus. Out of such conversations, with any suggested changes also being fully embraced, it is hoped that the Table may become truly converting, confirming, and connecting, actions "that connect us with one another and with God's world."[61]

A NEW PERSPECTIVE ON AN OLD PROBLEM

The call to open the Table to all who would come is not a new question to consider; however an example of its performance comes from an unlikely source. Namely, The Salvation Army (TSA), where the practice of the dominical sacraments was officially discontinued in 1883. In their place,

---

60. *APBA*, 113, 29, 77, etc., citing Matt 26:27.
61. Chilcote, *Recapturing the Wesleys' Vision*, 86.

TSA has employed the use of its own symbols and ceremonies, which I have elsewhere named as *neo*-sacraments.[62] Of particular significance to TSA worship is the use of the Mercy Seat, which performs an important role in TSA worship.[63] It is central to its shared identity and serves a functional purpose in the combined emphases on the conversion of new Christians and the sanctification of existing ones. Sitting at the front and center of the worship space, it is a focal point in both a visual sense and a liturgical sense, placing "salvation," in the fullest sense of the term, at the heart of Salvation Army worship. While TSA does not practice the sacraments of Eucharist or baptism, the heart of its worship, indeed all its efforts, is symbolized by the presence of the Mercy Seat at the front and center of its worship space. William Bramwell Burrows stated, in 1951, that "the focal point towards which all Army activities drive is still the [Mercy Seat]. No Sunday ends in any Salvation Army hall without a prayer battle in which men and women are urged to make a decision for Christ."[64] This continues to be true of its worship today.

In practical terms, after the sermon, the preacher will call for a response from those present. Individuals who choose to respond do so by coming and kneeling at the Mercy Seat and praying. Another person present may come and pray with them during this time for a specific need, and this may or may not be a person specifically trained for that task. A direct appeal may be given to those present who are not yet Christians to come forward, an action which reflects the influence of the nineteenth-century revivalism upon the founders of TSA, William and Catherine Booth. When a person comes to the Mercy Seat, they will be invited to recite a form of a "sinner's prayer." While there is no set form of this prayer, it would generally include a recognition of one's sinfulness, a request for forgiveness from God, and an acceptance of God's rule over the person's life from this point onward. Having prayed such a prayer, the person rises from the Mercy Seat a new person in Christ and is welcomed into the fellowship of the church immediately.

There are no special requirements concerning the materials from which the Mercy Seat is constructed. It may be a carefully crafted wooden

---

62. Couchman, "Neo-Sacramental Theology."

63. This section has been published as Couchman, "'Not My Will but Yours Be Done': The Use of the Mercy Seat in Theodramatic Perspective."

64. Burrows, *Mercy Seat*, 20–21. Here, for the sake of clarity, I have adjusted Burrows's use of the term "Penitent Form." The Mercy Seat is also known by this and several other names. For this book, though, the term "Mercy Seat" will be used.

bench, or it may simply be few chairs gathered together at the front of the worship space. It can be used for personal or corporate prayer during any moment of the worship gatherings, or it may be used during a special ceremony such as the enrollment of a soldier or the dedication of a child. Historically, its use was intended solely as a place for new converts to come and receive Christ and sat alongside the Holiness Table, a second piece of symbolic furniture used by those seeking sanctification. Over time, the two distinct purposes have melded into one. Even so, the significant role that this simple item of furniture performs is very important for the identity of TSA across the world.

TSA was birthed in the east end of London during Victorian England when life as a poor person was particularly bleak. TSA took worship to the streets, holding open air worship wherever people could be found, particularly targeting the poor. In these circumstances the bass drum was used to keep the beat during the march, and then, when the group stopped to preach to those listening, it was laid on its side in the center of the gathering to become an impromptu Mercy Seat. In over 134 countries TSA can be found and in every setting a Mercy Seat will be there. General Shaw Clifton once wrote:

> At the heart of Salvationism is the symbol of the human soul encountering its Redeemer-Creator, the Mercy Seat (Exodus 25:17; 26:34). No Salvation Army place of worship is complete without a Mercy Seat. It is our pulse, our heartbeat. There the sinner finds forgiveness and the saint still further grace.[65]

Within the Australian context, the church in general and TSA in particular is in decline. Reactions to Royal Commissions that have brought to light the atrocities performed in the name of the church against children in institutional care have eroded trust of religious movements. Simultaneously, TSA in many locations in Australia moved toward embracing a seeker sensitive approach to preparing worship. While this approach may seem in line with its history, it lacked the broader context in which "Salvation" meetings for seekers (as they were known in early days) were complemented by "Holiness" meetings for existing Christians. Holiness meetings encouraged Christians to move on in their faith and pursue full salvation in Christ. While embracing seeker sensitivity, there was a simultaneous reduction in meeting times from two to one; in many instances holiness meetings were dropped altogether and

65. Clifton, *New Love*, 22.

in place repetitive reproductions of watered-down worship experiences were offered up week after week to appeal to those not accustomed to the seemingly deterring rituals of Christian worship.

The result of this over time has led to a situation where the call to the use of the Mercy Seat after the sermon is seen by many in the congregation to be a call to "someone else," a call to the hypothetical seeker in their midst. That hypothetical seeker, in the context of Australia where the church is in decline, rarely exists. Furthermore, the appeal for response is often made *individually*, not *interpersonally*, meaning that the importance of the gathered people of God meeting together in the presence of God is turned into a transactional exchange of the goods of salvation for individuals who happen to be sitting in the same space. So, the powerful symbol of the "human soul encountering its Redeemer-Creator" sits dormant at the center of the worship space, like the proverbial elephant in the room.[66] Unused for weeks, or sometimes months, on end, a tragic reminder of the glory days of the past and of the impending doom of fading into insignificance unless something changes.

When considered from a theo-dramatic perspective, the act of praying at the Mercy Seat becomes a contemporary, and improvised, performance of Christ's Gethsemane prayer, "Not my will, but yours be done" (Luke 22:42). The broadening of the understanding of this act to become a deliberately repeated and embodied performance of Jesus' prayer may help to overcome the loss of use of this symbol.

Picturing Wesley's theology of an open Table in performative practice, it is not difficult to imagine Wesley extending an invitation to a gathered congregation to come to "receive Christ" at the Table, and that the invitation made would be intended to include everyone present, even those who were not yet Christians. The open invitation to "receive Christ" at the Table in Wesley's eucharistic practice influences TSA's open invitation for all to "receive Christ" at the Mercy Seat. The same theology fuels both performances.

The Mercy Seat has performed an important task in TSA worship, but it is necessary for a reimagining of its purpose in theo-dramatic terms. Drawing upon the scene above in "Gethsemane in Performance," here we recall that the church joins in the prayer of Jesus through contemporary, embodied performances in accordance with the *Logos*-script. So, the Mercy Seat can function as a location of personal Gethsemane for

66. Clifton, *New Love*, 22.

repentant sinners who kneel at this place of prayer in the center of TSA worship spaces and join with Christ in an embodied performance of his prayer. They can still declare their personal need of God's salvation and affirm their decision to live their lives according to God's will and not their own.

Thomas Torrance's warning against unmediated prayer is helpful to consider at this point.

> In a profound and proper sense, therefore, we must speak of Jesus Christ as constituting in himself the very substance of our conversion, so that we must think of him as taking our place even in our acts of repentance and personal decision, for without him all so-called repentance and conversion are empty. Since a conversion in that truly evangelical sense is a turning away from ourselves to Christ, it calls for a conversion from our in-turned notions of conversion to one which is grounded and sustained in Christ Jesus himself.[67]

The theo-dramatic interpretation of Jesus' Gethsemane prayer responds to Torrance's warning by seeing Jesus as the *Logos*-script of prayer. When the sinner prays at a Mercy Seat or elsewhere, they are joining in with Jesus' prayer as he joins with them. They pray *to, through,* and *with* Jesus Christ. Like Jesus, the sinner kneels before the Father, and in a time of great personal need, declares "not my will but yours be done." In practical terms, there is nothing new here. Appeals from preachers after sermons will still be performed in much the same way. In theological terms, though, that appeal from the preacher and response from the penitent sinner is grounded and sustained in Christ Jesus himself.

This also presents a new perspective on the question of the open Table. Like Wesley's open Table, the Mercy Seat is both a *confirming* and *converting* place of meeting with God, not just for the "hypothetical sinner" but also the "actual saints" in our midst. The Mercy Seat is a means of conveying grace (preventing, justifying, or sanctifying) to all people, according to whatever their need may be. Grace is available to all who respond to the call to receive it, to renew them in the image of God. The invitation to come to the Mercy Seat requires no previous preparation, only a desire to receive whatsoever God pleases to give. Everyone may come, and come again, and join with Christ in praying "not my will, but yours be done."

---

67. Torrance, *Mediation of Christ*, 86.

CONCLUSION

Despite TSA's ban upon the use of the dominical sacraments, its use of the Mercy Seat can become an example of improvisation upon the *Logos*-script that could inform liturgies that do use them. TSA's open invitation to everyone to come, be they sinner or saint, without prior preparation, shows that the call to "receive Christ" can be universal. Whether that reception of Christ is in the eucharistic elements or at the Mercy Seat (or elsewhere) is unimportant. Rather, the open invitation, extended to all, is an ongoing performance of Christ's invitation to receive him. Further, this opens the way to consider greater expressions of the equality that is fundamental to the *liturgia Dei*. In embracing this opportunity, the prayer of Christ in Gethsemane is performed by his disciples and his prayer becomes theirs. The Mercy Seat, the Lord's Table, and other liturgical performances can become places where the *Logos*-script is performed and re-performed by the company of believers. As they perform the *Logos*-script, Jesus becomes the characterization of the company, a characterization that reveals and embodies the nature of the Triune God. The church becomes a place where all people perform the eternal glorification that extends from, and returns to, Father, Son, and Mother Spirit. This they do *to*, *through*, and *with* Jesus Christ.

In response to the sample of feminist critiques above, it is not suggested that this theological framework provides a definitive solution to the significant issues raised by these authors. Rather, it is incumbent upon authors, particularly male authors, to amplify, listen to, and contribute positively to amplifying the voice of others, particularly those who have been historically marginalized. In theo-dramatic terms, male authors should exit the stage so that other actors may come into the spotlight. In this way, the invitation to an open Table and other liturgical performances is offered as a contribution to an ongoing conversation in this important debate. As part of the ongoing theo-drama, this offer may well be responded to with a "no." However, it is hoped it is received with a "yes, and" and so, together, the company of believers creates and discovers new meaning as it joins in the ongoing performance of the glorification of God, Father, Son, and Mother Spirit.

8

The Final Curtain

THE TASK NOW PRESENTS itself to draw this book to a close, yet also recognize that beyond it the theo-drama continues. More specifically, the *liturgia Dei* continues. The definition of worship offered and defended here is that it is the eternal glorification of God that extends from, and returns to, Father, Son and Mother Spirit, the *liturgia Dei*. The church joins in this *to*, *through*, and *with* Jesus Christ. Throughout this book, it has been demonstrated how anthropocentric definitions of worship are unable to sufficiently account for Jesus' worshiping. They fail to sufficiently account for his humanity and divinity, hypostatically united in his one person. Instead, either implicitly or explicitly, they have suggested that worship extends from Jesus' humanity alone. The failure of this view of Jesus' worshiping is that it divides that which is eternally united, and a central tenet of Chal is sacrificed. Instead, this book has shown that when Jesus worships he does so from his person, not just his human nature. Through this, he is revealing worship that is taking place eternally within the Trinity. The *liturgia ad extra* is revealing the *liturgia ad intra*. Further, the glimpses that the Scriptural text offer reveal that the Father and Mother Spirit are also worshiping. The Father glorifies the Son. The Son glorifies Mother Spirit. Mother Spirit glorifies the Father and so on. This is an eternal glorification of God that extends from and returns to the Father, Son, and Mother Spirit. This is the *liturgia Dei*.

From this theological foundation, consideration was given to theological anthropology, what it means to be human in the light of the *liturgia Dei*. This book drew upon the concept of *homo liturgicus*; humans are, by nature, worshiping beings because they are ultimately lovers. Given this, humans will love something or someone and the way this love is expressed is worship, even if that worship is directed somewhere other than God. Humans are created to love God and neighbor as themselves (Matt 22:37–40), and liturgical performances serve the purpose of enacting and shaping humans to be who they are created to be. Humans are created in the image of God and reflect God upon the stage of the world. That is, *homo liturgicus* is a reflection (*imago Dei*) of the *liturgia Dei*.

BEING OF THE SAME MIND

Attention returns, now, to the Christological hymn of Phil 2. It was stated above that Paul's intent at this point is connected to Christ:

> Be of the same mind, having the same love, being in full accord and of one mind. Do nothing from selfish ambition or empty conceit, but in humility regard others as better than yourselves. Let each of you look not to your own interests but to the interests of others. Let the same mind be in you that was in Christ Jesus. (Phil 2:2b–5)

The intent of Paul's use of this hymn at this point in the letter is not just to make a statement about Jesus Christ but to encourage the Philippians to have the "same mind" as Christ and each other. In addition to being of the "same mind," they should have the "same love," like-minded and like-lovers. Here, Paul wants the Philippians to think the same way, to love the same way, and specifically to do as Christ does.

The hymn that follows was shown to be a theo-dramatic performance of the *liturgia Dei* where the Son glorifies the Father through kenotic obedience and the Father glorifies the Son through giving him a share in the name that is above all names. Hurtado notes that the hymn does not contain anything that points to the salvific purposes of the Son and Father's actions; "The redemptive efficacy of his actions are not in view in these verses."[1] Instead, Hurtado suggests that the story is "complete in itself" and the telling of it serves the point of the "glory of God" (3:11).[2] It seems important to respond to Hurtado's claim here with "yes, and." Hurtado skips over Paul's explicitly stated point in the introduction to the hymn. The hymn is not just a Christological or doxological

---
1. Hurtado, *How on Earth Did Jesus Become a God?*, 104.
2. Hurtado, *How on Earth Did Jesus Become a God?*, 105.

statement. It is also an ecclesiological one. Paul calls for the Philippians to be the kind of people who have the same mind as Christ and love in the same way as Christ does. As the Son glorifies the Father, and the Father glorifies the Son, the company of believers are to be like-minded, like-lovers, and like-worshipers. They are, in humility, to regard others as better than themselves, and to look to the interests of others beyond their own. The example of this is Christ who "sets aside his interests *completely* for the sake of others."[3] Or, as has already been expressed, they are *homo liturgicus* reflecting the *liturgia Dei* through the *imago Dei*. The church is to be a people who join in the ongoing and eternal performance of the glorification of God that extends from, and returns to, Father, Son, and Mother Spirit. They join in this *to*, *through*, and *with* Jesus Christ.

Such fitting performances are not restricted to verbatim recitals of pre-prescribed liturgical scripts. Even where the same script is followed in each liturgical performance week in, week out, each performance is new every time. Every performance is a contextual improvisation of the *liturgia Dei* upon the stage of the world, where the church gives and receives glory to and from God. The glory is never held on to but rather, looking away from themselves to the needs of others, just as Christ did, they give the glory away. This is what fitting performances of the *liturgia Dei* look like in the church. Here, a scene demonstrates this reality.

SCENE: IMPROVISATION ON AN IMPROVISATION

At The Salvation Army Gosford Corps, where I served as Corps Officer from 2013 to 2016, the usual pattern of liturgical performance included a time in the service when the children were invited to come forward for a children's story. The story was usually targeted at them but occurred in front of the rest of the congregation. This was not an invention that I introduced but had been a regular part of worship there for many years. Similarly, it was commonplace among other Salvation Army Corps and indeed other church traditions as well. At the end of the story, the children were led out of the main hall into an adjoining room where they participated in Sunday School with authorized and trained leaders.

The intent of doing this, week in and week out, was to provide a space for the children to be themselves and to learn the gospel in an age-appropriate way. The danger, however, was that this intent would be

---

3. Holloway, *Philippians*, 113. Emphasis in original.

misunderstood by the adults who remained in the main hall and continued with the corporate gathering. I feared that it communicated something completely different to what was intended. I was concerned that the action of gathering the children at the front of the church, teaching them a Bible story or life lesson in front of the adults, and then parading them off into a separate space would communicate to everyone else, and the children, that they were being removed so that the adults could get on with the important business of church, without the children interrupting. What was needed was a disruption to the status quo, a change in the performance to ensure the intended meaning was communicated effectively.

To achieve this, I arranged ahead of time for the leaders to be ready for the whole church gathering to join the children in Sunday School. Normally they would have about ten children; this week they would have an additional 120 adults. They set up the room where Sunday School took place with tables and chairs, enough for the whole church. There were craft activities, colored pencils and paper, scissors, glue, and all the activities associated with Sunday School.

When the day arrived, the first part of the corporate gathering took place in the main hall, as it usually would. All of the gathered people performed worship in the usual way: singing, reading the Scriptures, praying together, and so on. Then the children were called forward for the children's time, as per the usual pattern. I asked the children if they had any stories from their week; a couple of them shared. The adults watched on with interest as they always did, settling in for what they expected would be a normal part of the service. After a few minutes, I described to the children how each week we watch them head off to Sunday School while the adults must stay behind and do adult things. Talking to the children I wondered aloud what they got up to, and so I asked them if it was okay if we all came with them. The children picked up what was happening a second or two before the adults did. They were eager to see this happen. At that moment I turned to the adults in the room and invited them to join the children in the room next door for Sunday School. Hesitantly at first, but then in increasing numbers, the adults stood from their seats, walked out of the main hall, and joined all the children and Sunday School teachers for the rest of the corporate gathering. On this Sunday, in a planned yet still improvised performance of the usual liturgical script, the adults responded to the offer with "yes, and" and joined with the children in their performance space.

In theo-dramatic terms, my concerns had arisen from an observation that, at the time of the children's story each week, the adults were being treated solely as *audience* and the children the *personae*. The disruption to the usual pattern of performance was a "breaking of the fourth wall" that invited the *audience* to join the children as *personae* in the drama of that worship event, and specifically in their space, on their stage. It was a planned moment where an offer was extended to the adults to *improvise* their response. They could have chosen to say "No," refused to stand from their seats, and demand that the usual way of things be maintained. This response would block the improvisation, and thus the performance would have ended in that moment. They could have chosen to say "Yes," stood from their seats, and moved into the other room but ultimately refuse to participate in any of the activities, remaining instead as *audience*. This response recognizes the offer to join in the performance but functionally limits the drama and so remains another kind of block. Fortunately, the adults followed the children's lead and responded with a "Yes, and." They embraced the opportunity given to them to move beyond being *audience* and become a part of the *personae*. They entered fully into the theo-drama and, together, everyone created new meaning. Together, we looked away from ourselves to the needs of others. Together, we had the same mind, and the same love, and together performed the *liturgia Dei* that day.

One surprising twist in the drama, that was only revealed to me later, was the story of one of the elderly worshipers who did, in fact, choose to say "No." He remained in his seat in the main hall and, for reasons unknown, blocked the offer that was extended to him. Having seen the elderly gentleman sitting in the main hall on his own, a young fifteen-year-old, Rachel, took it upon herself to walk back into that space, sit down beside him, and have a conversation with him until the time came for the service to conclude. Boldly ignoring the group activities taking place in the "all-in" Sunday School, she went back into the main hall and sat with the elderly worshiper for the remainder of the time. In this way, this young female worshiper, like the Canaanite woman whose story was told above, took a "No" and turned it into a "Yes, and." She looked away from herself and saw the needs of another and, with the mind and love of Christ, humbled herself and, through her actions, gave glory to God. This is the *liturgia Dei*. This is the ongoing performance of the eternal glorification of God that extends from, and returns to, Father, Son, and Mother Spirit. Rachel did so *to*, *through*, and *with* Christ.

In that moment, Rachel's act was not only a fitting improvisation of the *liturgia Dei*; it was also a living echo of the woman who anointed Jesus, of whom he said, "wherever the gospel is preached throughout the world, what she has done will also be told in memory of her" (Mark 14:9). Elisabeth Schüssler Fiorenza, in her seminal work *In Memory of Her*, insists that this is more than a passing commendation. It is a call to remember and re-member the women whose acts of worship, courage, and theological insight have too often been forgotten or marginalized in the telling of the church's story. Fiorenza challenges the church to recover its identity as a "discipleship of equals," where the theo-drama is not performed by a privileged few, but by the whole company of worshipers—young and old, male and female, every voice contributing a verse.[4]

Rachel's quiet improvisation on the expected script, her turning of a "No" into a "Yes, and," is precisely the kind of liturgical memory Fiorenza urges us to preserve. It is a memory that does not merely recall the past but reconfigures the present. Despite the anonymity of the women who anointed Jesus, it is in the actions of worshipers of the present, like Rachel, who re-tell her story through their worship. Not through spectacle, but through self-giving love, improvising the eternal glorification of God in a way that was both deeply human and profoundly divine. This is the *liturgia Dei*: not confined to the sanctuary, but alive in the spontaneous, Spirit-led acts of those who, like Christ, look not to their own interests but to the interests of others.

AN OPEN INVITATION TO JOIN IN THE PERFORMANCE

A final comment needs to be made about the *liturgia Dei*, and particularly its ongoing performance. Assumed within this definition of worship, specifically in the word "eternal," is an invitation to join in the ongoing performance of worship. It is astonishing to suggest that God worships God, that this activity is essential to the divine nature, and that there is an eternal glorification extending and returning from person to person

---

4. Schüssler Fiorenza, *In Memory of Her*, 97–104.

within the Trinity. These are remarkable claims. Even more remarkable is the invitation extended to humanity, through its very creation in the image of the divine nature, to join in the performance. We are invited to step upon the stage of creation, look away from ourselves, and, just like Christ, join in giving glory to God. In this, we too are "glorified" (Rom 8:28) but we do not hold onto the glory. Rather, we continue to give it away, joining in the eternal glorification of God that extends from, and returns to, Father, Son, and Mother Spirit. This we do to, *through*, and *with* Christ.

A scene from the movie *Dead Poet's Society* eloquently expresses this invitation. In this scene, John Keating, portrayed by Robin Williams, speaks of poetry, beauty, romance, and love as the things that we stay alive for. He could well have been speaking of the *liturgia Dei*, for the glorification of God is to love, to love God with all of our being and to love our neighbor as ourselves. To love just as Christ loved. To glorify God just as Christ glorified God. To worship God just as God worships God.

> We don't read and write poetry because it's cute. We read and write poetry, because we are members of the human race. And the human race is filled with passion. Medicine, law, business, engineering; these are noble pursuits, necessary to sustain life. But poetry, beauty, romance, love, these are what we stay alive for. To quote from Whitman. "O me, O life, of the questions of these recurring. Of the endless trains of the faithless. Of cities filled with the foolish. What good, amid these, O me, O Life? Answer: That you are here. That life exists, and identity. That the powerful play goes on and you may contribute a verse." That the powerful play goes on and you may contribute a verse. What will your verse be?[5]

The *liturgia Dei* calls forth for such a response from the church; "what will your verse be?" The company of worshipers responds with "yes, and" when they "sing to the Lord a new song" (Ps 96:1). They respond with "yes, and" when the nations are drawn to the glory God gives to them; "Now you shall call nations that you do not know, and nations that do not know you shall run to you, because of the Lord your God, the Holy One of Israel, for he has glorified you" (Isa 55:5). They respond with "yes, and" when they recognize that the glorification of God is not a performance that is restricted to fixed times, in fixed locations, using fixed words and actions. Rather, it is an eternal, improvised, and ongoing

---

5. Weir, *Dead Poet's Society*.

performance of the eternal glorification of God, that extends from and returns to, Father, Son, and Mother Spirit. The company of worshipers join in this performance the only way they can, *to*, *through*, and *with* Jesus Christ. This is the *liturgia Dei*. Worshiping the worshiping God.

> Therefore we do as our Savior has commanded:
> proclaiming his offering of himself
> made once for all upon the cross,
> his mighty resurrection and glorious ascension,
> and looking for his coming again,
> we celebrate, with this bread and this cup,
> his one perfect and sufficient sacrifice
> for the sins of the whole world.
> Renew us by your Holy Spirit,
> unite us in the body of your Son,
> and bring us with all your people
> into the joy of your eternal kingdom;
> through Jesus Christ our Lord,
> with whom, and in whom,
> in the fellowship of the Holy Spirit,
> we worship you, Father,
> in songs of never-ending praise:
>
> Blessing and honor and glory and power
> are yours for ever and ever. Amen.[6]

---

6. *APBA*, 129.

Credits

Ahmed, Sara. *Living a Feminist Life*. Durham, NC: Duke University Press, 2017.
Allmen, Jean-Jacques von. *Worship: Its Theology and Practice*. Translated by Harold Knight and Wilfred Fletcher Fleet. London: Lutterworth, 1965.
Anderson, Cynthia Peters. *Reclaiming Participation: Christ as God's Life for All*. Minneapolis: Fortress, 2014.
Anglican Church of Australia. *Admission to Holy Communion Canon 1973*. 1973. https://anglican.org.au/wp-content/uploads/2019/03/Admission_to_Holy_Communion_Canon_1973.pdf.
———. *An Australian Prayer Book*. Sydney: Broughton, 1978.
———. *A Prayer Book for Australia*. Mulgrave: Broughton, 1995.
"The Apostles' Creed." In *Creeds and Confessions of Faith in the Christian Tradition*, edited by Jaroslav Pelikan and Valerie Hotchkiss, 1:667–69. New Haven, CT: Yale University Press, 2003.
Aquinas, Thomas. *Summa Theologica*. Milton Keynes: Authentic Media, 2012.
Arcadi, James M. "'You Shall Be Holy': A Speech Act Theoretic Theological Interpretation." *Journal of Theological Interpretation* 12.2 (Fall 2018) 183–99.
Augustine. *Confessions*. Vol. 1: *Books 1–8*. Edited and translated by Carolyn J. B. Hammond. Cambridge, MA: Harvard University Press, 2014.
Bach, Johann Sebastian. "Matthäus-Passion Bwv 244." Bach Cantatas Website. https://www.bach-cantatas.com/Texts/BWV244-Eng3.htm.
Balthasar, Hans Urs von. *First Glance at Adrienne Von Speyr*. San Francisco: Ignatius, 1981.
———. *The Glory of the Lord: A Theological Aesthetics*. Translated by Brian McNeil and John Riches. 7 vols. Edinburgh: T&T Clark, 1989.
———. *Mysterium Paschale: The Mystery of Easter*. Translated by Aidan Nichols. Grand Rapids: Eerdmans, 1990.
———. *Our Task: A Report and a Plan*. San Francisco: Ignatius, 1994.
———. *Prayer*. Translated by Graham Harrison. San Francisco: Ignatius, 1986.
———. "A Resume of My Thought." *Communio: International Catholic Review* 15 (Winter 1988) 468–73.
———. *Theo-Drama*. Translated by Graham Harrison. 5 vols. San Francisco: Ignatius, 1988–98.
———. *Theo-Dramatik*. 5 vols. Einsiedeln: Johannes, 1973.
Baptism, Eucharist and Ministry. Geneva: World Council of Churches, 1982.

Barker, Kit. *Imprecation as Divine Discourse: Speech-Act Theory, Dual Authorship, and Theological Interpretation*. Journal of Theological Interpretation Supplements. Winona Lake, IN: Eisenbrauns, 2016.
Barth, Karl. *Church Dogmatics*. Edited by G. W. Bromiley and T. F. Torrance; translated by G. W. Bromiley. 14 vols. Peabody, MA: Hendrickson, 2010.
———. *The Epistle to the Romans*. Translated by Edwyn C. Hoskyns. Oxford: Oxford University Press, 1968.
———. *God Here and Now*. London: Routledge, 2003.
Basil the Great, St. *On the Holy Spirit*. Translated by Stephen Hildebrand. Popular Patristics Series. Yonkers, NY: St. Vladimir's Seminary Press, 2011.
Bauckham, Richard J. "The Worship of Jesus in Philippians 2:9–11." In *Where Christology Began: Essays on Philippians 2*, edited by Brian J. Dodd and Ralph P. Martin, 128–39. Louisville: Westminster John Knox, 1998.
Black, C. Clifton. *Reading Scripture with the Saints*. Cambridge: Lutterworth, 2015.
Block, Daniel Isaac. *For the Glory of God: Recovering a Biblical Theology of Worship*. Grand Rapids: Baker Academic, 2014.
Bloesch, Donald G. *The Church—Sacraments, Worship, Ministry, Mission*. Downers Grove, IL: InterVarsity, 2002.
Blowers, Paul M. *Drama of the Divine Economy: Creator and Creation in Early Christian Theology and Piety*. Oxford: Oxford University Press, 2012.
———. "The Regula Fidei and the Narrative Character of Early Christian Faith." *Pro Ecclesia* 6.2 (1997) 199–228.
Bockmuehl, Markus. *Seeing the Word: Refocusing New Testament Study*. Studies in Theological Interpretation. Grand Rapids: Baker, 2006.
Bokedal, Tomas. "The Rule of Faith: Tracing Its Origins." *Journal of Theological Interpretation* 7.2 (Fall 2013) 233–55.
Bonhoeffer, Dietrich. *Prayerbook of the Bible: An Introduction to the Psalms*. Translated by James H. Burtness. Dietrich Boenhoeffer Works 5. Minneapolis: Fortress, 2005.
Bonikowsky, Kay. "Also a Mother: Asian Feminist Theology Promotes God Also as Mother." *Priscilla Papers* 35.1 (2021) 19–25.
The Book of Common Prayer and Administration of the Sacraments and Other Rites and Ceremonies of the Church According to the Use of the Church of England. London: Oxford University Press, 1662.
Booth, William. "The General's New Year Address to Officers. *The War Cry*, January 17, 1883." In *Called to Be God's People*, edited by Robert Street, 135–37. London: The Salvation Army, 1999.
Borchert, Gerald L. *Worship in the New Testament: Divine Mystery and Human Response*. St. Louis, MO: Chalice, 2008.
Bouyer, Louis. *The Christian Mystery*. Translated by Illtyd Trethowan. London: T&T Clark, 1990.
Bowald, Mark Alan. "The Character of Theological Interpretation of Scripture." *International Journal of Systematic Theology* 12.2 (2010) 162–83.
———. *Rendering the Word in Theological Hermeneutics: Mapping Divine and Human Agency*. Ashland, OR: Lexham, 2015.
Brook, Peter. *The Empty Space*. New York: Touchstone, 1996.
Brueggemann, Walter. *Redescribing Reality: What We Do When We Read the Bible*. London: SCM, 2009.

Bucur, Bogdan G. "Exegesis of Biblical Theophanies in Byzantine Hymnography: Rewritten Bible?" *Theological Studies* 68.1 (2007) 92–112.
Burrows, William Bramwell. *The Mercy Seat*. London: Salvationist Publishing and Supplies, 1951.
Butterworth, Liam. "Pastor Resigns After Incorrectly Performing Thousands of Baptisms." *New York Times*, Feb. 14 2022. https://www.nytimes.com/2022/02/14/us/catholic-priest-baptisms-phoenix.html?smid=url-share.
Byrne, Lavinia. *Women Before God*. Rev. ed. London: S.P.C.K., 1995.
Calvin, John. *Institutes of the Christian Religion*. Translated by Ford Lewis Battles. Edited by John T. McNeill. Philadelphia: Westminster, 1960.
Castleman, Robbie F. *Story-Shaped Worship: Following Patterns from the Bible and History*. Downers Grove, IL: InterVarsity, 2013.
The Catechism of the Catholic Church. Popular rev. ed. London: Bloomsbury Continuum, 2000.
Chan, Simon. *Liturgical Theology: The Church as Worshiping Community*. Downers Grove, IL: IVP Academic, 2006.
Chilcote, Paul Wesley. *Recapturing the Wesleys' Vision—An Introduction to the Faith of John and Charles Wesley*. Westmont, IL: InterVarsity, 2004.
Clement of Alexandria. "The Stromata, or Miscellanies." In *Ante-Nicene Fathers*, edited by Alexander Roberts and James Donaldson, 299–567. Peabody, MA: Hendrickson, 2012.
Clement of Rome. "The First Epistle of Clement to the Corinthians." In *The Apostolic Fathers—Early Christian Writings*, translated by Maxwell Staniforth and Andrew Louth, 17–51. London: Penguin, 1987.
Clifton, Shaw. *New Love: Thinking Aloud About Practical Holiness*. Wellington: Flag Publications, 2004.
———. "Our God-Given Position on Sacraments—A Candid Reflection." *The Officer* (Mar./Apr. 2007) 2–7.
———. "Salvationism—Holiness and the Non-Negotiables of Salvationism." In *New Love—Thinking Aloud About Practical Holiness*, 19–41. Wellington: Flag Publications, 2004.
———. "Thinking Aloud and Candidly About the Salvation Army and the Sacraments." In *Called to Be God's People*, edited by Robert Street, 117–26. London: The Salvation Army, 1999.
Coakley, Sarah. *God, Sexuality and the Self: An Essay 'on the Trinity.'* Cambridge: Cambridge University Press, 2013.
Cochand, Nicholas, Isaïa Gazzola, and Job Getcha. "Formed Ecumenically Through Liturgy." *Studia Liturgica* 54 (Dec. 21, 2023). https://doi.org/10.1177/00393207231214385.
Cockayne, Joshua, and Gideon Salter. "Liturgical Anthropology." *TheoLogica* 6.1 (2021) 72–106.
Cocksworth, Ashley. "When Prayer Goes Wrong: A Negative Theology of Prayer." *Scottish Journal of Theology* 76.1 (2023) 10–23.
Cocksworth, Ashley, and John C. McDowell. "Introduction: Prayer in the School of Discipleship." In *T&T Clark Handbook of Christian Prayer*, edited by Ashley Cocksworth and John C. McDowell, 1–8. London: T&T Clark, 2021.
Cocksworth, Christopher J. *Holy, Holy, Holy: Worshipping the Trinitarian God*. Trinity and Truth Series. London: Darton, Longman & Todd, 1997.

Cole, Graham A. *He Who Gives Life: The Doctrine of the Holy Spirit*. Foundations of Evangelical Theology. Wheaton, IL: Crossway, 2007.

Collins, Kenneth J. *The Theology of John Wesley: Holy Love and the Shape of Grace*. Nashville: Abingdon, 2007.

Collins, Mary. "Naming God in Prayer." *Worship* 59.4 (1985) 291–304.

Conzelmann, Hans. *A Commentary on the First Epistle to the Corinthians*. Translated by James W. Leitch. Hermeneia. Philadelphia: Fortress, 1975.

Couchman, Adam. *In the Image of the Image: Gregory of Nyssa's Opposition to Slavery*. Oxford: SLG, 2023.

———. "The Neo-Sacramental Theology of the Salvation Army." Bachelor's thesis, Charles Sturt University, 2007.

———. "'Not My Will but Yours Be Done': The Use of the Mercy Seat in Theodramatic Perspective." *Studia Liturgica* 51.2 (2021) 217–29.

———. "Performing in the Theodrama: A Theocentric Vision of Worship." *Australian Journal of Liturgy* 16.4 (2019) 232–42.

Craigo-Snell, Shannon. *The Empty Church: Theater, Theology, and Bodily Hope*. Oxford: Oxford University Press, 2014.

"The Creed of Nicaea." In *Creeds and Confessions of Faith in the Christian Tradition*, edited by Jaroslav Pelikan and Valerie Hotchkiss, 1:156–59. New Haven, CT: Yale University Press, 2003.

Cross, Richard. *Communicatio Idiomatum: Reformation Christological Debates*. Oxford: Oxford University Press, 2019.

Cyril of Alexandria. *Commentary on John*. Translated by David Maxwell, edited by Joel C. Elowsky. Ancient Christian Texts. Downers Grove, IL: IVP Academic, 2013.

———. *On the Unity of Christ*. Popular Patristics Series. Crestwood, NY: St. Vladimir's Seminary Press, 1995.

Dahl, Nils Alstrup. "A New and Living Way: The Approach to God According to Heb 10:19–25." *Interpretation* 5.4 (1951) 401–12.

Danneels, Godfried Cardinal. "Liturgy Thirty Years After the Council: High Point or Recession?" In *Traditions and Transitions*, edited by Eleanor Bernstein and Martin Connell, 8–28. Chicago: Liturgy Training Publications, 1998.

"The Definition of Faith of the Council of Chalcedon." In *Creeds and Confessions of Faith in the Christian Tradition*, edited by Jaroslav Pelikan and Valerie Hotchkiss, 1:172–81. New Haven, CT: Yale University Press, 2003.

Dix, Gregory. *The Shape of the Liturgy*. 2nd ed. Westminster: Dacre, 1949.

Douglas, Brian. *A Companion to Anglican Eucharistic Theology. Vol. 1: The Reformation to the 19th Century*. Leiden: Brill, 2012.

Douglas, Sally. *Early Church Understandings of Jesus as the Female Divine: The Scandal of the Scandal of Particularity*. Library of New Testament Studies 557. London: Bloomsbury T&T Clark, 2016.

English Language Liturgical Consultation. "English Translation of the Lord's Prayer." 2007. https://www.englishtexts.org/the-lords-prayer.

———. "RCL Tables." https://www.englishtexts.org/rcl-tables.

Fagerberg, David W. *Liturgical Mysticism*. Steubenville, OH: Emmaus Academic, 2019.

———. "Liturgical Theology." In *T&T Clark Companion to Liturgy*, edited by Alcuin Reid, 3–20. London: Bloomsbury T&T Clark, 2015.

———. "Liturgy, Signs, and Sacraments." In *The Oxford Handbook of Sacramental Theology*, edited by Hans Boersma and Matthew Levering, 455–65. Oxford: Oxford University Press, 2015.

Farlow, Matthew S., and Paul Louis Metzger. *The Dramatizing of Theology: Humanity's Participation in God's Drama*. Eugene, OR: Pickwick, 2017. Kindle.

Fee, Gordon D. *The First Epistle to the Corinthians*. The New International Commentary on the New Testament. Grand Rapids: Eerdmans, 1987.

Ferguson, Everett. *The Rule of Faith: A Guide*. Cascade Companions. Eugene, OR: Cascade, 2015. Kindle.

Fiddes, Paul S. *Participating in God: A Pastoral Doctrine of the Trinity*. London: Darton Longman & Todd, 2000.

"First Fragments: Biblical Papyrus from Roman Egypt." Chester Beatty, 2023. https://chesterbeatty.ie/exhibitions/first-fragments/.

Fischer-Lichte, Erika, Ramona Mosse, and Minou Arjomand. *The Routledge Introduction to Theatre and Performance Studies*. English ed. London: Routledge, 2014.

"The Formula of Concord." In *Creeds and Confessions of Faith in the Christian Tradition*, edited by Jaroslav Pelikan and Valerie Hotchkiss, 2:166–203. New Haven, CT: Yale University Press, 2003.

Frost, Anthony, and Ralph Yarrow. *Improvisation in Drama*. New York: Macmillan Education, 1989.

Fulkerson, Mary McClintock. "The *Imago Dei* and a Reformed Logic for Feminist/Womanist Critique." In *Feminist and Womanist Essays in Reformed Dogmatics*, edited by Amy Plantinga Pauw and Serene Jones, 95–106. Louisville: Westminster/John Knox, 2006.

Garrett, Stephen M. "The Dazzling Darkness of God's Triune Love: Introducing Evangelicals to the Theology of Hans Urs Von Balthasar." *Themelios* 35.3 (2010) 413–30.

Geldhof, Joris. *Monotheism in Christian Liturgy*. Elements in Religion and Monotheism. Cambridge: Cambridge University Press, 2022.

Gifford, James D. *Perichoretic Salvation: The Believer's Union with Christ as a Third Type of Perichoresis*. Eugene, OR: Wipf & Stock, 2011.

Gorman, Michael J. *Becoming the Gospel: Paul, Participation, and Mission*. Grand Rapids: Eerdmans, 2015.

———. *Inhabiting the Cruciform God: Kenosis, Justification, and Theosis in Paul's Narrative Soteriology*. Grand Rapids: Eerdmans, 2009.

Gregory of Nazianzus. "Oration 31: On the Holy Spirit." In *Nicene and Post-Nicene Fathers*, edited by Philip Schaff and Henry Wace, 318–28. Peabody, MA: Hendrickson, 1994.

———. "Oration 40: On Holy Baptism." In *Nicene and Post-Nicene Fathers*, edited by Philip Schaff and Henry Wace, 360–77. Peabody, MA: Hendrickson, 1994.

Gregory of Nyssa. "The Great Catechism." In *Nicene and Post-Nicene Fathers*, edited by Philip Schaff, 471–509. New York: Christian Literature, 1892.

———. *Gregory of Nyssa's Treatise on the Inscriptions of the Psalms*. Translated by Ronald E. Heine. Oxford: Clarendon, 1995.

———. *The Life of Moses*. Translated by Abraham J. Malherbe and Everett Ferguson. New York: Paulist, 1978.

———. "On Perfection." Translated by Virginia Woods Callahan. In *Saint Gregory of Nyssa—Ascetical Works*, 95-122. Washington, DC: Catholic University of America Press, 1967.

———. "On the Holy Spirit." In *Nicene and Post-Nicene Fathers*, edited by Philip Schaff, 315-25. New York: Christian Literature, 1892.

———. "On the Making of Man." Translated by H. A. Wilson. In *Nicene and Post-Nicene Fathers*, edited by Philip Schaff, 387-427. New York: Christian Literature, 1892.

Gschwandtner, Christina M. "Mimesis or Metamorphosis? Eastern Orthodox Liturgical Practice and Its Philosophical Background." *Religions* 8.5 (2017) 1-22.

Gundry, Robert H. *Jesus the Word According to John the Sectarian: A Paleofundamentalist Manifesto for Contemporary Evangelicalism, Especially Its Elites, in North America.* Grand Rapids: Eerdmans, 2002.

Hahn, Scott. "Canon, Cult and Covenant: The Promise of Liturgical Hermeneutics." In *Canon and Biblical Interpretation*, edited by Craig G. Bartholomew, 207-29. Grand Rapids: Zondervan, 2006.

Hays, Richard B. "Continuing to Read Scripture with the Evangelists: A Response." *Journal of Theological Interpretation* 11.1 (Spring 2017) 85-99.

Heide, Gale. *Timeless Truth in the Hands of History: A Short History of System in Theology.* Eugene, OR: Pickwick, 2012.

Hernandez, Tamra. "Theological Interpretation of Scripture as a Trinitarian Enterprise." *Criswell Theological Review* 15.1 (Fall 2017) 47-60.

Hibbs, Pierce Taylor. *The Speaking Trinity and His Worded World: Why Language Is at the Center of Everything.* Eugene, OR: Wipf and Stock, 2018.

Hippolytus. "Against the Heresy of One Noetus." In *Ante-Nicene Fathers*, edited by Alexander Roberts and James Donaldson, 223-31. Peabody, MA: Hendrickson, 2012.

Holloway, Paul A. *Philippians.* Hermeneia. Minneapolis: Fortress, 2017.

Howsare, Rodney. *Balthasar: A Guide for the Perplexed.* London: T & T Clark, 2009.

Hurtado, Larry W. *At the Origins of Christian Worship: The Context and Character of Earliest Christian Devotion.* Grand Rapids: Eerdmans, 1999.

———. *How on Earth Did Jesus Become a God? Historical Questions About Earliest Devotion to Jesus.* Grand Rapids: Eerdmans, 2005.

Ignatius. "The Epistle to the Ephesians." In *The Apostolic Fathers—Early Christian Writings*, translated by Maxwell Staniforth and Andrew Louth, 59-68. London: Penguin, 1987.

Irenaeus. "Against Heresies." In *The Apostolic Fathers with Justin Martyr and Irenaeus*, edited by Alexander Roberts and James Donaldson, 1:305-567. Ante-Nicene Fathers. Peabody, MA: Hendrickson, 2012.

———. *On the Apostolic Preaching.* Translated by John Behr. Popular Patristic Series. Crestwood, NY: St. Vladimir's Seminary Press, 1997.

Jackelén, Antje. "The Image of God as *Techno Sapiens*." *Zygon* 37.2 (2002) 289-302.

Jenson, Robert W. *Canon and Creed.* Interpretation: Resources for the Use of Scripture in the Church. Louisville: Westminster John Knox, 2010.

———. "The Church and the Sacraments." In *The Cambridge Companion to Christian Doctrine*, edited by Colin E. Gunton, 207-25. Cambridge: Cambridge University Press, 1997.

Johnson, Dru. *Knowledge by Ritual: A Biblical Prolegomenon to Sacramental Theology*. Journal of Theological Interpretation Supplement 13. Winona Lake, IN: Eisenbraums, 2016.
Johnson, Elizabeth A. *She Who Is: The Mystery of God in Feminist Theological Discourse*. New York: Crossroad, 1992.
Jungmann, Josef A. *The Place of Christ in Liturgical Prayer*. Collegeville, MN: Liturgical, 1989.
Kavanagh, Aidan. *On Liturgical Theology*. Collegeville, MN: Liturgical, 1992.
Kittel, Gerhard. *Theological Dictionary of the New Testament*. Translated by Geoffrey W. Bromiley. 10 vols. Grand Rapids: Eerdmans, 1964.
Lavelle, Alex. "Shock, Horror, Treat: Halloween Kids R Ok." *The Age*, Oct. 30 2018. https://www.theage.com.au/national/shock-horror-treat-halloween-kids-r-ok-20181030-p50czd.html.
Laytham, D. Brent. "Interpretation on the Way to Emmaus: Jesus Performs His Story." *Journal of Theological Interpretation* 1.1 (2007) 101–15.
Leep, Jeanne. *Theatrical Improvisation: Short Form, Long Form, and Sketch-Based Improv*. New York: Palgrave Macmillan, 2008.
Legaspi, Michael C. *The Death of Scripture and the Rise of Biblical Studies*. Oxford: Oxford University Press, 2010.
Leim, Joshua E. "Worshiping the Father, Worshiping the Son: Cultic Language and the Identity of God in the Gospel of Matthew." *Journal of Theological Interpretation* 9.1 (2015) 65–84.
Lugt, Wesley Vander. *Living Theodrama: Reimagining Theological Ethics*. Ashgate Studies in Theology, Imagination and the Arts. London: Routledge, 2014.
Lugt, Wesley Vander, and Trevor A. Hart, eds. *Theatrical Theology: Explorations in Performing the Faith*. Cambridge: Lutterworth, 2015.
Martin, Jennifer Newsome. *Hans Urs Von Balthasar and the Critical Appropriation of Russian Religious Thought*. Notre Dame, IN: University of Notre Dame Press, 2015.
Mayer, Wendy. "The Homiletic Audience as Embodied Hermeneutic: Scripture and Its Interpretation in the Exegetical Preaching of John Chrysostom." In *Hymns, Homilies and Hermeneutics in Byzantium*, edited by Sarah Gador-Whyte and Andrew Mellas, 11–29. Byzantina Australiensia. Leiden: Brill, 2021.
Meredith, Anthony. *Gregory of Nyssa*. London: Routledge, 1999.
Moberly, R. W. L. "The Significance of the Church for Theological Interpretation: A Response to David Congdon." *Journal of Theological Interpretation* 12.2 (Fall 2018) 274–86.
Moltmann, Jürgen. *The Church in the Power of the Spirit: A Contribution of Messianic Ecclesiology*. London: SCM, 1977.
———. *The Trinity and the Kingdom of God: The Doctrine of God*. London: SCM, 1981.
Mongrain, Kevin. *The Systematic Thought of Hans Urs Von Balthasar: An Irenaean Retrieval*. New York: Crossroad, 2002.
Monro, Anita. "Alterity and the Canaanite Woman: A Postmodern Feminist Theological Reflection on Political Action." *Colloquium* 26.1 (1994) 32–43.
Moo, Douglas J. *The Epistle to the Romans*. The New International Commentary on the New Testament. Grand Rapids: Eerdmans, 1996.
Murphy, Michael P. *A Theology of Criticism: Balthasar, Postmodernism, and the Catholic Imagination*. Oxford: Oxford University Press, 2008.

Navarro, Kevin. *Trinitarian Doxology: T. F. and J. B. Torrance's Theology of Worship as Participation by the Spirit in the Son's Communion with the Father*. Eugene, OR: Pickwick, 2020. Kindle.

"The Niceno-Constantinopolitan Creed." In *Creeds and Confessions of Faith in the Christian Tradition*, edited by Jaroslav Pelikan and Valerie Hotchkiss, 1:160–63. New Haven, CT: Yale University Press, 2003.

Novation. "Treatise Concerning the Trinity." In *Ante-Nicene Fathers*, edited by Alexander Roberts and James Donaldson, 611–44. Peabody, MA: Hendrickson, 2012.

Oakes, S. J. Edward T., and David Moss, eds. *The Cambridge Companion to Hans Urs Von Balthasar*. Cambridge Companions to Religion. Cambridge: Cambridge University Press, 2004.

O'Day, Gail R. "The Gospel of John: Introduction, Commentary, and Reflections." In *Luke, John*, 491–865. New Interpreter's Bible 9. Nashville: Abingdon, 1995.

Olkinuora, Damaskinos. "John Damascene's Homily on the Withered Fig Tree (Cpg 8058) Parable in Action, or Exegetical and Panegyrical Preaching in Interaction." In *Hymns, Homilies and Hermeneutics in Byzantium*, edited by Sarah Gador-Whyte and Andrew Mellas, 30–46. Byzantina Australiensia. Leiden: Brill, 2021.

———. "Performance Theory and the Study of Byzantine Hymnography: Andrew of Crete's *Canon on Lazarus*." *Ortodoksia* 59.1 (2019) 7–31.

Origen. "De Principiis." In *Ante-Nicene Fathers*, edited by Alexander Roberts and James Donaldson, 239–382. Peabody, MA: Hendrickson, 2012.

Osborn, Eric. *Irenaeus of Lyons*. Cambridge: Cambridge University Press, 2001.

Parry, Kenneth. *Depicting the Word: Byzantine Iconophile Thought of the Eighth and Ninth Centuries*. The Medieval Mediterranean 12. Leiden: Brill, 1996.

Paul VI. *Gaudium et Spes: Pastoral Constitution on the Church in the Modern World*. Dec. 7, 1965. https://www.vatican.va/archive/hist_councils/ii_vatican_council/documents/vat-ii_const_19651207_gaudium-et-spes_en.html.

Pelikan, Jaroslav. *Credo: Historical and Theological Guide to Creeds and Confessions of Faith in the Christian Tradition*. New Haven, CT: Yale University Press, 2003.

———. *The Spirit of Eastern Christendom (600–1700)*. The Christian Tradition 2. Chicago: University of Chicago Press, 1974.

Pelikan, Jaroslav, and Valerie R. Hotchkiss, eds. *Creeds and Confessions of Faith in the Christian Tradition*. 4 vols. New Haven, CT: Yale University Press, 2003.

Peterson, David. *Engaging with God: A Biblical Theology of Worship*. Downers Grove, IL: IVP Academic, 1992.

Peterson, Paul Silas. *The Early Hans Urs Von Balthasar*. Berlin: de Gruyter, 2015.

Pinnock, Clark H. *Flame of Love: A Theology of the Holy Spirit*. Downers Grove, IL: IVP Academic, 1996.

Pomazansky, Michael. *Orthodox Dogmatic Theology: A Concise Exposition*. Translated by Seraphim Rose. 3rd ed. Platina, CA: St. Herman of Alaska Brotherhood, 2005.

Procter-Smith, Marjorie. *Praying with Our Eyes Open: Engendering Feminist Liturgical Prayer*. Nashville: Abingdon, 1995.

Quash, Ben. *Theology and the Drama of History*. Cambridge: Cambridge University Press, 2005.

Rhoads, David. "Jesus and the Syrophoenician Woman in Mark: A Narrative-Critical Study." *Journal of the American Academy of Religion* 62.2 (1994) 343–75.

Rhoads, David, and Joanna Dewey. "Performance Criticism: A Paradigm Shift in Biblical Studies." In *From Text to Performance: Narrative and Performance Criticisms in Dialogue and Debate*, edited by Kelly R. Iverson, 1–26. Biblical Performance Criticism Series. Cambridge: Lutterworth, 2015.

Rodrigues, Adriani Milli. "The Rule of Faith and Biblical Interpretation in Evangelical Theological Interpretation of Scripture." *Themelios* 43.2 (2018) 257–70.

Rodríguez, Rafael. *Structuring Early Christian Memory: Jesus in Tradition, Performance, and Text*. Library of New Testament Studies. London: T & T Clark, 2010.

Roten, Johann. "The Two Halves of the Moon: Marian Anthropological Dimensions in the Common Mission of Adrienne Von Speyr and Hans Urs Von Balthasar." In *Hans Urs Von Balthasar: His Life and Thought*, edited by David L. Schindler, 65–86. San Francisco: Communio, 1991.

Russell, Letty. *Church in the Round: Feminist Interpretation of the Church*. Louisville: Westminster John Knox, 1993.

The Salvation Army. *The Salvation Army Handbook of Doctrine*. London: Salvation, 2010.

———. *Salvation Story—Salvationist Handbook of Doctrine*. London: The Salvation Army International Headquarters, 1998.

Schechner, Richard. *Between Theater and Anthropology*. Philadelphia: University of Pennsylvania Press, 1985.

———. *Performance Theory*. Rev. and exp. ed. London: Routledge, 2003. Kindle.

Schmemann, Alexander. *For the Life of the World: Sacraments and Orthodoxy*. 2nd rev. and exp. ed. Crestwood, NY: St. Vladimir's Seminary Press, 1973.

Schumacher, Michele M. *A Trinitarian Anthropology: Adrienne Von Speyr and Hans Urs Von Balthasar in Dialogue with Thomas Aquinas*. Washington, DC: The Catholic University of America Press, 2014.

Schüssler Fiorenza, Elisabeth. *In Memory of Her: A Feminist Theological Reconstruction of Christian Origins*. 2nd ed. New York: Crossroad, 1995.

Seitz, Christopher R. "The Canonical Approach and Theological Interpretation." In *Canon and Biblical Interpretation*, edited by Craig G. Bartholomew et al., 58–110. Scripture and Hermeneutics Series. Grand Rapids: Zondervan, 2006.

Slee, Nicola. "Prayer, Gender and the Body." In *T&T Clark Handbook of Christian Prayer*, edited by Ashley Cocksworth and John C. McDowell, 649–65. London: T&T Clark, 2021.

———. *Praying Like a Woman*. London: SPCK, 2004.

Smith, James K. A. *Desiring the Kingdom: Worship, Worldview, and Cultural Formation*. Cultural Liturgies 1. Grand Rapids: Baker Academic, 2009.

———. *Imagining the Kingdom: How Worship Works*. Cultural Liturgies 2. Grand Rapids: Baker Academic, 2013.

———. *You Are What You Love: The Spiritual Power of Habit*. Grand Rapids: Brazos, 2016.

Smith, Mark S. "Like Deities, Like Temples (Like People)." In *Temple and Worship in Biblical Israel*, edited by Claudia V. Camp and Andrew Mein, 3–27. London: T&T Clark, 2007.

Smith, Philip, and Tim Phillips. "Popular Understandings of 'Unaustralian': An Investigation of the Un-National." *Journal of Sociology* 37.4 (2001) 323–39.

Speyr, Adrienne von. *The Boundless God*. Translated by Helena M. Tomko. San Francisco: Ignatius, 1955.

———. *The Countenance of the Father*. Translated by David Kipp. San Francisco: Ignatius, 1997.

———. *The Handmaid of the Lord*. Translated by Alexander Dru. London: Harvill, 1956.

———. *The World of Prayer*. San Francisco: Ignatius, 1951.

Stephenson, Barry. "Ritual as Action, Performance, and Practice." In *The Oxford Handbook of Early Christian Ritual*, edited by Ristro Uro et al., 38–54. Oxford: Oxford University Press, 2018.

Street, Robert, ed. *Called to Be God's People*. London: The Salvation Army, 1999.

Sutton, Matthew Lewis. *Heaven Opens: The Trinitarian Mysticism of Adrienne Von Speyr*. Minneapolis: Fortress, 2014.

Tanner, Kathryn. *Christ the Key*. Cambridge: Cambridge University Press, 2010.

———. *God and Creation in Christian Theology: Tyranny or Empowerment?* Minneapolis: Fortress, 2005.

———. "In the Image of the Invisible." In *Apophatic Bodies: Negative Theology, Incarnation, and Relationality*, edited by Chris Boesel and Catherine Keller, 117–34. New York: Fordham University Press, 2010.

———. *Jesus, Humanity and the Trinity: A Brief Systematic Theology*. Edinburgh: T&T Clark, 2001.

Tanton, Tobias. *Corporeal Theology: Accommodating Theological Understanding to Embodied Thinkers*. Oxford: Oxford University Press, 2023.

Tertullian. "Against Praxeas." In *Latin Christianity: Its Founder, Tertullian*, edited by Alexander Roberts and James Donaldson, 3:597–620. *Ante-Nicene Fathers*. Peabody, MA: Hendrickson, 2012.

———. "On Prescription Against Heresies." In *Latin Christianity: Its Founder, Tertullian*, edited by Alexander Roberts and James Donaldson, 243–65. *Ante-Nicene Fathers*. Peabody, MA: Hendrickson, 2012.

Thomson, James G. S. S. *The Praying Christ: A Study of Jesus' Doctrine and Practice of Prayer*. Vancouver: Regent College Publishing, 1959.

Torrance, Alan. "Introduction." *Participatio* 3 (Supplemental) (2014) 1–14.

Torrance, James B. "Christ in Our Place." In *A Passion for Christ: The Vision That Ignites Ministry*, 35–51. Edinburgh: Handsel, 1999.

———. "Contemplating the Trinitarian Mystery of Christ." In *Exploring Christian Spirituality: An Ecumenical Reader*, edited by Kenneth J. Collins, 296–307. Grand Rapids: Baker Academic, 2000.

———. "The Place of Jesus Christ in Worship." In *Theological Foundations for Ministry*, edited by Ray S. Anderson, 348–69. Edinburgh: T&T Clark, 1979.

———. *Worship, Community, and the Triune God of Grace*. Downers Grove, IL: IVP Academic, 1996.

Torrance, Thomas F. "The Christ Who Loves Us." In *A Passion for Christ: The Vision That Ignites Ministry*, edited by Gerrit Dawson and Jock Stein, 9–20. Eugene, OR: Wipf & Stock, 1999.

———. *Incarnation: The Person and Life of Christ*. Edited by Robert T. Walker. Downers Grove, IL: IVP Academic, 2008.

———. *The Mediation of Christ*. Rev. ed. Colorado Springs: Helmers & Howard, 1992.

———. *Theology in Reconciliation: Essays Towards Evangelical and Catholic Unity in East and West*. Eugene, OR: Wipf & Stock, 1996.

Treier, Daniel J. "What Is Theological Interpretation? An Ecclesiological Reduction." *International Journal of Systematic Theology* 12.2 (2010) 144–61.
Tucker, Karen B. Westerfield. *American Methodist Worship*. Oxford: Oxford University Press, 2001.
Unkel, Jill. *First Fragments: Biblical Papyrus from Roman Egypt*. Dublin: Chester Beatty Library, 2022.
Van Dyk, Leanne. "The Gifts of God for the People of God: Christian Feminism and Sacramental Theology." In *Feminist and Womanist Essays in Reformed Dogmatics*, edited by Amy Plantinga Pauw and Serene Jones, 204–20. Louisville: Westminster John Knox, 2006.
Vanhoozer, Kevin J., ed. *The Cambridge Companion to Postmodern Theology*. Cambridge: Cambridge University Press, 2003.
———. "Continuing the Dialogue: A Theological Offering." *Edification—The Transdisciplinary Journal of Christian Psychology* 4.1 (2010) 41–46.
———. *The Drama of Doctrine: A Canonical-Linguistic Approach to Christian Theology*. Louisville: Westminster John Knox, 2005.
———. *Faith Speaking Understanding: Performing the Drama of Doctrine*. Louisville: Westminster John Knox, 2014.
———. *First Theology: God, Scripture and Hermeneutics*. Downers Grove, IL: InterVarsity, 2002.
———. "Imprisoned or Free? Text, Status and Theological Interpretation in the Master/Slave Discourse of Philemon." In *Reading Scripture with the Church: Toward a Hermeneutic for Theological Interpretation*, edited by A. K. M. Adam et al., 52–93. Grand Rapids: Baker Academic, 2006.
———. *Is There a Meaning in This Text? The Bible, the Reader, and the Morality of Literary Knowledge*. Leicester: Apollos, 1998.
———. "'One Rule to Rule Them All?' Theological Method in an Era of World Christianity." In *Globalizing Theology: Belief and Practice in an Era of World Christianity*, edited by Craig Ott and Harold A. Netland, 85–126. Grand Rapids: Baker Academic, 2006.
———. *Pictures at a Theological Exhibition: Scenes of the Church's Worship, Witness, and Wisdom*. Downers Grove, IL: InterVarsity, 2016.
———. *Remythologizing Theology: Divine Action, Passion, and Authorship*. Cambridge: Cambridge University Press, 2010.
———. "Triune Discourse." In *Trinitarian Theology for the Church: Scripture, Community, Worship*, edited by Daniel J. Treier and David Lauber, 25–78. Downers Grove, IL: IVP Academic, 2009.
Vanhoozer, Kevin J., James K. A. Smith, and Bruce Ellis Benson. *Hermeneutics at the Crossroads*. Bloomington: Indiana University Press, 2006.
Wainwright, Elaine M. *Towards a Feminist Critical Reading of the Gospel According to Matthew*. Berlin: de Gruyter, 1991.
Wainwright, Geoffrey. *Doxology: The Praise of God in Worship, Doctrine and Life: A Systematic Theology*. New York: Oxford University Press, 1980.
Webber, Robert, ed. *The Complete Library of Christian Worship*. 7 vols. Nashville: Starsong, 1993–94.
Webster, John. *Word and Church: Essays in Christian Dogmatics*. Edinburgh: T & T Clark, 2001.
Weir, Peter, dir. *Dead Poet's Society*. Burbank, CA: Buena Vista Pictures, 1989.

Wesley, John. "Journal Entry—June 28, 1740." In *The Works of John Wesley*, vol. 19, edited by W. Reginald Ward and Richard P. Heitzenrater. Nashville: Abingdon, 1990.

———. "The Means of Grace." In *The Works of John Wesley*, edited by Albert Outler, 1:387–97. Nashville: Abingdon, 1984.

Wesley, John, and Charles Wesley. *Hymns on the Lord's Supper*. 2nd ed. Bristol: Felix Farley, 1747.

"The Westminster Shorter Catechism." In *Creeds and Confessions of Faith in the Christian Tradition*, edited by Jaroslav Pelikan and Valerie Hotchkiss, 2:650–52. New Haven, CT: Yale University Press, 2003.

White, Susan J. *Groundwork of Christian Worship*. Peterborough: Epworth, 1997.

Williamson, H. G. M. "Temple and Worship in Isaiah 6." In *Temple and Worship in Biblical Israel*, edited by Claudia V. Camp and Andrew Mein, 123–44. London: T&T Clark, 2007.

Winner, Lauren F. *The Dangers of Christian Practice: On Wayward Gifts, Characteristic Damage, and Sin*. New Haven, CT: Yale University Press, 2018.

Witherington, Ben, III. *We Have Seen His Glory: A Vision of Kingdom Worship*. Grand Rapids: Eerdmans, 2010.

Wright, N. T. *The Lord and His Prayer*. London: Triangle, 1996.

———. *Romans*. The New Interpreter's Bible 10. Nashville: Abingdon, 2002.

Young, Frances. "The 'Mind' of Scripture: Theological Readings of the Bible in the Fathers." *International Journal of Systematic Theology* 7.2 (2005) 126–41.

Name (Author) Index

Ahmed, Sara, 141
Allmen, Jean-Jacques von, 11
Aquinas, Thomas, 66–67
Augustine, Saint, 129–32

Balthasar, Hans Urs von, 18, 21–33, 39–40, 54n, 71, 99–101, 104, 106n, 108–9, 113, 117, 133, 136–38
Barth, Karl, 12, 26, 72–73, 117, 120
Basil of Caesarea, 102–5
Block, Daniel, 11–12
Bloesch, Donald G., 11–12
Blowers, Paul, 56, 62
Bonhoeffer, Dietrich, 14–15
Bonikowsky, Kay, 6, 8, 155
Bucur, Bogdan G., 35–36

Calvin, John, 132
Chilcote, Paul Wesley, 155
Coakley, Sarah, 7–8
Collins, Mary, 6–7
Cyril of Alexandria, 81–82, 111
Cyril of Jerusalem, 61–62

Dahl, Nils Alstrup, 13

Fagerberg, David, 15–16, 58, 72, 97, 101–4, 126
Fee, Gordon, 146–47
Fiddes, Paul, 55
Fiorenza, Elisabeth Schüssler, 169
Frost, Anthony, 40–41

Geldhof, Joris, 15–16
Gorman, Michael, 116–18
Gregory of Nazianzus, 7–8
Gregory of Nyssa, 18–19, 105–8, 132–34
Gschwandtner, Christina, 46

Hurtado, Larry, 4, 115, 165

Ignatius of Antioch, 63
Irenaeus of Lyons, 18, 62–63, 137–39

John of Damascus (John Damascene), 36–38
Johnson, Dru, 125
Johnson, Elizabeth A., 6, 150–51

Kavanagh, Aidan, 58
Kittel, Gerhard, 17

Lugt, Martyn, 50
Luther, Martin, 70–72, 79, 81

Maximus the Confessor, 128–29
Mayer, Wendy, 38
Mongrain, Kevin, 25
Monro, Anita, 41–44
Moss, David, 26–27

Navarro, Kevin, 82–83

Oakes, Edward T., 26–27
Olkinuora, Damaskinos, 34–36, 38–39, 46, 109

Palamas, Gregory, 38
Parry, Robin, 128–29
Pelikan, Jaroslav, 58–59, 65, 67, 128–29, 145
Peterson, David, 11, 82, 102, 139
Peterson, Paul Silas, 26
Pomazansky, Michael, 132
Procter-Smith, Marjorie, 6, 152, 154–55

Quash, Ben, 32–33

Rodríguez, Rafael, 51–52

Schechner, Richard, 22, 34–37, 46–47, 112
Schmemann, Alexander, 125–26
Slee, Nicola, 19, 149–51
Smith, James K. A., 12, 123, 125–33
Speyr, Adrienne von, 22–27, 31, 70, 88, 93–94, 97–102, 104, 108, 113, 118, 120–21, 134–37

Stephenson, Barry, 37
Sutton, Matthew, 26, 98

Tanner, Kathryn, 45–47, 78–85
Torrance, Alan, 83–84
Torrance, James B., 72, 82–85, 88–89
Torrance, Thomas F., 10, 72–73, 81–85, 162

Vanhoozer, Kevin, 19–20, 21–22, 31–34, 40, 50–52, 64, 86, 111

Wesley, John, 140, 155–58, 161–62
White, Susan J., 13–14
Williams, Rowan, 26
Williamson, H. G. M., 109
Witherington III, Ben, 12
Wright, N. T., 119

Subject Index

A Prayer Book for Australia (APBA), 1–3, 9, 11, 48, 50, 65, 144–49, 157–58, 171

baptism, 3, 10, 38n, 58, 73, 103–4, 119, 141–43, 149, 157, 159
Bible. *See* Scripture
Book of Common Prayer (BCP), 9, 146–48, 158

communicatio idiomatum, 59, 70–73, 79
Holy Communion, 13, 37, 84, 87–88, 126–27, 135, 140–52, 155–59, 161, 163
  body of Christ, 145–48
  open table, 140, 155–58
confession, 4, 18, 83, 149, 155–56, 161–63
creeds, 3, 22, 33, 45, 56, 57–68, 78, 80, 85, 97, 114, 123
  Chalcedon, Definition of Faith (Chal), 5–6, 9, 66–69, 70–71, 80, 92, 95–96, 116, 139, 164
  Niceno-Constantinopolitan Creed (N-CP), 2–3, 9, 16, 54, 64–67, 85, 92, 98, 105, 110, 116
  Apostles' Creed (Ap), 3
crucifixion, 74, 92

English Language Liturgical Consultation (ELLC), 50n
Eucharist. *See* Holy Communion

feminist theology and liturgy, 8, 17, 140–41, 149–55, 157–58, 163

Gethsemane, 89–91, 161–63
glory (*doxa*); glorification, 2–5, 8, 11, 16–20, 24, 30, 32, 47, 60, 72–73, 77, 83, 85–86, 89, 93–95, 99, 102–6, 108–9, 112, 112–18, 120–22, 123, 128, 131, 134–39, 140, 149, 155, 161, 163, 164–66, 168–71
gospel, the, 2–3, 10–11, 35, 43, 48, 60–65, 81, 86–87, 89, 145, 166, 169

Holy Spirit. See Mother (Holy) Spirit
homo liturgicus, 12, 123–40, 155, 164–66
hypostatic union, 4, 6, 11, 14, 16, 19–20, 27, 46, 59, 65–73, 79, 82, 89, 111, 137, 164

imago Dei, 4, 12, 20, 111, 122, 123, 127, 131–34, 136–39, 150, 165–66
improvisation, 33, 40–44, 46, 50–53, 56, 73–76, 87–88, 92, 105–6, 108, 110, 112, 117, 131, 135, 138, 161, 163, 166–70
incarnation, 6, 16, 27–28, 33, 45, 62, 66, 69, 71, 73, 77, 79, 84–85, 95, 98, 107, 117, 120–21, 131–32, 136

Jesus, 2–7, 10–16, 19–20, 21–22, 27–34, 39, 41–55, 57–70, 72–77, 78–96, 97, 100–102, 107, 112–22,

Jesus (continued), 123, 128, 131, 135–39, 140–41, 144–45, 149, 156, 158, 161–63, 164–66, 169, 171
  Logos-script, 67, 87, 92, 113, 161–63

lex orandi, lex credendi, 31, 57–58, 103
liturgia ad intra/ad extra, 121, 164
liturgia Dei, 5–6, 12, 20, 30, 34, 37, 39, 47, 55–56, 85–86, 89, 94, 105, 114–15, 117–18, 121–22, 123, 126, 128–29, 134–37, 139, 140–41, 149, 155, 157, 163, 164–66, 168–71
liturgy, 1–2, 12–13, 15–16, 21–22, 31, 35–39, 46, 48, 50, 55, 57–58, 65, 72, 82, 101, 104–5, 126–28, 130, 133, 135, 141, 145–46, 150, 154
Lord's Prayer (Our Father), 6, 50–55, 58, 112
Lord's Supper. *See* Holy Communion

Mother (Holy) Spirit, 3–8, 11, 14–20, 21, 27, 29–34, 38–40, 51, 53–56, 66, 68–69, 73, 77, 82–86, 88–89, 94–96, 97–99, 101–6, 110, 112–13, 118–21, 123, 131, 134–38, 140–41, 143n, 155, 163, 164, 166, 169–71

performance, 3–6, 10, 13–16, 20, 21–22, 28–31, 40–56, 58–59, 61, 63–64, 69, 71–77, 78, 80, 83, 85–92, 94–96, 99–102, 105–7, 109–13, 115, 117–18, 123–24, 127, 133–39, 141, 149–50, 152, 154–55, 158, 161–63, 166–71
  fitting performance, 22, 40, 51, 55–56, 67, 81, 92, 138–39, 166, 169
  performance theory, 34–40
perichoresis. *See* Trinity, *perichoresis*
prayer, 3, 5–6, 9, 12, 14–15, 25, 30, 32, 36–38, 47, 49, 50–55, 58–59, 65, 69 – 70, 83–86, 88–94, 97–98, 101–4, 112, 113, 117, 118–21, 127, 131–32, 134–37, 142, 146, 151–52, 154–55, 159–63

regula/e fidei (rule of faith), 59, 61–65
resurrection, 4, 54, 61–62, 73–74, 76–77, 92, 115, 117, 171

sacraments, 58, 142–46, 149, 151, 156–59, 163
sacramental theology, 82, 142–44, 145–50, 156–58
salvation, 3, 21, 29, 50, 55, 62, 87–88, 92, 94, 128–29, 159–62, 166
Salvation Army, The (TSA), 142–43, 158–63
Scripture, 2–3, 5, 7–8, 13–14, 17, 19, 21–23, 28–29, 32–33, 35–36, 38, 49–56, 57–65, 76–77, 84, 87, 91–92, 102, 110, 115, 117, 127–29, 142, 145–46, 148, 152–53, 164, 167
  interpretation, 17, 21, 33, 50–56, 60, 62, 64–65, 75, 76–77, 87, 147–49, 155, 158, 162
  distinction between "Bible" and "Scripture", 49–50
  "rewritten Bible", 35–36
Societas Liturgica, 141–44, 152

theo-drama, 4–6, 10, 14–15, 20, 21–22, 27–34, 38–40, 42, 44, 46, 50–56, 57, 61–64, 67, 69, 71, 77, 85–86, 89, 95, 97, 101, 106–13, 115, 118, 121, 128–29, 131, 134, 152–55, 158–59, 161–65, 168–69
Trinity, 3–8, 10, 15–16, 18, 20–21, 24, 27, 31, 33, 39, 46–47, 50, 55, 59, 68–70, 78–79, 82, 85–86, 89, 95, 97–122, 123, 134, 136, 139, 141, 149–51, 155, 158, 163–64, 170
  perichoresis, 15–16, 18, 59, 68–70, 101–2

worship, 1–16, 19–20, 21–22, 24, 27, 30, 32–37, 39, 46–47, 55–56, 57–60, 65, 68–69, 71–73, 77, 78–85, 88–89, 93–96, 97–104, 106, 110–22, 123, 126, 128–32, 135, 137–39, 141–42, 149, 152, 154–55, 159–62, 164–71

Scripture Index

OLD TESTAMENT / HEBREW BIBLE

Genesis
1:2	106
1:3	105
1:26–27	107
1:31	105
2:2	106
2:7	106
16:13	108
21	153
34	143
38	153
48:15	108

Exodus
3:14	10
12:14	87
19:9	110
25:17	160
33:22	110

2 Samuel
12	44

1 Kings
8:11	109

Psalms
35:22–24	110
96:1	170

Isaiah
6	109
42	153
43:19	108
55:5	170

Jeremiah
4	153

Ezekiel
43:1–5	17

Joel
2:28	76

NEW TESTAMENT

Matthew
3:13–17	10
3:17	30
4:15	44
4:23	10
5:17	35–36
6:5–15	10
6:9	55
6:10	92
8:4–13	43
9:27	41
10	43–44

Matthew (continued)

10:19	40
12:31	104
15:21–28	41–44
17:5	30
17:15	41
20:30–31	41
22:37–40	165
26:17–29	87
26:25–29	149
26:26	88
26:27	158n
26:39	56, 58, 89–91
28:16–19	44

Mark

1:9–11	10
1:11	119
1:38	134–35
7:24–30	41–44
8:38	103
9:6	119
10	43–44
10:45	30
14:1–25	149
14:9	169
14:12–25	87–88
14:36	118

Luke

2:46	10
3	10
4:16–27	10
6:12	10
8:56	76
9:51	90
11:1–4	10
15:2	149
20:1	10
22:7–38	87–88
22:8	10
22:21	149
22:42	90, 92, 94, 161
22:44	91
23:27—24:22	73–76
24:10	76

24:25	76
24:35	77, 92

John

1:1–18	10, 106
2:5	135
2:11	135
2:23	87
4:22	81
4:26	30
6:4	87
10:30	69
11:27	30
16	121
16:14	120
17	3, 10, 85–86, 88–89, 92–94, 115, 117, 121
17:1–11	2
17:1	5
17:5	5
17:22–23	138
20:28	32

Acts

2:17	76

Romans

1:4	60
8	118–21
8:22–27	5, 89, 118–21
8:26–27	69, 94, 118–21, 170
8:29–30	138
10:4	36
13:14	21, 53, 55, 69

1 Corinthians

2:7	17
10:17	148
11	145, 155, 158
11:7	17
11:17–29	145–49
11:24–26	88
12:12–27	148
12:27	53
15	60

15:3	65	**Philippians**
		1:27 60
2 Corinthians		2 114–18, 121, 128, 165
1:19–20	138	2:9–11 5
3:18	17	
4	17, 60	**Colossians**
		1:15 111, 132
Galatians		
1:9, 12	60	**1 Timothy**
2:20	69	2:5 135
3:8	60	
3:28	107	**2 Peter**
		1:4 131, 133
Ephesians		
4:15	27	**1 John**
4:3	141	4:8 132

www.ingramcontent.com/pod-product-compliance
Lightning Source LLC
Chambersburg PA
CBHW070328230426
43663CB00011B/2250